NO VISIBLE INJURIES
Growing up with a Narcissistic Mother

A Memoir
by
Sylvia Clare

Thanks

My gratitude goes most of all to David, my husband, for getting me through some of the history told in this story, for keeping me alive, and most of all for a 'second half of life' partnership that has enhanced both our lives enormously and provided each other with the mutual support and collaboration to move forwards with all our creative endeavours.

To my two sons who have also struggled with the fallout from this history of our family and have been loving and wonderful teachers for me, for us all to heal together.

To all the friends who accept me as I am and do not feel any need to control or suppress me, and especially the friends who helped me to get this book as good as possible for amateurs, especially Cathrine, Gaye, Erika, Emma, Jane.

Although this is very much my story in the raw, I have told much of it elsewhere in snippets. To write it like all out in such detail this took a lot of emotional and mental effort and David's editorial and emotional support cannot be underestimated.

Sometimes I include a poem I have written about an experience, which often conveys much more how it felt than prose would do.

'You own everything that happened to you. Tell your stories. If people wanted you to write warmly about them, they should have behaved better.'

Anne Lamott

'I grew up on a diet of jealousy and unkindness – violence, one way or another. It took me decades to learn how to feast upon love and revel in happiness.'

Sylvia Clare

REVIEWS

No Visible Injuries

This book is a very clear account of the effects of PTSD because of childhood trauma of physical and emotional abuse, which can then result in dysfunctional behaviour in adulthood.

It also shows very clearly how to learn to understand yourself and become the person you want to be, how you need to revisit and make sense of what happened in those traumatic situations. It is not an easy thing to ask of yourself and may not be possible to do. However over time, with love and patience from yourself, and those around, you can learn to find positive ways that help you manage in the present and the future.

Sylvia has shown her pathway with immense courage and determination. She has never said it was easy or been prescriptive but has said and shown it can be done with support and love, and hopes that it will give encouragement to others.

Jane Edmunds
Psychodramatist and Group Analytic Psychotherapist Retired.

'I found this book absolutely riveting. An insightful, heartbreaking and ultimately uplifting analysis of the damage caused by narcissistic parenting.' Sophie Hannah, Crime Writer and Novelist.

On writing memoir

My cautious pen scrawls across the page,
a thirsty book, drinking in my energy
as I sink deeper into its story,
sink deeper into this sorrowful chair,
sun glinting through smiling windows.

I amble through my own backstory,
write this memoir, searching for the moments of light.
I sip tea and chew on a rough biscuit,
its texture against my tongue slowly melting, softening.
Its honey flavour sinks in, a new memory comes
One of softness, sweetness, new inspiration.

Later that evening, a smug moon and stars
watch me through the same window
as now I edit, reread, cut and paste, delete.
I remove sections of my life from this book
as easily as I cut a slice of bread from a new loaf,
to be consumed elsewhere, else left to grow stale
Discarded, no longer digestible.
It is all as lived, but not all to share,
Editing my life as if it is just a fiction.

Royalties

Fifty percent of all royalties go to

Anti-Slavery International is the only UK-based charity exclusively working to eliminate all forms of slavery throughout the world by investigating and exposing current cases of slavery, campaigning for its eradication, supporting the initiatives of local organisations to secure the freedom of those in slavery or vulnerable to it, and pressing for more effective implementation of national and international laws against slavery. Founded in 1839 by British abolitionists, it is the world's oldest international human rights organisation.

Also by the Authors

Non-fiction
Raising the Successful Child by Sylvia Clare

Trust your Intuition by Sylvia Clare illustrations by David Hughes

Releasing your Child's Potential by Sylvia Clare

Living the life You Want by Sylvia Clare & David Hughes

Heaven Sent Parents by Sylvia Clare & Kelly McKain, illustrations by David Hughes

The Well-Mannered Penis by Sylvia Clare, illustrations by David Hughes

Travelling the Alphabet – Emotionally by Sylvia Clare

Living well with ADHD by Sylvia Clare and David Hughes, illustrations by David Hughes

Poetry by Sylvia Clare
The Musicians Muse

Black and White

Love and Chocolate

Gaia's Angry Daughter

Fiction
Julia - a novel of narcissism, family relationships and murder based on the Isle of Wight by Sylvia Clare and David Hughes

Panchevsky - a spy thriller novel by David Hughes

In the pipelines and due out soon:
Travelling the Alphabet – Spiritually, by Sylvia Clare

INDEX

INTRODUCTION

When and how I met Sylvia are aptly covered in her book, so I won't repeat what she will explain in due course. Instead I will give you a potted version of a few random events as I saw them. Not many, for that would take far too long. Just one or two incidents that I hope add to the readers understanding of who Sylvia was when I met her and who she turned out to be.

My first impressions of Sylvia (apart from her obvious intelligence and good looks) was that of someone going somewhere. She had a counselling practice, a very smart home on the outskirts of London, two handsome sons, and had just acquired a book contract. As she will explain in the book, I used to visit her one weekend in two, and she would reciprocate. One of these weekends I was driving us somewhere near Croydon, an area with which I was unfamiliar. Sylvia was giving the directions. Everything seemed fine until quite out of the blue Sylvia undid her seat belt and ducked down into the footwell of the car.
'What's the matter?' I asked. I was taken aback by this random act.
'My mother might see me,' she replied.
'What do you mean?'
'She lives round here, and she might see me.'
'What about it?'
'She can't. She mustn't see me.'
All of a sudden, I had a child in the car. The vivacious career woman had disappeared somewhere in the footwell and I was left with her child.

Explanations were given but in truth the great unfolding of the story took twenty years and more.

In the meantime we got on with life, which involved a shared love of music, writing and art, endless discussions about spirituality and, before long, Sylvia's decision to move to the Isle of Wight from outer London. The plan had been that we carried on seeing each other at the weekends because her counselling practice and contacts were in London, but Sylvia soon found that travelling backwards and forwards was too much. We would pool our resources and buy a large house and Sylvia would run her businesses from there until we were able to develop it into a fully-fledged retreat centre, at which point I would retire...

We looked at numerous places including one with the grand name or some might say peculiar name of Clatterford House. It was a semi derelict, though visually attractive, Georgian dump. Thirteen bedrooms including a Coach house. Dry rot, mould, leaky roof, dog poo, you name it. I was deeply unimpressed; Sylvia saw it's potential. I should say here that it was my fault in the first place that we had looked at it. Having dismissed it ,after three viewings with the estate agent, I was soundly asleep one morning when Sylvia shot up in bed and in her usual outrageously boisterous manner when wired, she shouted out.
'We have to buy that house!'
Being awoken from a deep slumber is bad enough but being awoken to the thought of buying 'The Money Pit' was something else again.

Need I say more than that we did buy it? I realise in retrospect that in those days I could not resist Sylvia's dynamism, her apparent utter lack of fear in the face of utterly daunting prospects. I needed that, I needed someone who 'went for it' against the odds to prove to me that it could be done, for I had never had the nerve. What I did not realise was that behind her driven nature and the ability to 'face things off' was a stark reality that would only come out later. I also did not realise that I would become a builder, a janitor, a foster parent for 'looked after' young people, a small business owner…but that is another story.

Let me step back a moment though.
We meet one lunchtime outside my workplace. Not uncommon in the early years of our relationship. The house is underway with the roof being fixed by two of the most reluctant roofers the world has ever known. It is a sunny day and Sylvia clings to my arm in a girlish way, how wonderful. All of a sudden, she starts punching my arm in a manner that is only just mock.
'Why won't you marry me!!!' She shouts out.
It is that Clatterford moment all over again. I recognise the pattern from a number of similar outbursts since we first met.

The only discussion we have had about marriage was when we first met, when we both agreed we didn't need 'that piece of paper from the city hall' as Joni Mitchell called it. Along with Valentine's Day, Birthdays, Mother's Day etc., etc., I had become used to Sylvia's list of things she didn't do anymore. So, this was a surprise. I recognised the importance of it right away because it was so off the wall. Note made to self, early on in our relationship, if it appears out of the blue, treat it with respect, it actually means something to her.

We marry. A wacky DIY, borrowed Bentley, scaffold climbing, bonfire under the stars wedding where we jump the broomstick. All Sylvia's ideas, adding up to a wedding no one would forget for all the right reasons. No wonder I love her, she is a one off.

I won't steal the story Sylvia needs to tell but several things happen that conspire to not only drop her into the footwell once again but this time a total car crash takes place. Six years of penury followed by several more of recovery. To come out of penury we break the law together, we both take Class A drugs. The experience rates as one of the strangest and the most profound in my life and embeds Sylvia and I in a relationship that is as close as I can imagine one to be. I say this now but there is one more episode which again I will only touch upon for fear of treading on Sylvia's literary toes. As part of her recovery she goes on retreat and comes back in a very strange state. Serene and detached, she has left me, left us. If it was not for my understanding that transformative states seldom last for long when the person returns to their normal life then when she says to me 'I could leave you today and it wouldn't matter' I might have taken her at her word. Fortunately, even though it takes around six months or so she does come back, albeit with an abiding awareness of another state of being.

I am not the long-suffering hero I might appear to be in this book. I know there were plenty of occasions over the years where I felt angry, lost, afraid, frustrated, and even betrayed but the fact is I knew something was deeply wrong. I knew that Sylvia was struggling with a huge problem she had never been able to resolve. That problem came out of her childhood and she needed space, safety, and love to be able to explore it. I am humbled that I was chosen to help her find some of these things. In letting me share her life she helped me to become someone different and I am not afraid to say it, I like that person a lot more than the one she met. So, thank you Sylvia.

Finally, I would ask the reader to understand that writing this book took Sylvia immense courage and fortitude. Revisiting the past, and particularly a difficult past, re-ignites the emotions and the opens up the wounds. Sylvia is a funny, happy, loving, compassionate person in her everyday life. If you ever get the chance to meet her you will not recognise the person she describes in her book. Such is the way we right past wrongs, by proving the wrongdoers false in their description of us. Through our positive behaviour we negate negative narratives. Ok too much alliteration, but I'm allowed, I'm not the author.

David Hughes

1. THE UNRAVELLING OF TIGHTLY KNOTTED BINDINGS

The air is soft against my skin, not yet too hot in the year. I glow and buzz with a sense of achievement at my efforts during this day, both in the garden and in the house. But now it is time to meander along the lane to meet my beloved David. He will be walking the other way, coming home from his day job, one he hates and resents, but stoically continues with, to make sure we can always pay the bills. His day job is not who he is.

Millers Lane is just off our own and involves me walking down Clatterford Shute to cross over the small footbridge at the side of the ford. Here I always linger for a few moments and look westwards across the valley floor, the Lukely Brook meandering so lazily along its path. Much of the water is pumped off upstream nowadays but historically it was a strong riverway which allowed several large industrial mills to turn their water wheels along its course.

I carry on ahead once more, continue up the last of the Shute and then left turn up a steep incline into Millers Lane itself.

I love the Shute and Millers Lane. It is like walking into another century, one that is still full of insects, fields, and wildflowers. There are sheep calling across the field above, an ancient horned breed kept by the Carisbrooke Castle English Heritage staff to maintain the grass in the field and to be in keeping with the historic building itself. The castle looks across the valley at us in our home. We see the sun rising behind it and setting facing it, slowly putting the castle into a spotlight and then into darkness. We watch it every day from our bedroom window.

Though the castle looms high above me as I walk, I am not considering its presence at all. I can't see it due to the incline of the hill above me and I am walking down the lane, my nose, ears and eyes fully connected to the spring fragrances, sounds and sights. It's a charming single carriageway, with high banks on one side, full of wildflowers, mostly campions at this spring-time of year, a few dandelions, and my favourites, the stitchwort, so dainty, a delicate white with its five tiny pairs of petals fanning out like stars. I often wonder why they are called stitchwort. I remind myself to look it up later.

The lane undulates and meanders gently along its winding route. Occasional cute cottages emerge around a bend here or there, always on the left as I am walking, facing the steep banking of the castle hill, all so familiar. I have walked this same lane almost every weekday evening for nearly a year now. It takes me roughly 20 minutes to reach our meeting point, the place that means we cannot miss each other accidentally by taking a slight detour. There is no alternative from here, it is straight home.

About a mile from home, just coming around the corner I see David's distinctive outline and speed up, impatient to take his hands in mine and re-connect after a day busy working, apart from each other. A few yards more and I break into a small run come skip motion to get there even more quickly. Always impatient and enthusiastic, I throw myself into his arms. We stand for a moment or so holding each other, connecting, not thinking how it might look if others are around, just being with each other.

'Hi how was your day?' I speak first.

'Nothing special, over, gone, history. How about yours?'

I start giving him a list of everything I've done that day as we are slowly walking towards home again, our arms around each other. He listens quietly for a few items.

'Hey! Stop. You don't have to tell me an inventory of everything you've done, you don't have to justify yourself to me.'

'Yes, I do, or I'll have to kill myself.'

The words come out of my mouth in a sort of choking motion and I am instantly stunned and silenced. David is too. He stops walking and pulls me around to look at him,

'What on earth do you mean, what have you just said?'

I stand there, mouth opening and closing, making no sound, still in slight shock. I don't know where these words come from, but they just came out of my mouth. I know it isn't a joke, and so does he. Somewhere deep down I have just let slip a truth which I have no idea ever even existed in my psyche.

'I d d don't know'. I stammer, confused and slightly ashamed at my own words.

David takes my hand once more and we continue walking.

'Let's get home and talk this one through,' he says. We continue in shocked silence.

Our house is only slightly less derelict than it was when we bought it a year ago. When we get back, dinner is ready. No one else is in tonight. We take our plates up into the garden and sit in the last of the evening light to eat. We're still not really saying much beyond functional exchanges and negotiations, still both in some state of shock about what happened in the lane. Our meal is completed in companionable silence, with the odd word here or there. Neither of us know how to start the conversation we know we must have. Once we have completed our meal, I take the plates inside and come back out to where David is still sitting.

'Can I show you what I've done today?'

'I can see my love, you've cleared masses, the garden is really taking shape now.'

'No, inside too. George and I worked hard this morning to get that back corridor cleared. I think it's beginning to look a little like a proper house once more, kind of connected up with itself.'

George is the builder who stayed on once all the other trades left. He is a jack of all trades, sufficient to meet our needs to complete this massive project we took on, a thirteen-bedroom, twenty-eight roomed derelict Georgian property which we want to turn into a retreat mindfulness meditation centre. Before us it had been a small hotel, then a pub for a few years, and before that, for most of its life, a slightly grand country family home.

The original half cellars at the back of the house, built into the slope of the hill we reside on, had been mostly destroyed in the process and been broken down into men's urinals and beer storage, with false walls, steps and general mess. It was mostly smashed through and cleared out when the plumbing was re-done but left pretty full of rubble and messed up. George and I had started planning out how we would manage the various levels and prop up where original walls had been removed with not enough support left behind. It was early days but the shape of things to come was now clear.

'You have been working hard today haven't you.'

'Yup, really pleased. We can start to get on with this area now, it's been such a grotty spot.'

'I didn't realise how much you really did today when you were giving me the list.'

And it was back. My list. My need to make this list.

'Shall we go and sit down and talk about it.'

David gently takes my hand and leads me into our general living room, the first room we managed to make habitable a mere seven months after we'd moved in, a room with new carpet, rehashed curtains and furniture we could relax in.

'OK so where did that come from?'

He looks at me with his big gentle blue eyes, direct and piercingly honest.

'I don't know, I suppose I must believe it. It must come from my childhood, everything does it seems, but which part I don't know.'

I'm still genuinely confused by what had come out of my mouth a couple of hours earlier but not yet ready to realise its full significance.

'I guess we shall have to explore that and try and work it out won't we.'

I hear a distant voice coming from somewhere deep down – 'don't trust, you don't deserve this, he will realise his mistake in time'. David takes both my hands in his and looks me straight in the face, his eyes full of love and softness.

'What you have to understand Sylvia is that I didn't marry you for any other reason than that I wanted you in my life. You don't have to do anything to be a joy to me. You can spend a whole day doing nothing and I shall be just as pleased to see you in Millers Lane waiting for me, or even not bothering to wait for me there, but staying here until I get home.

He pauses briefly to see if his words are sinking in.

'How can I make you understand how much I love you and want to be with you, whatever you do? There is no list you have to fulfil to please me, no agenda waiting to trip you up and make you fail once more. That is all gone, all in the past. We are here together. I know how hard you work. I see it every day. You don't need to tell me anything, I can see it myself. You have never let me down once in the last four years and I hope I've never let you down either.'

I listen to his short speech and realise the words are wonderful.

I've always longed to hear them, I love them, I ache for them, but I cannot take them in. I just cannot believe that this could apply to me, that this wonderful man who I married a few months ago and whom I met three years earlier in the most unexpected ways possible, could really feel that way about me. It just does not compute, not for me. I shrug a little, releasing the intensity of the moment from my body.

'I know you say that. I just find it hard to remember. Sorry to be a pain.'

'You're not a pain,' he laughed gently. 'This is real. I'll just have to spend my life making you believe it, won't I.'

'Ok I do believe you, but I can't believe it relates to me, that's all. I'll work on it.'

I pause and think deeply for a few moments, wanting to give him something back, some re-assurance that it will be ok.

'I don't know why you love me but I'm really glad you do.'

'That's a start. I'll just have to keep telling you how much I do love you until you believe it for yourself, won't I.'

I nod, still feeling somewhat sheepish and lost, and give him a hug which he returns. We hold each other for a few moments until I pull away. I feel uncomfortable and want to change the subject. There are some bits we need to organise before George comes back the next morning, clearing some space and discussing the next stage. Do we want steps up to the courtyard door, to take into account the different levels, do we want full width steps or steps at the side and a small platform?

We opt for the latter. It is easier and provides small cupboards into which we can stuff everything we are storing in case we might find a use for it. There are boxes of old Victorian floor tiles piled up in the corner which we must move. I rescued these years before from a wonderful Victorian mansion in south London that was being destroyed to build a new block of flats. So much artistry went into those houses and it was all being broken into pieces, nothing being reclaimed. I broke in at a weekend and lifted as many as I could. These will go into the intended cupboards and eventually form the flooring in this back-corridor area, but for now we must repair the ceiling, put in some beams and generally make the space workable once more.

This project we have taken on is huge. The house plus cottage, a converted stable block, has roughly twenty eight rooms in total, including attics and bathrooms, though we have removed about five excess bathrooms which were ruining the feel of the original rooms, changing their classical dimensions and making them awkward where they should have been elegant. They are gradually becoming spacious and bright once more.

There is so much to do here that it can feel utterly overwhelming and it is all I do each day, more or less, work with George or work in the garden creating my heart's desire as I think it through in design and planting terms. I am also now aware of how little I know on all fronts. Ignorance can be an amazing boost to one's confidence at times though. You don't realise how much you don't know and can learn through experience, sometimes called the hard way, but that's ok too with gardening. Plants are quite forgiving.

Once the essential business is taken care of, we settle down for the rest of the evening, not a great deal of time left but that necessary break between day and night that allows restful sleep. David is playing his guitar and I'm just sitting listening adoringly as his soft gentle resonant voice sings to me, songs he has written and some we both just love. Sometimes I sing along. Even though I know my voice is not one to be generally heard, I do enjoy singing. It is such a joyful activity and he is very generous.

I'm still reflecting on our earlier discussion and feel slightly insecure, uncertain that my comment might undermine us, present a burden that he won't be able to maintain. I seek to reassure him and downplay my comment and what may lie beneath it.

'Don't worry about me my love, I'm just an old wobbly feelings thingy twit head.'

David immediately stops playing and roars with laughter.

'What did you just call yourself?'

'Old wobbly feelings thingy twit head - I think that's what I said anyway.'

David is still laughing, though less raucously now.

'I've never heard that before.'

'I made it up I guess. It's just what I'm like. You don't have to take too much notice of me and the things I say or do. It's not that important.'

'Hmmmm, well I might just disagree with you on that one, don't you think? We might have to agree to disagree.'

'Well what I mean is I'm full of rubbish and I don't think you need to take too much notice of it.'

'In that case we definitely disagree because I think I need to take a lot of notice of you and the things you say.'

I look at him doubtfully. Somewhere in the distant far reaches of my mind something, or someone, is still saying 'don't trust this, you don't deserve this kindness, it is not for you'. I shrug it off, but I am left looking at David as if from a distance, not quite able to plunge into the depths of trust he richly deserves from me.

He sees my doubtful face and reaches out a hand.

'You're important to me. When will you understand that? Do you want to talk about it more?'

'No. I just don't want to drag you down or bore you.'

'You won't. I am still right here and have no intention of going anywhere, whatever happens, whatever comes out of your mouth or head. I want to know it all.'

David pulls me into his arms and holds me for a while. I struggle to relax and accept his words. They are still not sitting comfortably, yet I know they should be. I know this man. I knew him deeply when we first met four years ago, as if we had already known each other forever. But something inside me is resisting his love and tenderness, his openness to me, to all of me, even those deep dark corners we all have but prefer not to acknowledge. They're showing themselves to us, baffling us both. Yet David is accepting of that and I'm not.

We lie in each other's arms a while longer, sprawled across the sofa, until it gets too uncomfortable and I stand up. We're both in our mid-forties and already backs are not as tolerant as they once were.

'Do you want a drink before we turn in?'

'No, I'm good thanks, you go ahead.'

I walk into the kitchen, make some fruit tea, and return to the sitting room where David is now reading. I watch him for a while and then I remember to look up stitchwort. I have a large collection of books about plants, herbs and gardening. It's one of my passions.

I eventually find a reference and read that it is called stitchwort because it is supposed to cure the strong pain called a stitch when you have exerted yourself too much. I love natural folklore and green witchery. I think about what I might do in the garden the next day. In my mind's eye it is already flourishing and abundant with plants, but the reality is there is a great deal more work to do before I reach that stage. I yawn loudly and stretch out my legs.

'I'm going up now.'

'OK just behind you'.

I'm woken in the morning with a cup of tea on the table next to my pillow. I sit up and my head touches something above me on the bed head. A piece of paper with 'Old Wobbly Feelings

Thingy Twit head' in large black print is now blu-tacked above my head. I roar with laughter too as he climbs back into bed with me for the last few moments before he must walk back down Millers Lane to go to work. George will be arriving shortly afterwards.

2. THE ACCUMULATION OF SMALL ACTS OF UNKINDNESS

I am born in March 1955, a time of year when it is no longer officially winter but feels much as if it still is. It has been a brutally cold winter in most of the country with high levels of snowfall. But it starts to warm up slightly by the time I am on the move. It is a time I still love in the gardening year, when snowdrops and crocus are flowering if not already going over and the bold bright yellow of daffodils pervade suburban gardens everywhere. A spring baby, arriving just after the spring equinox. From what I have been told I am a relatively calm baby, sleeping easily, feeding well, generally relaxed and content within myself. This all makes my Mother feel very good about herself as a Mother. But then I grow up, slightly.

'You were very much wanted. Your Mother went on and on about having a child since the time just after she and your father got married'.

My Mother's cousin Shirley is sitting in a cousin's garden relating this to me when I am in my early fifties and still apparently well and robust. She means well, she is saying this to me to make me feel better after we have just had a showdown with Mother, but it doesn't help at all. It feels glib, another denial of my own truth. She doesn't know how far off she is. My brother and sister are both also present and are also deeply upset. Mother has just dragged them off to inform them that I am cut out of her will and they must come and see her more often or they will be too. This is how she treats us as her children, commodities to be bought and sold, to put up against one another to coerce and bully in order to get her will done.

Shirley says she loved me once. Perhaps?

That was not what it seemed to me though, ever…….

Late Summer 1958

'You're not the child I wanted! I'm having another one and this will be my best child, the one I want. Not you, I don't want you anymore.'

She is standing over me, raging. She feels so tall, a giant looming. I feel so small, so vulnerable. I am taken totally by surprise.

I'm sitting on my bedroom floor, playing with something though I can't see exactly what. But her words are cutting through me like skewers through tenderised meat, causing sharp pains in my abdomen. I fold over, collapsing in on myself, and am now bent double on the floor looking up at her. I don't understand what I've done in that moment to make her change so suddenly. This is a new Mother; one I have not known before. Part of me steps aside and observes her closely, the other part is still lying on the floor in pain and confusion.

'Mother, Mother please stop, please don't – I'm sorry, please stop'. The child on the floor is talking, I am just watching now.

She laughs strangely and repeats it, over and over again, 'You - are - not - what - I - wanted, you - are – not - the - daughter I expected to have'. She enunciates each word very specifically.

The pain of the words, her contempt and vitriol going into my body intensifies. I feel as if I'm about to die. But I don't know what dying is. All I know is I feel very, very afraid and desperate to stop this raging torrent that pours out of her and onto me, clings to me, covers me and threatens to smother me, her thick choking dark slime coating me with a blanket of hatred and blocking out all light.

I cower even lower, not daring to look up, and ask once more, 'Mother I'm sorry, please stop, you're hurting me. Mother it hurts a lot'.

Amidst the suffering there is confusion. I don't know what it is I've done. I don't know what has changed.

I sneak a look at her once more. She is silent now, still standing over me, still foam at her mouth and a triumphant look in her eye. She's smiling. It's an ugly grimace spread across her face. Not a look of loving tenderness for her suffering child but a smile of triumphant glee, a gloat, a real, monstrous enjoyment of my distress, a sense of achievement. She has power and is now using it and experimenting with it.

I start to move slowly away from her, crawling across the floor.

'You - are - despicable.'

Her spittle flicks onto my face. She is now crouching down closer to me. I don't know what the word means but I know it isn't good. I eventually hear it so many times over the following years, I come to know it well.

I peek up at her once more. She looks like a slavering beast, spitting and screaming at me about something else but the words no longer mean anything to me. They are just repeated over and over again, a chant, a mantra.

She stands again, is dancing now, from one foot to the other, with glee. I remain curled on the floor, silent, as she demolishes my sense of self, my sense of worth, and my sense of belonging, being wanted and being loved.

'Just wait 'til your father gets home'.

Father, my sanctuary. My strong safe haven. The one who gives me a break from Mother at weekends. Perhaps all is not well between us already, though I cannot pinpoint it. I am always labelled a daddy's girl and told later how hurtful my Mother found that. But Fathers have scarcity value at weekends, and they do different things. They represent a break from weekday routines. When we go out as a family, if my hands are cold, he holds them in his huge hands and keeps them warm for me. I make him laugh and he makes me laugh, in good ways.

And now that is being threatened too. I can feel her anger and resentment of our relationship and know it is now under threat.

My pleading seems to spur her on to even greater triumphs of cruelty. I look up at her once more and see how impervious she is to my distress, to my existence, to my being.

I feel as if I'm now out of my body, watching this scene. I see that new ugly face of hers differently, more objectively. I know it, recognise it from deep down. It's strangely familiar, as if I'm expecting it. Intuitively I know it will always be like this from now on. I stop pleading, stop responding, stop being present. I instinctively suck in all my energy fields and withdraw from her. I let her carry on until she has finished. I'm quiet now, motionless, unresponsive, and eventually she gives up.

She walks away. But nothing for me will ever be the same again.

My confusion arises because until this point it seems Mother and I have got on well enough. I am a very curious individual and ask a lot of questions and mostly she answers them. She seems to enjoy being the wise knowing one

Her words though, 'you are not what I wanted'!

Coming after three years of feeling the central focus of the family, first grandchild, niece, they are a complete shock, and totally overturn my world.

I am writing this aged 64 and in the 23rd year of a relationship with the most loving tender husband you can imagine. We adore each other. This I know through and through. But those words still haunt me. I wonder how he came to feel that way about me. ME!!!! This worthless person. I still wonder when he will wake up and realise he too has been landed with a monster whom he thought was wonderful. I am always aware that the scales may suddenly fall from his eyes. They never seem to though. He just loves me more and more deeply.

These memories have been locked away from my consciousness until they are released in a total PTSD based breakdown in my early fifties. A series of events lead to a complete breakdown with complex PTSD. That probably originates from this point and was gradually built upon over the following weeks, months and years, until it became my experience of life, always this fear and terror in the shadows and always waiting to leap out on me.

The specific memory came as an episodic flashback, one of many hundreds, almost all recovered memories released by the breakdown which was more a breaking apart of my being. I was more than torn apart, I was shredded into millions of pieces. What would happen was that I would go to bed and attempt to sleep. Mostly I didn't sleep at all during this illness, but my body would get to a state of complete exhaustion, and just shut down. I would sleep for a couple of hours and then wake up gasping and in total shock trauma, often crying out loud and feeling nothing but pure blind terror and an intense desire to harm myself. My entire body would be in pain too, locked into muscle spasm and the skewers being pushed into me again and again and again. The illness took about six years to run its course and another four years to regain any confidence or sense of being. That process is still ongoing. Each flashback brought a new memory back to life in a state of complete shock, reliving all the horrors of them in entirety each time. That is what traumatic memory feels like. I had completely locked them all away and had no recollection of any of it until the breakdown released them all into the open. It was to become a great blessing and a huge nightmare to survive. It would test both of us to our total limits and we would make it.

But I didn't know that back then, I fought against the illness and breakdown and struggled to stay on top of it for as long as I could, until I realised that I had no choice but to surrender to it and see where it led me. Fighting was just making it worse and it wasn't helping anyway.

The how's and whys that all happened is the basis of my story though, and what I have learned from it since then. It has been and is simultaneously the worst and best part of my life. But without the husband you met in the first chapter, I wouldn't have made it through alive.

My father's Mother, 'little Grandma' we call her because she's barely five feet tall, also lives with us. She does most of the basic housework. Her husband, my Dad's dad, died before I am born, in 1951, and I suppose Dad just feels obliged to care for his Mother from there on. I am mostly discouraged from talking to her by Mother, but when I do, I recall nothing much occurring between us. She is a live-in non-person in that household already by the time I'm aware of her as a personality, and that becomes a greater and greater state of reality as time goes by.

We originally live in her house, a small semi-detached, three-bedroom house in Selsdon, a suburb of Croydon, south London. I live in her house for my first three years but remember little about it other than a deep rote learned memory of the address. Perhaps Mothers impending second child sparks the move, and we transfer to a much larger, 1920's detached four-bedroom house. It has dark foreboding oak veneer panelling around the hall walls and two large living rooms. That is how it feels to me, coming from a much smaller house and being small myself.

There is also a large enclosed garden where I'm allowed to go and play alone, which I love. Digging – always digging in the mud. Once I am a little older it is digging to the other side of the world, but at three it is just digging because it feels good to do it. It gives me a sense of escape from indoors, though I don't recognise this specifically, just that I prefer being outside. I want to dig a tunnel to the other side of the world, to arrive in the alternative reality that I feel deeply does exist. I feel it tangibly though cannot touch or taste it, but I do feel its presence strongly. I want to reach it on my own. A new world to be in.

The kitchen is the only reliably warm room in the house in winter as it contains the boiler and cooker. I like to sit in there at the kitchen table doing drawing or looking at books. I love books and learn to read very quickly indeed.

Memories of those very early days in the new house are scant, glimpses really, unclear in exact dates or times, but real nevertheless. Memory is unreliable when it is recall from history and is very different from relived traumatic memories which are clear and present and as powerful as they originally were lived, exactly as they were experienced.

I remember Mother through laundry days, with an open top electric washing machine. We also have a manual mangle stuck onto a tabletop, through which she winds all the clothes to squeeze the water out of them. I help her by catching them the other side and making sure they go into the basket and not onto the floor.

We get along ok as far as I can remember, though it is so long ago, and those ordinary memories are less vivid than those locked in by trauma and then released by breakdown. I have no recollection of ever having been difficult or contrary to her in those early days and rather remember enjoying sharing the chores with her, enjoying my roles and contributions. This is very much my nature nowadays too.

But now I am lying on the floor in pain, unable to move. She has stopped, gone and left me 'to think about it'.

I am.

I am thinking about it but can make no sense of what just happened. Mostly I feel numb with shock and a strong sense of not being in my body anymore, but watching myself lying on the floor, very still.

I now understand these sharp wounds were my chakras being assaulted with seriously destructive energy. Even as a child I am a very open and a highly intuitive individual who senses everything through the subtle energies. I still do.

I try to behave as normal when Dad came home. I hope he will be ok with me. But as soon as he gets inside the door, Mother takes him aside and tells him how much I have upset her. Even while he is taking his coat off, she is telling him. Though I can't hear the words she was saying, I feel them all. She can't wait to tell him how awful I am. When he comes into the kitchen his look of disapproval tells me everything, his words spoken coldly, to be good for my Mother and stop upsetting her when she is pregnant. He doesn't really look at me again that evening.

The four of us are sitting around the kitchen table having tea and no one looks at me. It feels as if I no longer exist to them.

I eat quietly and quickly, ask to be excused and retreat to my bedroom. I take myself to bed devastated, alone, confused. Mother comes up a little while later and checks I've cleaned my teeth. I have. That's it.

I sleep deeply, dreamlessly, almost a blacked out, comatose sleep: it drowns out the sorrow.

In the morning it is cold on my face, the draft coming from below the curtains. My bed is directly underneath the window. I lift the corner of my bedroom curtain. I can do all this without leaving the warmth of my covers. It is nearly light but still that grey of winter morning sunrise.

I notice the ice on the inside of my bedroom window, such finely detailed intricate patterns of lacework creeping up from the bottom of the wooden frames. It is so fragile and pretty. I trace its fine contours with my eyes, taking in each delicate spike or wave across its web like design.

Then I breathe on it and watch it slowly melt and disappear, a small trickle of water running down onto the sill below, a small pool lying there. So still and so complete, slightly raised. As I watch it, I feel I'm inside that globule of melted ice water, merging with it in one reality.

I hear my parents moving around in the rest of the house. I feel no inclination to bound out to them and greet them on this new day, so I stay put and study the ice, absorbed by its existence on my window.

Eventually Mother comes in.

'Get up then get dressed, you don't need me to baby you anymore'.

My clothes are underneath the eiderdown on my bed. I pull them into the bed with me and manage to shed my night clothes and dress without exposing my child flesh to the bitter cold of the icy morning in an unheated bedroom. I take a deep breath and go downstairs to find breakfast. Everything seems as if nothing had happened yesterday. Perhaps I'd imagined it all. Mother seems very brisk and cheerful, but distant, cold.

Dad eats his breakfast quickly before dashing off to catch his train to London, clad in a dark suit and tie already, his uniform of dark winter-lined raincoat, briefcase, and bowler hat all in place to grab on the way out. I can still smell his coat after all these decades, can still recall it hanging damp in the hallway every evening, disappearing as he leaves each day.

I always remember spending a lot of time in my bedroom alone even when very young and I wonder now that I was not allowed to spend more time with the adults in my life. Perhaps I did but have no recall of it. Ordinary memories of that time are very hazy and distorted by time and subsequent events. The flashbacks come back as whole memories though, complete with physical dimensions such as the noises, smells, the physical pain of those moments. The feeling of being shot through with arrows dipped in emotional venom so powerful they will paralyse me for much of the rest of my life.

3. FLOWERS ON FRIDAYS

The following Friday, as if the above never happened, I get my flowers.

Dad always brings me a bunch of anemones and Mother a bunch of freesias from a flower stand outside the station every Friday on his way home from work. I look forward to them each week.

I think 'it will be ok with Dad, at least he seems to love me still'.

Flowers mean love, it seems to me in our family. They make Mother smile too. I want freesias like hers but am told not to be so ungrateful and selfish, they are special flowers for Mother only. In my three years old mind, and after that outburst, this equates, to 'she is loved more than you'! Mother's flowers smell nice and mine have no fragrance. Mine are larger, in brash colours and clumsy in the vase, hers are elegant and dainty. My flowers are lesser than hers because I am worthless. That was what I've been told and shown.

To this day fragrance in flowers remains very important to me but I hate freesias; their smell especially I find cloying and sickly. They remind me of my Mother too much. They remind me of not being good enough.

After that episode Mother behaves as if it had never happened and things go back to 'some kind of normal' for a while. I continue to work the mangle with her on Mondays and read, dig or draw on other days. Afternoons, after lunch we watch children's TV. Tales from the Riverbank was my favourite, and Andy Pandy, and the Wooden tops. Then we watch Woman's Hour, on

TV in those days too. I take it all in with equal interest. My brain feels like a sponge for ideas and information.

I question my Mother,

'Do I have a good balanced diet?'

We have just been listening to the importance of that on the TV. She laughs

'Of course you do, I make sure you're well fed'.

It seems fairly normal once more. I slightly relax.

Little Grandma is dusting the house in the background every day, vacuuming afterwards. Mother seems mostly to do cooking and darning socks, sitting with her feet up because of her varicose veins. Unless it's laundry day.

It is never normal though. I know that even as a child. I just know what it is that I live with as being my own normal. But I feel deeply and intuitively that something is seriously wrong.

I have no way of expressing that sense. I'm terrified of this baby about to be born, big and blooming in my Mother's belly. What will happen to me when it arrives? Will I be cast out completely as Mother has suggested will happen?

How can a nearly four-year-old articulate these fears other than to just have general anxiety about everything that might happen next.

My sister is born in winter, in January 1959. I am immediately labelled jealous by Mother, but it seems everyone else is also joining in, everyone, whatever I do or do not do.

'She's just jealous.' Or 'It's jealousy.'

This jealousy is clearly a terrible thing, everyone seems to agree, but I don't really understand what it means yet. Does that mean I am also terrible too? I have no idea how I manifest this jealousy. I just feel abandoned.

And I am then summarily dismissed. By everyone. A total abandonment by my whole family.

The expectations are great. My Mother has just had my sister, her sister Mercia has my cousin Emma shortly afterwards and their cousin Shirley is around the same time too, to her first child, my second cousin Julia. We go from one to four girls in a few short months. Somehow I am now excluded from this gathering of family with all the babies. There is a family photo of me around this time. I see how disjointed I am from my face, how fearful too. I'm standing near my father in the photo.

Up until now I've been the only child of my generation, occupying that position for nearly four years, enough to get used to it. I feel very insecure and seek re-assurance from others, not Mother who now makes it clear she has little or no time for me beyond duties like meals. What might be called attention seeking, all labelled as jealousy.

No one knows I feel so fearful of my sister's arrival, how could they? And I did also love her greatly, my little sister. But I am terrified of the power her position gives her over me and I determine to make her an ally. Again, no words form in my mind, no active plan, just instinctive for a child, for her own survival. I feel somehow I'm responsible for her protection from the ravening monster I now know lives inside my Mother's frame.

If I show any emotion at all, that is the response. It's all I hear about myself, though to be honest jealousy is never really my thing and never has been. I can't say I've never felt jealous ever, of course I have, but it has been very rare and barely noticeable.

During the immediate time of my sister's birth, flowers arrive daily from Dad, but only for Mother.

I don't remember who is looking after me but I'm guessing my little Grandma did. For the next few days it seems I have dropped off the radar completely.

But then Mother comes home from hospital and Dad is back to normal. I tried my very best to be good and some days I seemingly manage it, though it's never clear why this day is OK and not that one too. There doesn't seem much of a difference to me. Every so often Mother suddenly and intermittently pronounces my badness to me, not quite as viciously as before, more as a matter of fact now well established between us.

I have since learned that this is a form of emotional manipulation called 'gaslighting' and is very common behaviour from people with Narcissistic Personality Disorder. The aim is to make you feel so uncertain that the perpetrator has you totally in their power and you turn to them for reassurance because they are the ones who make you feel so uncertain. It is an insidious system of making you doubt everything that you think, see, feel, or hear. Your entire experience is put into doubt and you are left utterly lost and defenceless against the perpetrator who now has total power. Couple that with the power of parental control and responsibility and it becomes a totalitarian experience of the most abusive kind. I end up both believing and doubting everything I am told about myself and everything I'm told about other people by Mother. I trust no one anywhere in my life about anything. I still struggle with that.

Life resumes a new rhythm for the following four months or so, but I am clearly out of favour with Mother and it isn't changing. She just sort of ignores me, and some days finds fault with me at every turn. Dad is given regular reports on how 'bad' I've been that day or how 'difficult' and I begin to just wait for his disapproval, as one waits for anything routinely in life. He is never given a good report though. No news is good news.

Friday is the best day though. Friday is flowers and they always put Mother in a good mood. Once more it seemingly makes us both happy

That gives me an idea!

How to win Mother back and show her I can be her wanted child too. My sister and I can share her. That seems reasonable to me. I just need to show her how kind I really am.

Flowers seem the obvious option but picking from our garden is not allowed. I come up with an amazing plan that makes complete sense in my four-year-old mind.

I decide to go around all the local gardens and 'borrow' a flower from here or there so no one would notice or miss anything, and this is how I can give my Mother a bunch of flowers. I imagine her smiling at me like she does at Dad when he brings her the Friday freesias.

Perhaps this will make it all ok with her again. She is ignoring me emotionally but goes through the motions of caring when anyone else is around. This confuses me. Does she or does she not love me? Perhaps I have a chance to win her back.

Finally, the day comes when I know I can put my inspirational plan into action. It's warm and sunny, a mild late spring day. I need no coat. Nothing to alert her to my secret plans to make her love me again, properly.

I sneak out of the side gate while she is busy with my sister and creep along the road, about four houses and stop. I watch to see if there is anybody around, then I edge myself into the corner of their front garden and take some polyanthus from one plant, just two stems, then race back to the pavement, heart pounding in case I am seen.

I wait, crouching down by the wall, and make my way carefully along to the next garden. Here are some forget-me-nots that go well with the deep velvety red of the polyanthus. Same stealth approach. Mission accomplished. From another garden I take a deep orange marigold. It looks too little. More flowers, more love.

I am completely absorbed in my task of collecting this beauty.

I move one garden further along. There are some more polyanthus in a row. I pick two more flower heads and decide my flowers are a big enough bunch to present.

The flowers fascinate me, their colours and textures. Why do they smell so different to each other? The petals seem to be made of the most amazing stuff, rich and subtle, delicate and fragile, so easily damaged and so very, very beautiful.

I feel pleased with my own ingenuity and intended offering. I am confident it will win her approval. I let myself in through the back gate once more and go into the kitchen to find her.

Mother hasn't noticed I've been gone. She's watching TV and

holding my sister. I don't know where my little Grandma is, though she rarely leaves the house and never has any visitors at all.

I walk into the sitting room and take a deep breath, full of hope and good intentions, wanting to feel that glow of being wanted once more.

'Hello Mother, here are some flowers I got for you so you can love me again.' I hold out my offering.

Instead of a nice sweet smile of loving recognition, suddenly the ravening monster returns.

'Thief, you little thief, how dare you, where did you get these, you despicable child, I can't trust you for anything. How did you get out? Where did you get these, did you pick these in our garden? We don't grow these flowers.'

And on and on, the monster looming over me and I cower, close myself in and wait for her to finish. She puts my four-month-old sister down onto the sofa, and Hazel immediately starts crying again.

I am not responding, not crying or looking at her. I am just silent.

This time, because I am not responding she picks me off the floor and shakes me by my shoulders, screaming into my face, 'look at me, tell me where you got these from'.

I stutter, 'I got them from the other gardens.'

She screams once more at me, puts my sister in her pushchair and drags me out of the door to show her where.

Then she begins knocking on doors and exposing me as a thief to anyone who is at home.

Most of all they looked bemused, shocked and unperturbed by my theft.

One says, 'What a sweet thought you had for your Mother.'

'Yes well' Mother stutters, momentarily stumped, 'that's no excuse for stealing'.

'It's hardly theft is it? Not in one so young. No harm in a couple of flowers is there,' says the kindly woman and turns to close the door.

We get to the end of her driveway and Mother turns on me once more,

'See how you show me up in public, you despicable child', this time hissing through clenched teeth so no one else can hear. She shakes me roughly by the arm and continues dragging me to the final door, determined to complete my humiliation and frustrated by the kindness of strangers.

Four houses along, as far as I had dared to go on my own at four years of age.

The woman who answered the door was initially shocked but then broke into a big friendly smile and said

'It doesn't matter, you can keep the flowers, we have plenty more. We've only just moved in so would your daughter like to play with mine, they look about the same age'. And she turned and called out 'Charlotte'.

Charlotte comes downstairs to meet me. She has long blond plaits, blue eyes and looks a little shy, as I am too. I immediately like her.

Charlotte Smith is my first ever friend of my own age, an only child who likes solitary activities, especially reading. We both learn to read before going to school and have a lot in common.

She immediately invites me to stay and play, for a couple of hours, and to go home at four o'clock.

My Mother reluctantly agrees, relieved to be rid of me but shocked and frustrated by how her intention to publicly humiliate me has backfired. Instead I've gained a friend and am invited to join them. It feels like someone is contradicting my Mother about me and I like it. Mother leaves me there, taking the flowers back home and putting them into a pot as 'evidence for my father to witness', she told me later.

Aunty Peggy, as Charlotte's Mother told me to call her, offers me cream soda and cake halfway through the afternoon. I have no idea such delights existed. We've never had anything like that at home. Plain bread and butter with jam or honey or cheese sometimes for tea but never a mid-afternoon snack unless we have visitors, and then not for children.

We're greedy and ungrateful for what we're given to eat if we show signs of wanting treats in front of other people, though cake is served for us all when guests were present. I look but never ask. It is still post war and there is still minor rationing around. I remember all food being a treat, a righteous indignation in my Mother's voice often underlying anything she spoke about regarding memories of rationing, as if it had been a direct deprivation for her, not a collective effort for all to survive.

Here with Aunty Peggy I feel safe, wanted, appreciated, encouraged. It feels good being in a house filled with love and warmth.

When Mother finally comes to collect me to come home, I feel such a great reluctance to go with her. I dread going back into the potential torture chamber. She tells me off for that too, and fearfully and reluctantly – interpreted as sulkily, I follow her home.

'Say thank you for having me' my Mother prompted.

'Thank you, Aunty Peggy for having me' I said.

'Not Peggy'- responded my Mother brusquely, 'that's not how to address your elders politely, Mrs ..' she looked up at Peggy who quietly said

'Aunty Peggy is fine'

We get home moments later. As soon as the front door is closed, with my baby sister still in her arms.

'How dare you show me up like that in front of my new friend, behaving so badly.'

She is screaming at me once more, the frothing, spitting monster returned, berating me for my reluctance to come home with her again, showing her up in public.

Hazel starts crying. Wailing. A seriously distressed sound. An infant in fear. I want to hold and comfort her.

'Now look, you've made your sister cry. Go to your room and wait until your father gets home'.

Dad is told about my theft and how much I've upset my sister and made her cry and I'm sent to bed without any love, or stories. I cry myself to sleep. Quietly. So no one can hear me.

4. STEPPING OUT
OF OLD SHELLS.

It is summer 2019 and the tenth Ventnor fringe is in full swing. I apply early in the year and am given a chance to take part as a poet in the free fringe. This suits me. It is my debut as a performing poet. David has come to support me as ever, and to film me.

I have been writing poetry covertly since a teenager but knew, at that time, I had not found a voice. Later on, I had a friendship with someone who also gets me back into poetry and although those attempts are also pretty dire, there were one or two lines that worked well. Some of those got kept on file but I mostly ignored and dismissed them.

Until a few years ago.

During my recovery, the writing and poems come pouring out of me. The muse has me in her grip and she isn't letting me go. I surrender and decide to have fun. I don't want to be the best poet in the world. I just want to write poems that people enjoy, that are accessible to people who might otherwise be intimidated by poetry, to invite people into how I think and feel about life and the world, if they want to join me.

I am reading at the Book Bus venue. It's a delightful old French single decker bus filled with second-hand books and stationed in the church yard and carpark of St Catherine's church in Ventnor. The view out across the bay is glorious. The day is sultry hot, with little breeze coming from the sea. You can see the calm flat surface glimmering in the sunlight, reflecting the sky back at you. You can see it above the roofs of the houses scattered and tumbling down the hillside which is Ventnor Bay. As a seaside town on the bottom point of the diamond shaped Island, it is one long sweeping hillside from the downs to the sea, and all built by the Victorians who saw the potential of this wonderful south facing sea cove and beach. Almost everything faces out to sea here. But the rock is full of holes, called vents, and every so often houses or parts of a house disappear down them. Living here really is on the edge in so many ways. A creative energy, a holiday all year round, a fun place to spend time. The ideal spot for an arts festival in all ways.

The churchyard has enough mature trees to create shade. They murmur and whisper in the minimal drafts that float up from the seafront, thermals rather than offshore wind, complete with conversational gulls gliding in circles.

There are wooden benches and rugs on the grass between the gravestones, provided by the organisers. The ambience gentle and comforting, we settle down to wait for my allocated slot. I'm not feeling nervous, though I expect to be. It is more like I feel this is my destiny, this is what I am meant to be doing, right here and now.

Finally, it's time for my slot. I clutch my poems and begin to read. My chocolate collection, some love poems and then some political ones. They go well enough. I know I am reading slightly too fast but cannot slow myself down any further. People laugh at the humorous ones, at my intended lines. This encourages me. David is filming me from one side. I'm determined not to have issues about my nose. I still have body dysmorphia and my nose sideways is one of them. I'm determined to shed all these last traits of fear and self-doubt and just be, do, absent of any self.

At the end I get applause and thanks for the chocolate which is passed around during the chocolate series. Several people come up and say how much they enjoyed my writing, how it made sense to them. That is what I want. Not to be a poet of great critical acclaim but a poet of accessibility. I feel successful in that small way. We pack up and wander down into town to wait until we go to the next gig where other friends of ours are touting their debut act too. Matt and Kat do regular food reviews of all the eateries on the island and their reputation is growing. They are very honest and sometimes a bit brutal but worth reading for the humour they include.

Their combined style works well on stage and the audience is mostly friendly faces. We really enjoy their show. I can see their nerves and slight speed reading also and realise I must develop presentation performance skills if I'm to continue this. I know I will. It feels right. Not ego based or self-promoting, just sharing insights with others for the sake of it. The words matter, not me.

We then go to a burger bar which has the most sublime vegetarian burgers of all time, at a venue called Stripped. This was one of the recommendations from Matt and Kat's food guide to the Isle of Wight

There are two more gigs to listen to before we go home, but my debut is over. I am relaxing in that knowledge. The other shows are mixed but that is the fun of the fringe, a hit and miss adventure into the arts. Many performers come here as a trial run before attempting Edinburgh fringe. We see one show that truly amazes us with the quality of the acting and the storytelling. From Brazil it is a story of double standards and prejudice against transgender people. One actress plays all parts with stunning virtuosity. It's interactive and the audience are the judge and jury. I am deeply inspired by both the writing and the performance.

That night we get home, late for us, nearly midnight. It's straight to bed and sleep, snuggled up against each other as we always are, in spite of the heat, though we do have to separate out later to keep cool.

Four a.m. and I'm fully awake. This is a common occurrence. I rise and slip on a bathrobe. In the sitting room my laptop awaits me, blinking its one red eye at me until I put the lamp on and lighten the whole room. There is almost daylight emerging from the gloom now and the light from the screen is a shock to my eyes. Now is the time I write. Whatever comes into my head, it is often my quiet insomniac hours that are the most productive.

I check and respond to any emails that came in yesterday, check my writing stats for previous online articles and poems and then settle down to the next piece of writing. This calms me and after a couple of hours I feel drowsy once more. I return to bed.

David is used to this routine and puts an arm out almost unconsciously and holds me as I lie with my head on his chest until I feel very sleepy once more. I turn over and fall soundly asleep.

I wake to him bringing me tea, saying it is 8.30 and I need to wake up now. He climbs back into bed and we watch the tops of the trees from our bedroom window. This has been our ritual for two decades now, early morning once but older age and retirement has allowed us more freedom. Before, it was the Castle we looked at every morning but now it is treetops at the bottom of our garden and the neighbours. We moved into a smaller house that was just our home and writing or music creating space, no longer at the beck and call of others, no business always in our home too, no other bodies filling up our space unless as guests. I have found this to be bliss on all levels. I still teach mindfulness elsewhere. It is something I believe in more profoundly than words can convey.

Through the window I can see there's not much happening though it's not too hot yet, you can see that it will be another relentlessly hot day ahead. Shortly I will go out and check my chickens and bees, my morning ritual.

Then I shall start writing again. I have really got back into writing and the words nowadays just seem to pour from me. It is almost as if they bypass my conscious brain and just come from a flow of consciousness. Often poems start off from an image or a sentence or even a pair of words that go well together. Then there are ideas for articles, which stack up on my laptop waiting for me to hit the moment of inspiration which means that is the next one I will work on. Then there are the books. Many of them start off as articles, then they form into books. This passion for writing has come from the aftermath of my breakdown.

So much stuff came up for me and I feel I need to keep some kind of record of it all. No logical reason but it just seems to be the point of everything I've gone through, to reclaim the territory, the narrative from my own experiences and to make it my own triumph. After all, David and I have both paid a high price for the decision to see my father once more, just before he died. That is what sparked off the breakdown which released all these traumatic memories buried so deeply within me for so many decades.

That was over ten years ago and I am still recovering from the fallout of that time, still slowly rebuilding some confidence on the inside, though now it is mostly working out how my, or our life, will go forwards. It is certainly along the creative lines for both of us. We are deeply happy and inspired by this and perhaps it is our reward for enduring and surviving that emotional holocaust.

But today we are working on our first joint novel. David has written most of the body, but I'm heavily involved in it too. It's loosely based on my own life story, a fictional and perhaps kinder version of what I am also trying to write with this memoir.

Life is good. We are more happily together than either of us ever thought possible and we have made this time for us as a couple from now on, though we do both still care for a lot of other people either by giving mutual support, or by being the carer or life assister system. I cannot imagine not wanting to help others.

We also regularly help as volunteers at our local arts centre and are part of a crack team of gallery installers and de-installers for each exhibition. Much of the artwork has featured in my poetry as I sit for three hours per week stewarding the gallery and looking at it. I also read whilst on duty, if there are no people in at any given point. It is a wonderful and productive time for me, for both of us, and we do get to meet some amazing people in the process.

Sometimes I look at David and a slight echo of doubt hovers darkly over me.

Am I really allowed to be this happy in my life?

But nowadays it goes quickly enough too.

Some weeks later David and I are returning from another open mic poetry evening at a new bar in Ryde. It is a strange affair. The owner has gone away and asked a friend to open up for us, but she works elsewhere so cannot arrive until after we should have started. The potential contributors to the evening are the only one's present, apart from two men who arrive later on and sit away from us all. David and I tried out something different tonight. He played guitar as a background to my poems. We weren't sure if it worked but our friend Donna Jones, an amazing poet in her own right, said it did so we have taken heart and are planning to do this a lot more.

This seems to spark a surge of creativity and inspiration in me. Poems written for people as a gift, the Gift of Poetry. Wow. I suddenly realise it doesn't matter if some or none of this comes off, it doesn't matter what I do or do not do. I can just enjoy having a mind that jumps all over the place and come up with all sorts of crazy ideas. I can just enjoy it all and there is no voice saying, 'don't bother, nothing you do is worth anything'. I start to recognise how free I am finally, how amazing it is and what fun life really can be. I feel as if I might burst with joyfulness.

5. THE BUILDING OF COMING STORMS

Mother is the eldest of three sisters, with four years between her (Lorna) and Mercia and 10 years between Mother and Gigi, her pet name, or Flavia. My Grandparents names are Alan and Violet.

There are four years between Lorna and Mercia and almost four years between me and my sister.

It takes me years to recognise the pattern and there is a reason why that four years is significant. But that is a story that needs its own chapter.

At this age of four though, I have no idea of my Mother's own history, what any of this means or why it is happening. All I know is that life is now terrifying, and I can never be sure of anything. One day it all seems fine and the next moment everything just explodes.

All certainty about all the things I'd previously felt confident about is being incrementally taken away from me. Mother is clever with words, and they don't show on the outside, don't leave scars and marks that other people can see. The signs are there of course, damaged children do tell you if you know how to read the signs. I know I still exhibit some of those sometimes when I watch people too closely, not feeling confident about their presence. This is a poem I wrote about it.

Frozen Child

I have a look, a certain kind of stare
that watches closely, intently.

A child monitoring her surroundings
for safety and unknown terrors.

The watching appears rude, invasive,
but I'm not watching you,
just your body, for sudden moves,
just your face, in case it changes
from light to darkness.
It is that instant I await.

Forewarned is forearmed
the child always ready,
prepared for the next attack,
never knowing where it will come from,
how it will manifest, just watching.

A kind of stare, not looking at you
looking beyond at what might be there.

I know I still do this, and I cannot help it.

Back to the historical narrative – 1959 later summer.

Mother takes me and my sister Hazel to see her parents about once a week and I love going there. Mother's Mother, Violet, is called 'big Grandma' since she is five feet nine inches tall. Functional but unflattering names for what should be a tender relationship, but it matches the reality. Tenderness is in short supply. And the loving potential? That is to end shortly.

One day we're just about to go out to visit them when she stops and turns to me.

'You know they don't really like you, don't you? They know what a horrible child you are to your Mother. They are just nice to you because they are nice people.'

Tears well up. Mother sees and continues,

'All of them, they are all just such nice people, you're just lucky to be part of this family', she pauses for effect, to check I'm listening, 'and they all feel so sorry for me having such an ungrateful, sulky moody child like you'.

Then she walks away.

Five minutes later it's time to leave to go to Grandma's house. My sister is laid in her carry cot on the back seat and I squeeze into the space next to it. I hate travelling in cars as I struggle with motion sickness, even on short journeys. I still do sometimes.

When we arrive, my 'big Grandma' throws the door open and picks me up with a great swoop and kisses me on both cheeks, her face beaming with love from ear to ear. I am still her first grandchild.

I am confused.

Mother had just said they don't love me. But that feels like being wanted at the very least. Is that love or not? What is love then?

I ask Grandma if Gigi is upstairs. She is. It's summer and she's home from university. I rush up the stairs to find her in her bedroom. She gives me a huge hug and lets me play with her jewellery; beads and costume broaches pinned all over my dress. I'm convinced I am royalty. She brushes my hair too then lets me brush hers. She has hair so long and thick she can sit on it. I love to play with her hair. Sometimes she plaits it up and I can twirl it around her head in all sorts of designs. Gigi's hair is a feature of some wonder for years in my life, it makes her magical.

When it's tea-time we're called downstairs and go together, hand in hand to Grandma's big cosy kitchen with the big table against the window where you can see the garden at the back of the house. It's a large garden which slopes uphill and has several separate areas. It feels very adventurous for me at four to go beyond the house and up into the outer reaches of the garden, amongst the apple trees at the top. I inherit my love of gardening from my Grandmother. Later in life we will spend a lot of time together out in her garden. But for now, it is still very big for me on my own.

In the kitchen her dog Pippa, a poodle, is snuffling around. They also have a soft fluffy tortoiseshell cat, Puffy, which stands on the sink worktop in the scullery, teasing the dog who can't reach her and just bounces and barks manically non-stop until they are both fed. Then Puffy will jump down right over Pippa's head and be away upstairs before the little dog knows what's happening. The stairgate stops him following her up and her preferred place is always the airing cupboard – well out of reach of small black poodles.

I love Puffy and Pippa and their antics.

We sit and have tea. I have a glass of milk and two biscuits on my plate. Mother is drinking a cup of tea and looking after Hazel.

It feels almost peaceful but there is some sort of a tension, I can always feel it when we're at Grandma's with Mother, a spring waiting to explode. I take another biscuit offered to me.

'Don't be greedy, you'll spoil your proper tea when you get home.'

Mother has started, though she is restrained, but her tone warns me.

'One more biscuit for a growing child won't hurt will it?' Grandma says.

I looked slowly from one to the other, not sure of my ground. There is some sort of contest going on between them, that I can see. Who to trust or believe? I decide to ask.

'Mother says you don't really like me, you're only nice to me because you're such nice people'.

There it is, stated simply and openly, a question perhaps, or a challenge. Mother erupts.

'I never said any such thing. You little liar, she is a liar, you can't trust her'.

She's exploding now and trying desperately not to. I can see that. She seems more worried about Grandma's face. I watch.

'Don't be too hard on the girl Lorna.' Grandma is looking at Mother now, right into her eyes, but Mother glares back and is clearly not going to back down, Eventually Grandma looks away and sort of shrugs.

Gigi leaves the room quickly to return to her bedroom. I try to follow her out but am told to stay where I am by Mother.

Grandma says 'Of course I love you, but you mustn't go upsetting your Mother like this when she has a new baby. AND you mustn't tell tales.'

I say nothing more. Perhaps she believes me and perhaps she believes Mother. Now I am a liar too. I don't know what liar means yet, though it sounds quite bad.

The commentary of how other people really feel about me continues after any visit to my grandparent's house, whenever we're not with Dad. She never says it in front of anyone else, just as a confidential between her and me. She likes to confide such things in me, as if it's our little secret. It almost feels like, if I am prepared to take what she says, I can sometimes have Mother back to myself, just occasionally.

A week later we're back. Gigi has gone out and I feel bereft. This time Grandma gets the flower fairy cards out of her special drawer in the kitchen table and I spend quite a long time gazing at both fairy and flower and wishing it were all real. I ache for the world of fairies and fantasy, gentleness and magical possibilities. It feels real but just beyond my reach all the time. I can sense it but not see or touch it, that magical world.

Grandma makes delicious fresh lemonade with her blender and I help her in the kitchen while Mother looks after Hazel's nappy. I'm not sure what I do but what Grandma tells me is that I am being a very good girl and helping her in the kitchen.

Then Grandad comes into the kitchen and asks as usual if I wanted to come for a walk with him and Pippa, in the park. We're gone for about half an hour I guess. It's a simple outing but when we get home my Mother seems very quiet and unhappy.

I sit at the kitchen table and ask Grandma,

'When will the lemonade be ready?'

'Stop showing off and behaving badly. Stop being so demanding.'

Mother has started on me with her words, telling me not to show her up. Every time I move, she's on me, but nothing specific.

I am so confused once more. I've had a great day with Grandad in the park. He let me go on the swings too. I've come home and walked quietly with him, held Pippa's lead sensibly, and now we were having drinks that Grandma had made for us specially, that I helped her to make. It's a hot day. I am thirsty so say yes when Grandma offers me a second glass of lemonade. I've hardly seen Mother so I can't work out what's wrong this time, but it's there, always waiting to blow up.

In retrospect I realise I represented a threat to her. They all made me feel welcome and loved but not her and her jealousy of me was insurmountable. How dare they like me and not her first. How dare they show me attention and time and affection. So it's all taken away from me with those simple little words. 'They're just nice people.'

When we get home they are restated with certainty, 'they don't like you because you are such a horrible child and so unkind to your Mother, but they are nice to you because they are nice people.'

But this time is different. There is no frothing monster, just cold plain words spoken matter of factly.

I love my aunt Gigi, very much. She gives me time and seems to care about me. She and I always spend time in her bedroom being girls together. I am devastated when a few weeks later we arrive for our regular visit and she has gone back to university. It's another form of sanctuary for me, time when I'm not so on edge and can relax and be myself and feel loved. But is this love? Or is it just nice people being nice to me? I don't understand anything anymore.

I wondered how Mother knew but did not doubt she might be right, after all they were nice people, to me at least they were. Even Gigi.

The next time we go to Grandma's house it's a Sunday afternoon and my other pregnant aunt, Mercia, the middle and favourite of the three sisters, is there with her new husband Colin. Grandad decides to tickle me for fun.

I'm ok at first. I don't like it but able to cope. But he just goes on and on. I can't help but laugh when being tickled. The laughter must seem like encouragement, but I am also begging him to stop and then the laughing becomes crying soon and he still doesn't know when to stop.

'Stop, stop, please stop' I beg, and continue to cry and giggle at the same time and he continues to tickle me mercilessly.

Everyone is watching, I feel their eyes all burning into me, but he just keeps on and on, tickling and tickling me. I'm desperate for him to stop.

Then I wet myself.

Grandad stops, perhaps in disgust.

I am only crying now, huge silent tears and sobs from the humiliation of it.

I 'd begged him to stop and he just couldn't seem to stop himself going on and on with the tickling. We must go home then. I don't have any dry clothes with me. It's all my fault.

'I don't expect to have to bring a change of clothes for you at your age,' Mother announces to me as we get in the car to leave, 'you've spoiled the day for everyone'.

Perhaps they didn't love me after all, I feel so bad, I never want to go there again.

When we get home, I'm quite severely told off by Mother for upsetting Grandad and disgracing myself, but not the usual raging monster- just a reminder that they don't like me anyway so I shouldn't upset them any further. It has become matter of fact to her now and she doesn't need the raging monster for a while. Cold iterations of her message are all that's needed. It feels like life is beginning to prove her point.

I secretly nickname my Grandad Mr Tickle. He also has a moustache which scratches when he kisses you, that tickles too.

By this time it's even hotter. The middle of July. I am fully four years old and it is Wimbledon finals weekend. I recall Mother watching the TV a lot, tennis. She has watched TV most of that week and ignored me for much of it, or that is how it feels.

Dad is out visiting his friends Jean and Johnny Hayden. I like going to visit them, but they don't have children, so I'm left behind that day. Dad doesn't like tennis. I hate being left behind at home on my own at weekends. It fills me with dread. Weekend visits with Dad to see other people are my respite, my time out from coping with Mother and trying to manage her irascible demands and pronouncements.

I come down from my bedroom.

'I'm hot, and bored, and lonely'.

Mother tells me,

'Go away, I'm busy with your sister and don't want you around her anymore. You upset her. Go and entertain yourself. Develop some initiative'.

I don't really know what initiative is, but I go back up to my own bedroom and try for a while and once again I feel empty, so alone and unwanted.

I decide to act on my own initiative, as has been suggested, though I didn't realise that's what I'm doing. I'm just trying to make my own life bearable.

Although it's Saturday, I very quietly let myself out of the front door and go to see my new friend Charlotte. I knock on the door and ask if I can play.

Peggy comes to the door, opens it and looks around for my Mother.

'Are you on your own?'

'Can I play with Charlotte?'

Aunty Peggy shakes her head, with a sad smile on her face, and said gently, 'no it's Saturday and we have family visiting'.

My hopefulness hits the floor. In desperation I try again.

'But my Mother says she doesn't want me any more now she has my sister and she told me to go away. She's busy watching TV and told me to find something to do, so I came here'.

I must look desperate because they let me in. Charlotte takes me up to her room to play. A little while later, Mother comes looking for me. About half an hour or so. Perhaps they phoned her.

I've always been a very literal person and am as a child. Social rules like tact and diplomacy pass me by. It is either this or not this, in a matter of fact way. I simply state truths which to me seem perfectly reasonable. I am still known as direct and blunt by friends but most of them like me for my open honesty and don't see it as a problem, though I understand as an adult that some people don't understand my way of being either. I don't understand theirs. The confusion is entirely mutual.

However for Mother, with her double life, I am her worst nightmare. I tell people what she says to me. Her only defence becomes that I am not to be trusted with anything, I am a liar. This is added firmly to the list of my deficits now, along with jealous, sullen, ungrateful and moody. By now I mostly just want to take every opportunity to get away from her.

Aunty Peggy is told all this with great seriousness. I am made to apologise for telling lies to our friends, then dragged back home.

The frothing monster is back. How dare I tell such lies and show her up in front of her friends. How dare I go out of the house without permission from her at my age. How dare I exist just to cause her such misery.

This time I feel little direct emotion. I am numb and stand there patiently waiting for her to finish the diatribe and then dismiss me. I go to my room and find a book and read as if nothing has happened, but inside there is just one feeling. Dread. Daddy coming home!

I hear her voice droning and whining about me as soon as he

comes in the door, no greeting just accosted with 'Why were you away for so long and left me with Sylvia again? Why didn't you take her with you?' and then the terrible account of how much damage I've done to her friendship with Peggy.

I'm listening from upstairs and realised it was not true, half of what she said was embellishment. Peggy was nice to both of us. She completely leaves out the parts where she'd told me to go away and sort myself out. I had done what she asked me to do after all. She is the one lying now, and I begin to understand what lying is. She takes no responsibility for how I might interpret her words but makes out I have gone specifically against her instructions instead of trying to meet them with my literal four-year-old view of the world.

A few minutes Dad comes bounding upstairs and into my room. He doesn't bother to look at me, he just picks me up and slaps me very hard across my bottom, puts me down and says, 'you know what that's for,' and left. I'm stunned that he would physically assault me, attack me in this way, without bothering to find out the whole story. I am devastated, frozen and cannot cry or feel anything. I just lay on my bed and read.

A few weeks later.

It is Saturday once more. My father has a weekend ritual to go and see big Grandma and Grandad himself and he takes me with him 'to give Mother a break from me'. Little do they know.

I love Saturday morning rituals, time off from Mother and time with Daddy when he would be nice to me, and so would Grandma and Grandad. Grandad never tickled me again, though he was always Mr Tickle to me after that.

I feel safer on this day than most times of the week. I'm away from Mother and it becomes a focus of my week, every day measured as a day closer to this day, a day out with Daddy.

This particular Saturday though, comes after a really tough week when I have been 'bad' every single day and had to 'wait 'til Daddy got home' every day too. The result is a distance between us both, Dad and I, that feels massive. Perhaps this is the chance to bridge that chasm, or at least get some respite with Gigi or Grandma.

Dad announces he's off and I jump up ready to go with him. But he says

'No, you haven't been good enough this week'.

I beg with him. I've endured so many showdowns with the monster that I also need the respite, but he could not know that. I beg and plead and even my Mother agrees I should go 'to give her a break from me too.'

I have a book to return to Charlotte whose house we pass on the way along the road. Daddy stops the car and I jump out and ring the front doorbell. No reply.

Dad winds down the window and calls out to me,

'Take it round and leave it by the back door where it'll be safe.'

I do as he suggests and then run back to the front. I stop and rub my eyes. Daddy is no longer there. I see him disappearing round the bend further along the road. He has forgotten to take me with him. I'm sure I can catch him up, so I start running along the road after him. The thought of going back home is too much for me to endure.

I reckon he could only be moments ahead of me and if I ran hard enough, I would surely catch him up. I run and run, as fast as my four-year-old legs will carry me and as hard as my beating heart will allow.

I start crying and then try to stop, so it doesn't slow me down, fighting down tears of betrayal and abandonment, fighting back fears of getting lost. I work through all the turnings and roads in my mind, tracking how I will follow him all the way to my grandmother's house if I must.

I get to the end of our road, sure I would see him waiting there to pull out. But he has gone on already. I run across roads and dodge traffic and cry as I run. My face feels tight from the salt water drying on my skin.

The next road is The Avenue, which is wider and busier than our own. I manage to cross this in between cars and thank my legs for running fast enough to get me safely across.

I'm getting tired, so I walk a little bit but then run again. I just know I have to go as fast as possible.

Eventually, at least a mile from home I am stopped by a busy road. The traffic is not slowing, and I stand there crying, knowing I am losing time. I'm fearful that I have so very far still to run and realise now I won't catch Daddy up. I wonder what his face will look like when I turn up at Grandma's house.

I stand there hopping from one leg to another in distress, hoping the cars would just stop in both directions enough for me to cross. I know how important it is to look both ways.

The house on the corner just behind me has a garden with a high hedge around it. Just then a man with hedge cutters comes out. He stops and looks at me for a few minutes, then comes over.

'What's up little girl? Why are you crying, where are you going, who is with you?'

'I'm chasing my Daddy in the car because he's gone and left me behind'.

'Where's he going?'

'To Grandma's house.'

'Do you know the address?'

'No. I know the roads to get there. Will you help me get there?'

'I don't think that's a good idea, do you?'

I'm still trying to cross the road while he's talking to me, still desperate that somehow he will help me get across so I can keep following Daddy.

'OK where do you live then?'

I tell him my home address. He takes my hand. 'Come in and have a drink and a biscuit, then I can take you home'.

Inside the house, his wife asks my name and looks very concerned at my story. I worry that I have done something wrong to them too. They give me the promised drink and biscuit. Then he pops me into his car and takes me home.

Mother is completely astonished when she opens the door. She gives the man a bewildered smile and then looks at me standing behind him.

'I think I have your daughter here.'

'Yes, that's my daughter but she's supposed to be with her father going to her grandparents. Why is she with you?'

'Apparently not – Sylvia says he went off without her and she tried to follow him. I found her at the crossing by Langley Way, trying to cross the road on her own and being very sensible waiting for it to clear both ways. But it didn't stop enough for her to cross, so she waited, crying. What a sensible little girl you have.'

He passes me over. I enter the family home once more, wishing I could stay with the nice man and his wife. I dread how this one would work out for me now.

'Thank you for bringing her home, I am sorry she put you to such trouble', Mother repeated once or twice more and then he says 'no trouble - goodbye,' and she closes the door.

I turn to go upstairs immediately, but she is surprisingly calm and asks me what has happened, then gives me a strange sort of hug. I go upstairs to my room, the nearest thing I have to sanctuary in that house and curl up on my bed with another book.

When Dad comes home, it all changes. The raised voices from below echo through the house. I stay in my room, waiting for the storm to pass as it invariably does, wondering what the outcome of this one will be for me.

But for once, instead of me, Dad is met by the wrath of Mother, the scorn and derision, and her fear of what those people would think of her family. Then it goes silent. I hear them moving around downstairs and my sister making the odd noise, as eight-month-old babies do.

Later he comes upstairs to see me and bring me down for a very late lunch. He scowls at me and tells me off for not returning home instead of trying to follow him. He doesn't look at me for the rest of that day.

How does a four-year-old make sense of that kind of experience?

Betrayed and confused—and a whole lot more.

There are a few more similar incidents along these lines from time to time but these specifically stand out in my mind as the beginning stages of what is to come next, and came back to me with a vengeance when I broke down with PTSD after Dad's death some fifty years later. It all came rushing back to the surface in glorious technicolour, as traumatic memories which have lain hidden for decades always do, as real as when they occurred with all the raw emotions still attached.

I often wondered if anybody recognised how much she was also lying all the time or just assumed she was the honest adult and I was the difficult child. I remember reading a quote by Jung once, 'there is no such thing as a difficult child, just a child being mismanaged'. That quote stayed with me for years before I was fully able to embrace its significance for myself.

This teaches me to be so different with young children myself where and when I can. It taught me so many lessons in life about how not to be and helped me find deeper dimensions than I might perhaps have done otherwise.

Playtime regrets – a poem

I love babies, little ones,
young children to play with,
to explore, go into make believe with
places where you can be anything.
My leg is a horse
for my grandson who likes to bounce.

A duvet the pregnant belly of a Mother dog
who would give birth to two pups,
my nieces, mewling, inventing this identity.
Me always the Mother dog, taking them on adventures
but always giving birth first.
And all of this under a large duvet,
where the best adventures come.

MY Mother though, did she ever play?

'Mother did you ever love me

Did I ever swing easy on your knee?'

My own sons, could I play for them?
Was I too busy coping to allow time out?
Too exhausted to do more with them,
endlessly loving to read to them.

Their memories are of the same.

We did go swimming and exploring for real
in mountains in France,
once in Egypt on camels, near the sphinx.

Perhaps I left it too late to play with them.
Perhaps Mothers cannot play
where aunts and grandmothers
have more room.

Please take this reminder for yourselves,
I wish someone had told me
when I was younger
when my babies were still wanting
to play with me.
I shall never forget to play again!

I was no sort of innocent 'butter wouldn't melt child', neither was I this awful creature my Mother perceived. I did have completely undiagnosed or unrecognised ADHD, more the inattentive kind but also physically energetic and restless. That does present its own set of challenges to any parent. I have two sons with ADHD. I know the reality, but I also know that I didn't deserve the treatment I got.

My brain was very literal and curious, and endlessly wanting to explore further than I was ever allowed – to find out about life and experiences of different kinds.

However, I must share one story which came back to me recently. I am close to five years old because I know I'm not yet at school when this happened.

We are driving to Grandma's house.

'What are you going to do at Grandmas today,' Mother asked, apparently in a pleasant, though unreliably placid mood.

'Play with Puffy if I can find her. She's usually in the airing cupboard.'

'Did you know cats have nine lives?'

'What does that mean?'

'Cats can survive all sorts of things. Like if they fall from very high up, they will always land on their feet and walk away. They're very supple and strong for their size, like acrobats.'

I am curious and consider this for the last few minutes of the journey.

We arrive at Grandma's house and I rush into her arms for a cuddle.

Mother has Hazel in her arms and pushes past us.

'Let me in will you!'

I rush upstairs, and Mother and Grandma take Hazel into the kitchen. I find Puffy hiding in her airing cupboard and pull her out. She is quite disgruntled and reluctant to be dragged from her warm dog free sleeping place. I try to play with her, putting her into the child play cot for dolls but she doesn't want to sleep there and tries to escape. I chase her into Grandma's bedroom above the kitchen. I close the door behind us.

Grandma's bedroom window is open.

Mother's words go round and round in my head, 'If cats fall from a high place, they are always alright and will land on their feet'.

I want to know if this is true.

I pick Puffy up and take her to the window. She tries to jump down inside. I put her back on the windowsill. She is reluctant still and struggles slightly with me to get away. Perhaps she knows what's coming but at this point even I don't. Not really, not consciously. I am just exploring what cats can do.

I pick her up and put her back on the windowsill, right on the outside of it again but she still does not fall down. I push her out and she goes over the edge. I try to look over at her to see how she fell but I am not tall enough to look out that far.

I hear this shout from the kitchen below, and footsteps come racing up the stairs.

Grandma and Mother come into the room and ask me 'What on earth is going on? We just saw the cat fly past the kitchen window. Did you push her out of the window or what?'

I tell them quite simply 'Mother told me cats have nine lives so you can't kill them and if they fall from high up, they always land on their feet. But I can't see properly from here. Did she land on four feet and walk away?'

I look at both adults who look back at me in shock and then also realise that I am just being literal, testing out what I have been told.

Mother starts on me.

'I don't tell you things so you can try them out, I tell you for information'.

'Perhaps you should be more careful what you say to her,' suggests Grandma, and for once nothing much more happens.

Most sadly for me though, every time Puffy saw me again she always ran away – it was years before I understood why. But Mother was right, she did land on her feet and did have a few lives left still. I had to be content with Pippa, taking him for walks, when Grandad was home.

Nowadays I truly regret hurting Puffy like that, but it's the kind of thing people with ADHD often do. They don't lack empathy but their literal interpretations of everything makes them do unexpected things. It's an example of my confusion in childhood and the mixed messages I was consistently given, not that I was a bad child.

6. WHEN THE STARS ALIGN FAVOURABLY

Meeting David was a complete turning point in my life. Transformation. When we got together it was one of those amazing coincidences that you know were just meant to happen. Pure synchronicity.

The relationship I'd escaped from previously had become unworkable. I was about two years clear of that realisation, though not of the time it took to extract myself from the games and prevarications, placed to make me hold on a little longer. Not that I was holding on. Once it was over for me, it was over. I had done with all my attempts to heal and grow together and had realised it was becoming abusive and destructive, to myself at least, and it wasn't going to change, other than for the worse. It took me a while longer to fully understand how I had completed my circle of NPD relationships. I'd been attracted to that energy yet again in my subconscious attempt to heal my childhood, only to be burned on those flames once more. I also had a minor breakdown and by the time he left I was on medication for panic attacks. How unconsciously we repeat our mistakes until we recognise them and grow past them to move on! I was walking wounded but certain I was now on a good path.

I had several friends at that time who went to Cambridge Folk Festival as a yearly pilgrimage to our shared love of music. The first year I went there was just myself and three other friends, all males, Chris, John and Steve, who were very gentle with me in my emotionally fragile and abused state. I totally loved it, having never attended a weekend festival before apart from some illicit one-day event Hyde Park trips in my teen years, without parental knowledge. I fell in love with the sense of freedom and the music was just amazing.

The following year I was getting my own life back up, my writing career was starting, with my first publishing contracts, and I was busy building up a private practice in therapy and meditation/emotional literacy workshops.

It was utterly nerve wracking on top of the big breakdown a year earlier. The decision to quit my safe teaching job came from a sense that everything was in a melting pot anyway so I may as well just throw caution to the wind and see what happened. I had thus far swum pretty well, but it was frantic doggie paddle under the smooth surface still.

Going to Cambridge the next year was something I was really looking forward to. John had previously moved to the Isle of Wight with his then girlfriend and made friends with my future David at work in the planning department of the local authority. They discovered a mutual interest in music, so that second year my David was invited to join the party and travel up with John. We meet and talk a little bit, but he is very quiet and shows no apparent interest in me, so I just see him as another bloke in the party, nothing more.

Until the last day.

We are packing up tents and sleeping bags, getting ready to go our separate ways, and just standing around talking casually about running and other forms of exercise, and how we mostly needed to do more. David confessed to be being a long-distance runner.

Then David says, 'I meditate a lot and have no anger anymore.'

That is like a saucer of cream for this cat, or a punch between the eyes, whichever analogy works for you. All I can say is that this comment is the greatest chat up line anyone could have thrown out at me just then. Here is a very lovely man who meditates and is self-aware enough to know about the destructive nature of anger. I poke and prod a little more and then suggest he might like to bring his daughter up for a weekend in London as a summer holiday trip. I give him my card and leave it at that, hoping I have given the hint that I might like to talk more about meditation experiences etc. Who am I kidding!!!

He didn't phone me.

But he got me thinking. I'd more or less decided not to allow myself any more relationships. I had two much loved teenaged sons who, with undiagnosed ADHD and trauma themselves, were a challenge, and a history of relationship disasters, with lovers, family and friends. I was single and thriving, just, so why risk that again?

Why risk anymore?

I see it at that time as my failure and evidence of my inherent worthlessness, though now I would say those were all experiences that taught me so much about life and love and myself. At the time I am in the process of writing and researching for my book Trusting Your Intuition, so I write a manifestation list for the universe, a sort of psychic email/ wish list /energy message- 'this is what I want to manifest in my life next please'. I write the following list in my notebook.

- I want someone who will love me for who I am and not for what they can get from me. I will do the same for them.
- who is on a conscious journey of spiritual and personal development, so we can travel together, for whom this is paramount, a deep plunge and not a shallow paddle.
- who is able and available to commit fully so that I can commit fully in return
- who is interested in music, the arts generally, travel, the politics of social justice and equality,
- tall and slim, and honestly likes loving tender sex
- who will embrace my sons as I might embrace any child they may have also
- I want someone for whom equality in a relationship is

an intentional goal

I write this list in one of my small notebooks and put it into a drawer next to my bed, and honestly completely forget about it. It is a demanding list and why should I get what I asked for?

The following July, I am busy for part of the Cambridge weekend with work commitments from my now developing business, but I can get away for one day and an overnight stay. I book my ticket, not knowing if I would see David again but hoping, secretly, he will be there. And if not, I would just have another great break with friends and music and beer. What could be better?

He is there.

I act supercool. I arrive just as they are all emerging from tents and preparing for a swim in a nearby school pool that opens for the use of weekend campers, all slightly the worse for wear of course.

The ritual of the morning swim also counts as ablutions and hangover cure. I just love swimming and had not wanted to miss this integral part of any weekend at Cambridge Folk Festival. We swim around a little and then I have the strangest experience in the pool. We are all standing around chatting a bit in between swimming a few lengths and I suddenly recognise something profound and unexpected. I know I will be resting my head on David's chest. I am not imagining it. I deeply know it. It actually feels as if I have already been doing this for a long long time, that is 'how it already is' between us. I dive off, swim away and climb out to dry off and get dressed again, feeling very self-conscious indeed. I am also acutely aware that he is watching me, so I do not dare look around.

I shrug it off as weird, but I'm used to that. We all emerge from the pool and head off to the breakfast tent for an all-day style meal, it will last until late afternoon. Then, replete, we carry on with our day, arriving at the main festival site around lunchtime when the music starts up again.

David and I barely stop talking to each other that day, sitting around on rugs, reading a little, listening to more music, going off to different tents together to find new music that appeals from the programme, and into the evening when we change to 'standing to listen' mode in the tightly packed arena, dancing when we can find space to move.

When it's time to go back to the campsite and tents, to sleep, David realises I haven't brought a tent with me. We all usually pile in with shared tents and if not, my car is an estate so I'm not too worried. But when we get back to the campsite that night, I'm told there isn't room in the shared tent. So, car it is, no worries. Then David very kindly and gallantly offers me his tent and he suggests he would sleep in the porch bit of it. By then I know he is a very gentle and intelligent man. I accept his offer with some persuasion and insist we should share his tent as there is room for both of us and we have our own sleeping bags. We spend the night together in extremely courteous and modest mode, very respectful of each other's boundaries, and that is it.

The following morning, we emerge and I have to leave more or less immediately. I risk offering him my card again and this time he takes it and apologises about losing the last one. I finally find out he'd washed it in his jeans and spent a whole year hoping John would invite me down to the Isle of Wight, so we could meet up again.

In the meantime, John tries to tease David about his 'conquest' at the weekend when they are back at work, but it doesn't go down well with David's colleagues who are also good friends.

John has also told me since that he and the others had planned not to let me sleep in the shared tent where there had in fact been room for me, but they were attempting matchmaking in their own way. We didn't need any help. All is forgiven and we are still good friends with John, though have not managed to attend any sleepover non-local festivals for some years now and have lost touch with the others. We have great festivals on our island anyway and can go home to sleep. At our age a necessity.

David phones me four days after getting home, on the Wednesday evening when his daughter is staying with her Mother. We chat for about three hours without realising it, and he invites me down. I only have part of that coming weekend free again and I am teaching my groups most weekends but I drive down to meet him and stay at his home.

David collects me from the passenger ferry and drives me to his house. We sit out on his decking in the early August afternoon sunshine. His garden looks across the island as far as the cliffs at Yaverland and the view is stunning, extensive and very green. It's extremely attractive but, as I later learn, a deep hazard in strong winds when you can barely stand up.

We are continuing to talk endlessly, as if we have a deep well of interest in each other, when I have this extraordinary experience. It feels as if I am being taken on some kind of an elevator which is taking me gently down, and down again, deeper and deeper, into some mysterious subterranean basement of consciousness. It is filled with golden light and peacefulness. Somehow our communication, our connection and simple talking is far deeper than anything I have ever known before. We don't stop talking then either, there just seems to be so much to share, but we are both still very respectful of each other's boundaries, where we'd both been burned badly before and are thus both wary to rush into anything.

Later that day he takes me to Ventnor beach. We walk along the shoreline and talk imaginary worlds among the rock pools. Then we lay on the beach for a while and I collect minute stones of different colours, making them into little piles.

Some years later I wrote this poem about that day. It remains clear in my mind, in both our minds. And I still have the poem David wrote and sent to me that week, the most wonderful thing I had ever experienced in my whole life up until that point.

Lost and found.

We discovered each other
in lost and found.

You were a treasure chest
washed up on the beach
when my toe stubbed against you.

Tentatively opening your lid,
I discovered many secrets -
many compartments concealed
from unappreciative eyes and minds
jewels dulled by non-use,
wrapped in oilcloth, fusty with age

I was broken on that beach
discards from other people's debris.
You carefully collected all my fragments
painstakingly re-assembled them
into a collage of unexpected beauty

Many years later I find still
there are secret compartments
located in the depths of your being.

We carefully light candles
for each other, to find
hands to hold in the dark.

We sleep apart again that weekend but later discover that neither of us have really been able to sleep much. He will go on the write a song about that too, called Sign Language, one of his band's regular numbers.

The next day he sees me off on the ferry. When I look out of the back of the boat and see he is sitting on the gate, watching the boat sail away, I know at that point I already love him deeply but that I will never 'fall in love with him'. It is way deeper than that immediately. There is no falling necessary.

We never look back, apart from joyful reminiscing, in spite of the many challenges from so many factors surrounding us. They don't seem to affect us and in fact often make us more determined to stay together. We do split up for two days, a few months later, over tensions to do with teenage offspring being hostile to our relationship, but we work through that and realise from that moment onwards that we won't let it happen again, come what may.

7. STEPPING FURTHER INTO THE FUTURE, MAKING COMMITMENTS

Two years of weekend commuting to see each other is becoming tiring and expensive. I have sold my house and bought a flat from which I can maintain my practice and workshops. In the process of moving, David comes to help me pack up and I find my notebook by chance. I flick through it to see if it's a keeper. I find my list.

We are sitting in bed this morning, planning our mode of attack of what to deal with next on the house packing front. There is still an enormous amount to do and we must be out by the time completion goes through. I hand him the list and he reads it.

'That's a description of me'.

'Now look at the date.'

'That was six months before we got together.'

'Yep – I think I put my order in and got what I asked for and some. You're like a treasure chest with lots of secret compartments and even after two years I am still finding out new and exciting treasures about you. You are my wonderful mystery gift man.'

We laugh and get on with the day. He is amazing. I realise I could not cope with the move without him.

Selling the house and buying the flat means I can spend more time on the island with David, I think we both want commitment, we both feel totally committed. There is a deep relief that comes with feeling one part of your life is now settled. Emotionally you can move on together, with all else that life brings, without fear of more heartache and breakups. I state early on that I didn't want any marriage or financial involvement again. I'd been badly hurt from previous relationships and knew from experience how people could get very angry, including myself, and take victim positions over possessions shared and then being divided, almost to the point that this was more significant than the loss of the relationship. I don't want to risk any repetitions.

David though. He has already pretty much completely won my trust and heart/soul commitment and loyalty. It feels fully reciprocal.

But I want him to want me and ache for him to take a risk and ask me. I want, or even need, to be wanted, I mean really wanted not just for now, while I meet someone's needs but deeply wanted through thick and thin. That is what my wish list meant to me and what I would offer in return. I'd never experienced anything like this before and I feel this is the time, but I need him to want me before I can risk anything deeper, though it is there welling up in me.

One weekend I'm down on the island for a longer stay and meet him from work for lunch on the Friday. We are walking back towards his office through Seaclose Park. Completely out of the blue, for me too, I suddenly round on him, started punching him on his shoulder, saying 'why won't you marry me'.

Like so often with me, things come from my deeper place of intuition. I have little or no conscious awareness until they happen. I had no idea this is going to happen or why at that moment, but that is what just happens. Not the most romantic marriage proposal of all time but typical of us.

David stops and simply says, 'I thought you didn't want to get married, but yes I'll marry you if you would like that'.

We laugh at my craziness, hug and walk him back to work. And that was that.

I go off to do some other stuff in town, to meet up again at the end of the afternoon. When I get back to our car there is a note on the windscreen. 'If you are free on the 12th August 2000, will you marry me?'

I can honestly say that the glow of happiness and joy spread through my whole body and I thought yes, yes, yes, thank you, thank you, thank you. I have never stopped feeling like that about our relationship.

It is a year until our wedding. We have so much to do, including making the decision for me to sell up completely in Beckenham and to move fully to the island. That choice of where one of us would move to hung mostly on his daughter still being at school and my youngest son being ready to leave school and go on to A levels at college. My son also states that he wants to go to college on the island, to make a new beginning in his life.

I sell up the flat I bought as a half-way move. Living between two homes does not suit me emotionally and practically. I am earning enough money to cover the running costs of the flat and travel, but nothing left over for myself. It isn't working. I am missing phone calls from new clients despite trying to work a remote answerphone. My publishers aren't signing anything new because the book publishing market has just changed massively with the arrival of Amazon and selling books at discounts. Libraries are slowly being closed by hard pressed local authorities, so there is less and less of a guaranteed selling market for my books and I am not enough of a best seller yet to make it through this change of affairs. When I work out I am working to cover the costs of travel and running the flat and nothing more, it seems like a common sense, no brainer decision to make the move completely and start up on the island instead.

The various stages of this life plan take time and it is utterly overwhelming for me. Several friends intimate I might be making a mistake and try to put serious doubts in my mind. I simply avoid them for a while, though some of those friendships never fully recover and now have dissolved, as friendship sometimes do. All relationships have their purpose in our life, and some will last for a long time, but others will pass on as we evolve.

I have some sadness for a time, yet also realise the old dynamics are no longer comfortable for me. But I know with a certainty that I must do this, however it works out. David is my destiny in this next stage of my life and who knows what will be next anyway. Make the changes and if it doesn't work out then move on, but don't thwart your potential development in life because of doubt and possibilities. That has become my motto unconsciously in life as an escape plan from my family and now it becomes a conscious approach to life, not unaided by my impulsive nature which I later learn is part of my undiagnosed ADHD. But the stress and upheaval leaves me breathless, floundering at times with the sheer logistics of it all. Unbeknownst to me, at the time, I have an undercurrent of deep anxiety and terror, always present, undermining everything I do.

It is around this time that I also become aware of the weight of other people's expectations of me and how much I don't want them. I just want to get on with my own life, not in any hedonistic way but just in a 'right to live as I choose' way, without hurting anybody directly. Those expectations mean I do hurt people, through no intended fault of my own and whilst I regret them, I have to make my way through this massive transformational stage of my life. It started with the breakdown of my previous relationship, my decision to resign my secure teaching post and take a chance on myself and my writing, which is not drying up for me, and on my teaching skills, to teach what I believe in and what seems far more important for life, rather than what an exam syllabus demands of young people.

Now I am selling up again, twice in nine months, and, moving away from everything I have known for a long time. It possibly is a huge gamble, but it feels utterly right. I am going with that single intuitive feeling. It is more of a risk in my mind not to give it a go. What might I miss out on? After all I have just published my book called Trusting your Intuition, so why not live according to that principle?

We tell my Mother about our marriage plans and she asks if she can come to our wedding. It will be the first of her three children's four weddings to date that she has ever attended. In the expansive and joyful mood of the time I said yes.

The next time we meet Mother and my stepdad Douglas is at my brother's house for a Sunday visit. Douglas closets himself and David in their living room while we all help with the lunch preparation and my brother does whatever he does. I check on them and they seem to be just chatting and getting on well. Mother is being her usually ingratiating self with my sister in law Kelly and her usual critical self with me, but I feel immune to it now I have David in my life. It isn't until we get into the car to go home again that he says to me how awful his experience has been, being grilled by Douglas as to his suitability to marry me, according to their value system, which is about as far removed from ours as it could be. I am horrified and shocked and terrified that it will affect 'us', in some way and yet again my Mother, or her influences, will wreck my life and relationships. But David is made of stronger stuff, wiser and deeper too; he acknowledges they are nothing like me or I like them.

I write a strong letter to Douglas and Mother and distance myself from them once more. That single incident makes me realise how terrified I am of her influence affecting or damaging my life ever again and we cut ourselves off and withdraw her inclusion in our wedding. On the journey home I realise I would rather not have a wedding, rather not even get married, than have her attend it. So great is my terror of her ability to destroy any positive relationships in my life, and so unconscious am I of that terror, until it arises and shows itself to me.

Douglas attempts to mediate with me by promising he won't let her speak to anyone, but I no longer trust him either. His value system is just as much at odds with ours anyway. I want to be free to have a wedding as I want it to be, without comment or intrusions or judgments from anyone in my family. I am getting to the end of being able to tolerate being treated as the loser, crazy woman with hippy values of love and ecosystem protection and peace. Heaven forbid after all if those values come to prove they are exactly what the world needs. They aren't about money and status and power.

She didn't come, and apart from my brother no one else in my family did either, in solidarity of her distress. No one bothered to ask me why I had taken that decision. My family just judge me for it and ignore my happiness. Surprisingly I feel relieved by that.

That is the point when I decide to not bother with my extended birth family ever again. They ignore us and from then I pretty much ignore them too, and it feels like a huge relief, a burden lifted, a liberation from the constraints that have dogged me for my entire life until this point.

Even though I love them all, and I know they are all good people in their own ways too, I know I don't belong with them. They don't value me, and I don't want to feel like the underdog in my life anymore. Our wedding teaches me and reveals to me so much of what freedom means and involves and it is good. I know that I want to see what might happen next, that this commitment means the world to both of us.

Wedding vows

So we will make this love of ours official to the world
A pronouncement of our intimacy and desire to be seen as one.
Yet I loved you gently and fiercely from when we first met
So this is just surface dressing
And confirmation that you are indeed the one I choose
to be my advocate if I cannot speak for myself

to be my other half.

When we are joined I cannot find the space between us,
Where you end, and I begin, have merged
We are one, yet there is so much spaciousness
to breathe, and to be who we each must be
who we are
the person that drew you into this union is still here
yet has melted into you too.

I promise to love you,
as if I can make a promise
for something that already overwhelms me,
fills me with more joy than I can express.
Can one make a promise to do something
like love? Can one pin it down to words and promises?

I promise to honour you,
To honour all that you are
and all that you have been
and all that you will become
I will love and honour you as one single stroke,
our emotional and spiritual journeys in parallel,
free to take their own intended courses

I will obey you as I must
since I have chosen you to be my true master
the mirror into which I will look
daily to see myself, to learn about who I am,
how I might grow and change.

How can I not obey you,
as I know you will obey me too?
The infinite mirror of true love.

The marriage itself takes place at the formal registry offices and
guests are invited to come if they want to or just to come to the

party afterwards which is going to be our true wedding, not just the legal one.

Why bother with the legal one? I have no family who bother to understand me or value me, and thus no one I can ever trust to do what is right for me. I know David 'got me' in those profound bottom elevator ways that I have recognised since the beginning, and I can trust him to listen to me deeply and recognise my rights if ever anything happens to me. I also trust him to do the right thing by my sons. He is insightful, gentle, wise, and generous, non-materialistic and utterly trustworthy. What more could I want than for this person to be my official legal next of kin on every level and unarguably, by anyone? Even my sons hold him in high regard.

So we do the legal bit and invite all those who we feel are on our side.

The house is still in early basic renovation and although we've warned people, many have chosen to stay with us for the weekend or longer. We ask people to bring sleeping bags and as they arrive, give some of them hammers and floor nails to replace floorboards with, so we can unroll carpet to put airbeds mattresses and sleeping bags on. It's a wonderful functional chaos and everyone seems to think it is fun.

I am doing all the catering so on the morning I get up at 5 am to start the preparations. David goes off in the car to collect cakes from a local bakery at 8 a.m. and generally caters breakfasts for our resident guests in the other kitchen. I stop at about 10 a.m., get changed into my wedding dress, which is a slinky purple and rose-pink twenties style evening dress, and go and get married legally.

Our neighbours at that time have an old Bentley and he puts ribbons on it and drives us there and back. David is in chinos and a black shirt, no tie, and we honestly look more like a gangster and his moll standing next to an open topped car with running boards than a couple about to get married.

After the official bit is over, we get home. The few friends who have offered to help have done wonders and I continue organising lunch for everyone, until everything is served on time, vegetarian of course, though we do provide some cold meats for those who feel they cannot survive without eating dead animal. After lunch most people get changed and come for walks down the lane to visit the stream, or laze around in the garden playing barrel walking with old aluminium beer barrels that were left behind from when the house had been a pub for a while.

I also want our own ceremony. I put together some ideas from handfasting and Buddhist teachings, and we have our own designed wedding circle, complete with our official princess and fairy attendants, these roles fulfilled and indeed insisted upon by two five year old daughters of friends.

In the evening we have a bonfire, as huge as is possible, at least fifteen feet or more, burning all the beams and old roof timbers filled with damp and dry rot. Everyone sits around on the old carpets we laid out from the house and it is very chilled and relaxed.

Some people go home at the end of the weekend and some stay on for up to a week but in total we have accommodated 28 residentially, plus lots of day visitors, a try out for our future retreat centre, and it has worked well.

It is the best day of my life in so many ways, my sons are both there as is my first husband and his Mother. Friends surround us with positive vibes of all sorts, including comments on how much they are enjoying our wedding, how chilled it is and how memorable and very, very different.

8. LEARNING LESSONS OF A DIFFERENT KIND.

At five years old school is starting. What a relief. It means I am away from Mother for five whole days a week. I am feeling optimistic and wondering how things might change for me. To begin with it seems pretty good. I enjoy doing things, though much of it confuses me and appears pointless. In the classroom is a pretend shop where we can learn about money but once you have played in there for a while, it is utterly boring. The newness wears off pretty quickly and I just want to retreat into books once more. I think I am near the top in reading if nothing else.

I don't make friends much though and this is noted at every opportunity. I have already become a people watcher, not a joiner. I've been taught that no one will like me anyway so why bother. I am already a frozen child.

Within lesson times, I am very good at picking up basic concepts but not very good at developing them because I get bored and don't concentrate, apparently. I have no idea what all this means but it is interpreted as laziness and bad behaviour on my part and thus my parents are notified of it and I'm punished for it.

My first parents evening comes.

I have no idea what will happen when my parents go to the school. No one has warned me how they will gang up on me even more, that teachers became united common enemies. There is no respite from the endless crush of criticism and expectations and rejections. According to Mother and Dad when they get home, with disappointment written all over their faces, I am already all wrong there too.

The evening is not fun.

'So, you're as bad at school as you are at home.'

I look at them in turn, with a sort of impassive mask on my face, showing nothing but confusion and a frozen defence, masquerading as feigned indifference. What do I say? What can I say or do? I am powerless on every level. I just see stone cold faces and hard cruel eyes looking back at me. I wait for the next comment.

'Why can't you be normal and do things people ask you to do?'

I don't actually know what it is that I have or haven't done, and no one ever asks me how I feel about anything. Could I tell them anyway? I doubt it.

I listen passively to their list of complaints from school, with their own disappointment overlaid for emphasis. I continue to say nothing. Not to protest or respond in any way. It seems to work, and they run out of words to throw at me.

'You insolent child. Go to you room now. We'll talk to you tomorrow.'

A new word to describe me. Insolent. I don't know what that means but I'll come to understand it eventually.

That day is a sort of victory for me though. I learn how to be utterly passive as a defence mechanism from then on, if I can manage it. I am born at the end of March and have a fiery passionate nature when roused, and can be very forceful myself, but I learn how to be immobile, shut down, cut off, and that feels safer for now.

The following morning Mother starts on me again.

'Have you got anything to say for yourself this morning, how much you let us and yourself down?'

We are at the kitchen table having breakfast. Dad has gone off to catch his train, brief case and bowler in place, his male commuter's uniform in those days. Uniformity, conformity, fitting in. 'What would the neighbours say, think'.

I come to understand how massively important these things are for people and for my parents also. It is that era. I also feel them as a constraining prison, false values, empty and dishonest. They dominate my life through my parents in the most negative ways.

Mother continues.

'When are you going to behave like you're supposed to, when are you going to learn to be nice to other children and make friends like normal people do?'

I say nothing again, shrug, and leave the kitchen. I start upstairs to finish dressing for school. She follows me out and stands in the hallway, grabbing my arm through the bannisters. She jerks me to a standstill and wrenches my shoulder.

'Look at me when I am talking to you, how dare you walk away like that,' she is spitting now. Her grip on my arm feels ice cold, like iron. I am captured and held fast by my torturer. I manage to shake her off my arm by moving backwards so she is bent painfully against the bannister. We tussle and I cannot break free. My shoulder is hurting now.

'Don't you be so insolent to me like that, don't you try to shake me off like that, how dare you treat your Mother like this.'

I look at her, straight in the eyes and say,' I hate you as much as I hate eating dog pooh.'

She lets me go then and I run upstairs, desperate to get away from her physically. I can hear her laughing at me now with some sort of manic cackle, as I imagine evil witches to have. I later learn how much I love witches as healers, a magical and wise ancient race of women. But up until now I have only met the fictional kind in Hansel and Gretel, or Snow White, and Mother fits that bill so well.

'You can't hate me, I'm your Mother, you have to love me,' she retorts, and continues cackling.

It is so bizarre. I have just delivered my killing words and she is laughing as if she is drunk with parental power. I can tell it is power, because she's got a response from me. I vow from then on to give her nothing at all if I can help it, nothing.

My shoulder hurts for the rest of that day.

I don't mention it to anyone.

My struggles at school continue unabated. I can always get the initial concepts for any subject given to us to learn but I can never concentrate enough to show I understand or take it to the next level. My brain is already wanting something new instead. I consistently get things wrong and feel more and more stupid and worthless in all aspects of my life. I am also finding it very hard to know how to relate to the other children and my attempts are thwarted by my own sense of worthlessness and diffidence. When you are told endlessly 'you can't make friends', then you assume whatever skills you do have are inadequate in the extreme.

The parents start to get me additional English and maths workbooks to supplement my school lessons. I am given these to complete at weekends, shut into the dining room to do them on my own after minimal instructions, the assumption being I have already learned the lessons at school, I guess. A cold unfriendly unheated room with austere Edwardian furniture from my Little Grandmother's previous house. I mostly cry and cry, silently, then do my best.

Dad comes in to check on me.

'Here Daddy I've done this page,' tentatively offering to show him but fearing a negative response, not knowing what is expected of me.

He takes a cursory glance, 'Not good enough! You haven't done what's asked of you. Can't you see what is in front of you, can't you just concentrate and get on with it.'

'What is concentrate?' I ask cautiously. This is the first time I've been told this word or that it applies to me.

Mother comes in to see what is happening.

'She hasn't got it right again. She'll have to do it again.' Dad leaves the room and Mother turns on me once more.

'What is wrong with you, why can't you just do the work like normal children do?'

I try to respond.

'I do try, I don't understand what I'm meant to do.'

'But we sat down and went through it with you first. What is wrong with you, why won't you listen properly, just concentrate?'

That word again.

'What is concentrate?'

She starts shouting and waving her arms around, punching the air between us.

'Concentrate, concentrate, concentrate, you just do it, you look at the page and concentrate on it.'

Her voice is getting louder. She is starting to turn red. Spittle is forming at the corners of her mouth. I am watching very closely. I need to know what I am doing wrong so I can try harder, as she keeps telling me to, but I don't understand what this concentration thing is.

I try again.

'Mother I want to concentrate but I don't know what it is or how to do it.'

I am trying to stay calm, to keep her calm, to be compliant and willing to please. I'm desperate not to attract Dad's attention back from the other room and have him come in to punish me again.

'Just show me what concentration means and I will do it,' I say, encouraging her.

'I can't show you concentration. You just do it. Now do this page again and do it properly before you can join us in the living room. If it wasn't for you the whole family would be happy.'

She stands over me watching while I start to look at the page again, but it swims before my eyes and I can't make out what I've got wrong.

'Concentrate,' she shouts at me, 'concentrate, concentrate'.

'But how Mother, please show me how,' I am crying now and pleading with her. I just don't understand. I try to reach out to her, but she shakes me off.

'Just do it,' she hisses, 'what's wrong with you? Just do it like any normal child would. If it wasn't for you, the whole family would be happy.'

She turns her back on me and walks out and harshly closes the door again, clearly announcing her irritation and displeasure with me.

Closing the door on me and shutting me out from the family, my little Grandma, Dad and Hazel in the living room. I am punished, unwanted and rejected.

All her words come back, 'if it wasn't for me'. That is a new announcement. Her parting shot leaves me feeling worthless, that I have no right to live because now my very existence makes everyone unhappy. I don't cry, just have a frozen realisation of what she said to me.

I go over to the door and listen to the rest of the family in the other room. They seem fine without me. I want to open it but daren't. Anyway, I can't easily reach to open the handle as it is high up and pretty stiff to pull down. If I do open it there will be even worse trouble. I return to the table. I feel imprisoned in this unheated room, trying to make sense of what this word concentration means and how I am supposed to do it, and trying not to think of the other words she just gave me.

Concentrate, concentrate – the word goes round and round, in my very muddled and confused, scattered mind. Then I look back at the page of English homework before me. My mind goes numb once more. I can't make sense of what it means. I can read the words, but they don't make sense. My brain just can't understand what I am supposed to be doing and I don't know how to make it.

I take a deep breath and start again.

This time I can begin to understand, but then my mind goes off once more.

Again, I take deep breaths and find I can return to the page once more, and gradually I manage to work through it. The effort it takes me is extra-ordinary and by the end I feel exhausted. I am crying through much of it, from the exertion, and my face is now sticky with dried tears, my skin feels taught. Eventually I finish the page I'd been allotted for that Sunday.

I knock on the door to be let out.

No one comes.

I knocked harder and this time Dad comes in. His face expresses pure disappointment with me. I shrivel further inside.

I show him my work.

'Finally. Why couldn't you just do that in the first place? Come on then.'

There is no recognition of the super-human effort it has taken me to achieve that work page. No one ever knows how hard I try.

I realise looking back that this is when I first realised my brain just didn't work properly. Half a century later I find myself receiving the diagnosis of ADHD with such relief and recognition. I also realise I'd taught myself mindfulness and concentration skills, using the breath to concentrate, back at six years old. I will never know how I learned to make it work for me but that is how I cope, though it is some decades before I recognise what I need to do. Take a deep breath before every little task, sentence, whatever, and somehow that will help my mind to work properly. It takes me such effort and is exhausting but when I do, it works.

The effort, the remembering to do it doesn't come regularly. Mostly, as a child, I forget.

I remember at about seven years of age, just one day knowing that no matter how hard I try I will never be able to meet expectations, either at home or at school. School has become another venue for ego demolition and institutional bullying and I just give up on everything, including myself.

I am depressed, though in those days, depression is barely acknowledged in adults, let alone children. I am seriously depressed and it's beginning to show at home too. This becomes a new source of bullying from Mother. Now I am sullen, moody and ungrateful. My extended family all swallow that explanation, nagging me, chastising me for it whenever I see them, and I am not bright and jolly.

One day Dad stands in front of me and shouts at me to pull myself together and be happy. I clearly remember the effort it takes to push down my feelings of despair and worthlessness and pretend. I continue to survive like this for many more years until my deepest healing begins.

It is many decades later, after the worst of my breakdown has passed, that I realise this had possibly been a positive in my life. That in fact I gradually realise how many of my so-called failures, rejections, and losses have been protecting me from negative influences that might have ended up with me in a far worse state emotionally, or as a clone of my parents in line with their wishes. For me, that latter is the worst thought. I am grateful to them for rejecting me so whole heartedly.

But at four, five and six – right up until I have that breakdown, it feels like it is the only truth about me; I am indeed this horrific, worthless, failure of a human being that no one could ever possibly love, or value, or want.

Now I believe that being the failure made me a better person. But where do their expectations come from. That is also an interesting story.

When I was born the midwife who helped deliver me later became my godmother, Pat. She liked to relate how she remarked to my Mother what an intelligent look I had already in my eyes and the shape of my head, at birth. She is the first person to ever see me alive. Maybe that was the beginning of the high expectations they had for me. After all they never put my sister in that position. It is an unanswerable question but one that I do ponder.

But my parents are not normal. Their relationship is deeply dysfunctional, mostly due to my Mother's un-diagnosed mental health issues, my father's lack of emotional literacy and his inability to cope with Mother. He has been turning to Alan and Violet, my grandparents, for support and is told to discipline me so that Mother can be happy again. They will not listen to his concerns that something is seriously wrong with Mother, they will not countenance that at all. His support system is closing against him too. His sense of aloneness with this nightmare is increasingly desperate, though no one is recognising it.

Mother has very fixed ideals of how everyone should treat her. She must always be the centre of attention. But I am too intelligent and curious about life, I ask and challenge her on everything that doesn't make sense to me. I do this more as I get older, even though it will attract more abuse. By then I have worked out the abuse will happen regardless, so I don't bother to be careful anymore.

I am also frequently bored and need a lot of stimulation but was not and still am not a great socialiser, more of a loner who prefers one on one. Mother once sent me to a local mother who ran a small playgroup for 3-4 yr. olds in her kitchen. Apparently I was being observed for social interactions then, though I don't remember much about it, just going and being collected afterwards. To be honest 'playing' is just boring too. I want to be doing things actively throughout my whole life, my whole childhood too— favourites are digging in the garden, climbing trees, going for walks, watching insects and plants and birds. All this is deemed unnatural. And this is pretty much how I still am, it's my normal.

Reading is my only respite. Life at home goes from bad to worse, violence has crept into our family on a regular basis, mostly, as they described it 'if they didn't give me a good thrashing every month or so I'm not very nice to live with'. I am already so traumatised by my Mother I am in pretty much constant 'frozen emotion' mode.

School continues like this, with more and more punishment making no difference until I take the eleven plus. I do incredibly well. That surprises everyone.

It doesn't change anything at school other than make it harder for me to slip under the radar. No one investigates why I'm underperforming as my test scores suggest I should or could be doing better. If anything, it is taken as evidence that I am wilfully lazy. The pressure to perform so my parents can show off about me is huge. They make no secret of how ashamed they are of me. I fail and fail again in my parent's eyes and no matter what I do, it is no use. Unless I am top of the class in something, I am worthless to them. If I do achieve top marks, then I should have always been doing it. Never any encouragement or recognition of how challenging the process of school style learning is for me.

The family paradigm is about success academically and financially, in property terms. It is about status and visible bragging rights. I brought none. On top of that I am now the unwanted child, the family scapegoat and my reputation has been thoroughly ruined by my Mother's version of me, to cover her tracks. I am counted as sullen, ungrateful and lazy. The cause of all the family problems. I learn how to 'pull myself together' in front of other people and this is my survival for the next few decades. Every time I try to say I'm not ok, I am shut down, one way or another.

For a while I also believe all of it, about myself and about what makes you worth something in life. I scrape through because I am intelligent. But my brain has ADHD and trauma, so it doesn't work for me at school. But I finally get 7 O levels and 2 A levels. Something, but not good enough. I accept all their evaluations.

Until I realise, they are wrong.

About it all.

As I grow up, through books and other life changing experiences I realise there are other ways of looking at the world.

I start looking. It takes me a long time to unravel all that I have been brainwashed with. Decades really. But I am freed from their values before I get fully free from the rest.

I look back now from my age of retirement.

I am so grateful to my younger self for failing, and not getting myself onto their treadmill. I could have been an academic success, a career success, all sorts of things if I had not been made to believe I was worthless and had nothing to offer anyone.

I am so glad that I was made to look the other way. I looked inside myself and found my qualities of compassion and kindness.

I found love and gentleness and a spiritual approach to life which my family do not like or respect. I found deep, deep happiness, perhaps more than they will ever know.

I have enough — a good life and a nice home. I have friends and family who love me, my own sons and grandson, and a soulmate husband. I write and create — poetry, gardens, my own designs in knitwear.

I have fun and laugh a lot. I am nothing to boast about, no great success story other than that of survival and living on my own terms.

I have enough.

Letter to my Younger Self.

What I would like to say to my inner younger self.

You were awesome to get through all that. I must take my hat off to you. Even now I find it so hard to go back there and to think about what you endured, all the while knowing others have it far worse too. That thought horrifies me and drives me on still, to make this public and recognised. You are far more resilient than I feel nowadays, and without you I would not now be able to experience the strange phenomenon of being loved for who I am—warts and all.

You were pretty good looking back then too, though you could not see, or feel it, and hated it when people gave you compliments. You could never trust them, until you learned how to. But you also knew that beauty does not mean anything about who you are as a person. It is just a further burden of projections and expectations from others for you to cope with. What they wanted from you. You never wanted it after all. All you wanted was to be accepted and seen, just seen for who you are. It takes you a long time to get there but you will.

So, hang on in there girl, make it through. Let me welcome you with open arms into the future where you hair is white and your body is crumbling from all that strain, but where you are truly happy, and surrounded by sons, a grandson, and a husband who all truly love you for all you give them and all you have struggled with too. Between them they give you the greatest gift, which is to know you can love someone, the four of them, unreservedly, and without fear.

Hang on in there kiddo, it is worth that struggle to get through and you will make it, I promise. But I think you intuitively know that anyway—don't you?

9. SURVIVAL SKILLS ON THE HOME FRONT

Life at home goes from bad to worse. Violence has crept further and further into our family on a regular basis, both emotional/verbal and physical.

I am regularly informed that without friends I am even more worthless. Friends are a measure of your social value. If you are bullied, as I was at school, for being odd and different, that is yet another sign of your worthlessness and you deserve it. Once Mother comes into school to talk to a teacher about one particular girl who'd made it almost impossible for me to come to school. My refusal forces her to act. Mother had felt herself bullied at school, so there is a modicum of recognition in her for my experiences. But the girl denies it and thus it is put back onto me.

One day after school, I am looking out of my bedroom window, feeling very bored as usual, and I see some girls, who look about my age, along the street playing and talking together in a front garden. I go downstairs to find Mother in the kitchen, preparing tea. My sister is colouring in at the kitchen table, aged about 4 by now, I am about 8.

'Mother can I go and make friends with those girls up the road?'

It seems like a reasonable request, one that will win approval and make her happy since she repeatedly tells me how unsocial I am.

'Who are they?'

'Just some girls up the road hanging out in the front garden.'

'I don't want you hanging out with people like that, playing on the street. NO. Go and find something productive to do. Tea's ready in half an hour.'

I don't argue but slip quietly out of the house to go and find out what they are like, intending to ask them if I could play in future, reporting back and perhaps being allowed to play another day. I must be gone longer than I realise.

The house is a corner one, just the other side of a turning, The Crescent, which is next door but one to our house. I have crossed the road safely many times before.

I introduce myself and feel a comfortable reception developing, curiosity about the new girl, if nothing more, and it only feels like less than a minute. Mother comes raging down the street,

'What are you doing out here? How dare you cross that road without my permission, I thought I'd told you to go and do something productive in your own room.'

I quickly say sorry to the new friends, to minimise the embarrassment. They are friendly but look at Mother with astonishment. I feel utterly humiliated, smile bleakly and follow Mother back home.

She is in a mood now and it's my fault. But I'd only been gone for a few minutes to find out about them, I hadn't gone to play with them. And they were nice to me. I sat and ate my tea in silence.

When dad comes home, I've already retreated to my bedroom, hoping the fallout won't be too bad. I hear them having words downstairs though, Mother whining and Dad shouting. Then I hear him bounding up the stairs.

The bedroom door crashes open. He comes into my room in a fury, grabs me by my hair and drags me downstairs. I struggle to keep my footing on the stairwell. He isn't slowing down for me. I just about make it on my feet, held up in part by his grasp of my hair.

Dad flings open the front door and drags me into the front garden. There he yanks off my lower clothing and proceeds to 'thrash me', his terminology, my naked lower areas in full view so that 'all the neighbours could see what a terrible child he had to deal with'.

Dad is a very solid, strongly built man. Built like an ox I heard Mother say once. He is using his full strength on my body and his hands lay blow after blow on me. I can feel his anger and hatred - his desire to destroy me once and for all. He is shouting at me, 'how dare I go and upset my Mother yet again, why does he have to come home from work every day and be faced with me?'

When his anger has subsided enough to let me go, I gather my clothes and run inside, completely in shock from his assault. He has hit me before but this time I know he wants to kill me, to destroy me, to silence me forever. Something has changed, he hates me in that moment of hitting, hates me beyond his own recognition. His fury is so intense I can feel it as his hand cuts through the air before landing on my flesh. I will never feel safe with him again. Even though I am obliged to live with him as a daughter, I can never allow myself to feel anything with him, ever. Another part of me freezes.

I remember so clearly, when the flashback nightmare for this one arrives, I am shouting out in terror, shaking, and it isn't until several years after his death that I am ever again able to recall any good times with him. I ache for the father I once knew but the father I now have cannot be trusted either. I am utterly alone, living with the enemy and only eight years old.

The Chosen One

I was the first
the centre of attention
a trophy to bestow
upon novice aunts and grandparents,
A new generation begun.

I was the chosen one
to fulfil your desires
your needs, your dreams

selected for success
by the shape of my head
my brow
an alertness in my eyes.

I became Daddy's girl
chosen to sit on his knee
to place my cold hand inside his gloves
against his huge warm hands.

Hands that held me, guided me
showed me that I was the chosen one.
But when the light in my eyes
and the sense in my brow
failed to meet approval,
your hand turned hard against me
dizzying my thoughts
with headaches that lasted for days.

I again the chosen one,
your wrath against life's injustices
fell heavily against my flesh.

I the chosen one, the first
of a new generation
carrying the responsibility
for all who came later
who learned to stay quiet
to sit in fear
of becoming a chosen one.

Then I grew beyond your reach
beyond the venom of your words,
chosen now for excommunication
rejection upon a whim
never revoked.

I chose to learn the strength
of forgiveness, to love the lessons.
I learned to trust the senses
in my brow,
the light in my eyes
I found the words to say
I am the chosen one
And I choose myself—today.

The 'discipline' continues, more or less as before - scary – confusing – erratic and usually unconnected to much of what I do or don't do - to be endured until they both calm down but never to be responded to. As I write this memoir, I'm not pretending I was some kind of perfect innocent darling - no child is - but when the rules change constantly you don't have a decipherable stable code of behaviour to learn from. I was left confused and lost for much the time. The great positive is that I learn to trust my own intuitive instincts more than any other human alive. Even when they are under threat from Mother's gaslighting techniques, making me doubt everything I experience as real, I learn to trust something deeper than her reality.

I don't know where that comes from though, it's as if I know something outside my own experience. It is greatly assisted by reading and being read to from books that have a fantasy or mystical quality to them. There seems to be a genuine something beyond this nightmare reality, so I decide to look there for salvation. This did and still does stand me in good stead. I remember being read the first part of The Lion, the Witch and the Wardrobe by C.S. Lewis by a temporary teacher we had for a couple of weeks, in year four as it would be called now.

I can still remember the classroom, sitting at the back, craning my ears to catch every word and feeling spellbound, transported. It speaks to me so deeply.

I want to know Aslan, to be protected by him. I want to read that book badly but don't know how to find it, until much later, by a series of synchronous events such as those that lead you to the places and things you need to reach, it is handed to me as a gift. I now understand Aslan represents Jesus but that source of solace is denied me because of Mother's church involvement.

But back to age eight coping strategies, another traumatic flashback memory, and trusting instinct and intuition above anything else.

I'm in my bedroom, probably reading and I hear Mother screaming on the landing outside. I open my bedroom door to see my sister cowering beneath Mother's raging monster, crumpled in a heap on the floor. Mother was her usual hissing, screaming, terrifying, spittle flecking, red-faced monster, but now inflicting herself on my little sister as she had a few years earlier on me.

'Why won't you hug me and give me the love I want?' she is screaming words to that effect, 'I am your Mother, you should love me, you must love me. Why are you being wicked like your sister?'

I intervene immediately and stand between my sister and my Mother. I put my body between them so she cannot hit or shake my sister, then I calmly look her in the face and tell her

'You have to earn love, it's not something that can be demanded. You kill the love people have by screaming like that.'

I am calm and clear and know I am speaking truth. I never know where that courage or wisdom comes from. It flows through me, like melting butter through holes in toast, bright, deliciously real, and trustworthy.

To this day I don't know where that wisdom came from in me, but I knew in the instant I saw my sister starting to be abused, as I'd been, that love is never possible if people behave like that. The fear they create destroys the possibility of love and trust developing or even when it is there, it cannot be given safely, or freely. Love never grows from fear and abuse. I began to understand why I could not love my Mother and Father as church told us to do, as the vicar told us to.

I know I always want to love my Mother and I want her to love me, but I know she makes it unsafe and impossible for either of her daughters to do so. I want to help her to understand that.

I then simply take Hazel into my bedroom for the rest of the day. My presence is her protection for now.

When Dad gets home, I hear their voices, then the usual storming upstairs. I'm dragged out onto the landing and given a good thrashing for my sister to see because I am trying to turn her against my Mother. That is Mother's justification for that day's rage. Hazel watches and says nothing to help me, she is too afraid she might be next. But I still remember her eyes and the shame and guilt she felt. We both knew I was taking this one for her.

After that Hazel starts to suck up to Mother a bit more, a defensive move I am sure, but it leaves me even more isolated rather than being allies as sisters. That dynamic between us never leaves, always polluting any attempts we have at making a relationship.

Another thing I often wonder now is what my Little Grandmother, Ada Mabel, thought, said or did about it. She must have known how badly Mother treated us when Dad was at work, but as far as I know she never said anything. Perhaps she was too afraid of Mother herself. Afraid to come between husband and wife. Lorna was pretty unkind to her too.

I think it was some time around then, maybe slightly before or afterwards, that we are suddenly whisked away for two weeks to go and stay with Mother's old school friend Freda and her kids. Hazel and I both sleep on her children's bedroom floors and I guess Mother has a spare room or sofa or something. Mother tries later in life to suggest that Dad was violent to her and she was afraid of him herself, always placing herself as the victim, but then NPD works exactly like that. The individual with NPD is never responsible for anything, it is always someone else, even if that someone else is a young child.

But if it is before the outdoor thrashing, that might explain why it was suddenly stepped up so much against me. He still smacks my sister occasionally, but she is mostly too afraid to do anything much. She is a very nervous child and bites her fingers up to the elbow, and anyway she is Mother's 'good girl' alternative to me.

We leave without discussion or explanation and then we return two weeks later or thereabouts. I don't know why we don't go to my grandparents. They have a big enough four bedroom house where we could all have had beds. Such are the mysteries of dysfunctional families and their goings on. As a child I just accept what we're doing. Mother is nicer, more reasonable during that time at Freda's and I remember sort of hoping we could stay there. I don't remember missing Dad at all.

During the time I am writing this book and my aunt Mercia is now able to listen to my story properly, Mercia comments how they brought out the absolute worst in each other. I think that is true. Mother was much better with Douglas, her second husband. He kept her under control through approval, but there were no children at home by then either, no scapegoats. Douglas sort of ignored and joked about Mother's tendency to shout out loud when alone in the kitchen. She would get louder and louder, increasingly heated and angry about the injustices the world heaped upon her, aka Shirley Valentine on steroids.

We come home and nine months later my brother is born so I think there is some sort of reconciliation between them. Life is easier for a while. But she can never stop herself exploding so I have no doubt that it continues, maybe less severely, due to the positive hormones of pregnancy.

I have my ninth birthday in March of that year and during summer we move to Nottinghamshire for Dad's work. He becomes assistant branch manager of the big regional branch. That opens a whole new chapter in my life.

10. THE HEALING WORLD OF DREAMS

I was growing up in a family with no genuinely healthy, engaged, relating patterns, and no safe attachments or love. So I think it natural my mind would turn towards the magical to find sanctuary. As mentioned, I come across it in books, my other form of sanctuary, and perhaps unconsciously I seek it in the material world too, as a salve, a healing, a possible rescue even.

That I am by now frozen and traumatised by my parents is evident. My unconscious mind sought so many ways to protect me and dreams are one of them. No one really understands the full purpose of dreaming as a human brain function but in part it is deemed to be a way of working through the events of the day.

My recollected dreams start around age five as far as I can remember. These dreams are vivid, repetitive and often lucid in that I can add to the narrative sometimes, as if I can interact or negotiate and converse with some of the characters.

My entire life has been on two levels, the normal, material, practical level and another one. I am not that unusual, but I am also not that 'normal'. I am deeply sensitive to things beyond this material world. I sense things, energies and intuitions, people's emotions even. These lead me to write my first books. They also send me on a deeply spiritual journey which is both a deepening of that influence in my life and my healing from Mother's fallout. Dreams have played a huge part in my life and here are the ones relevant to this part of my story. They both comfort and inform me during the terror years. Other dreams come later, in the healing times. Always very prophetic.

<u>The crab dream.</u>

This dream haunts me nightly for several years in early middle childhood, roughly between four and eight years of age.

The basic premise of the dream is this. I am running across the fences of the back gardens of Goodhart Way. I need to get to the other side of the street. I need to cross the road, and for some reason that will be my salvation. But I cannot get across that road because every time I try to sneak between the houses, creep down their side passages and put on full speed across the road until my heart pumps itself to the maximum, I am always thwarted. I am trapped, outsmarted, jeered at, blocked, made to feel inadequate and a failure. The giant crab is always there waving its claws and threatening me with destruction in the clench of its huge pincers.

Sometimes I make it part way across the road and am slightly ahead of the crab, but it always sees me before I can make it all the way and I'm chased back into the world of back gardens. On occasions I also see the remains of other victims on the road, those who are caught. Their carcasses lie mangled and rotting, twisted into knots and blackened by decay. These sightings are truly horrific. I am at least successful in remaining alive and not being caught. I am too quick, and that brings some relief and makes me redouble my efforts. I think the carcasses are my Little Grandma, and possibly my father himself. They are both laid waste by Mother's verbal assaults and denigrations. And possibly my younger sister, because I remember in some dreams trying to get my sister to run with me and try to escape with me, but she won't. She is too small or too weak or too slow or something, but she will always succumb and just stay put in one back garden, not trying to escape but accepting her captivity.

I return again and again, to my frantic racing across the back gardens alone, always alone, trying to outsmart the crab – to get ahead of it, to escape it, anything so that I can cross that road. I will be hurdling fences and climbing trees, almost flying across these gardens but unable to get to the other side. I always feel both deeply frustrated and simply sad for those other people in my family, all of us trapped by the monster my Mother has become in her little power realm, wielding her cruelty like a battle axe over our heads continuously and then wanting us all to pretend to the world that we are a happy successful family and everyone must collude with the lie that protects her.

Salvation simply means getting to the other side, on which there are pretty much identical houses. It seems to be that outsmarting the crab will save me, getting past it, winning the contest. But I never do. My child sized body and life experience can never outsmart this huge menacing crab of which I am terrified. It seems to know my every move, my every hope and dream and aspiration, and be ready to smash them with its huge claws.

I wake every night in a heated sweat, my heart thumping as if it will break out of my chest. It takes me a long time to get back to sleep. Every time I wake, I'm left with the residual of that dream, sometimes more than once in a night and I always feel tired during the day, every single day for years. The terror I feel rarely goes away, since I am simply dreaming a story version of my actual life.

This dream is obvious though isn't it? My Mother is the crab and I am desperate, wanting to get away from her, get past her, get some kind of advantage in my own life, to escape her waving giant claws, her taunting and aggression and crushing power over me. I am the desperate haunted child, powerless and trapped.

This dream overlaps with the next one which has become a lucid form of dreaming. Now I can have actual conversations with the characters and do deals on the outcomes, thus gaining some personal empowerment and insights.

The Shaman

From very early on I feel there is something fundamentally wrong about the way native Americans, or 'Indians' are portrayed in western films. I instinctively feel they are the good but wronged peoples. The cowboys feel wrong, as if they are the real baddies. I also identify more with their culture than the American western dream being peddled in these films, creating justifications for something which in later life I realise is mass murder and genocide - nothing more, nothing less. The fact that this comes up in my dreams is of no surprise to me, but what happened later was!

The premise of the dream is that I am a white girl whose family home is being ransacked by Indian tribes defending their rights to land that has been stolen from them. I am always taken captive with the rest of the white people in this dream, but because of my youth and gender I am held apart, not immediately killed but kept for possible use by the tribe.

I am always in solitary confinement, sometimes a tepee, sometimes a wooden shed, awaiting the decision whether to kill me or enslave me. I keep trying to tell them I'm on their side, how I feel their fight is just, their culture wonderful, and not all whites are bad. I want them to understand how killing us just makes the European narrative more justifiable, they were more easily viewed as savages. I want them to understand peacefulness and co-operation.

This always leaves the elders confused, am I to be trusted or am I just being a double agent forked tongue, even as a child of about eight to twelve years of age.

In this dream however, the situation is not so finite or desperate. Although I am very afraid, there is a shaman in these tribes who sees the truth in my heart. He befriends me.

He cannot overtly support me for fear of those baying for my blood. He would lose his standing in the tribe. But he will find a way of helping me to escape when all is quiet. Not only this but he finds ways to help me overcome my fear, to understand about waiting my time, not rushing around and wasting energy but waiting for an opportunity when I can make my move and go free. This means I will run alone as a fugitive, but I would be alive and go on to live my life.

So, night after night I am held captive, my life at risk, but I always have one friend, the Shaman who sees my true heart and helps me to escape, to overcome fear. He is teaching me how to manage fear.

There is so much fear in my life daily, I become dependent upon this shaman during the day too and often find myself talking to him as I go upstairs to bed 'you will come and help me again tonight, won't you?' and other such questions, that I even sometimes speak out loud albeit very quietly, to this shadow presence in my life as I go upstairs to the terrors the night always holds.

Again, the meaning of this dream is very clear. It is a progression from the crab narrative, taking episodes from my normal life and creating them into dream narratives that help me to work myself through the trauma of life with my Mother and Father. Wait your time, learn to overcome your fear, your time will come, know your own truth. It suggests there is more to my story than the one my Mother tells, that I have value other people can see even if she would or could not.
Eventually this dream is superseded, but that is another stage of my early life.

A few years later, I am in my early forties, yet to meet David, at another crossroads, looking for answers to the endless deep, dark feeling of worthlessness and failure that my life represents, a non-stop struggle just to survive. I find myself being led in all sorts of psychological and spiritual directions. Many of them are a bit mad in the early days but all part of the journey to understand myself. I am trying to reconnect with that deeper intuitive side, the part of my experience of life that I learned to bury for fear of its power to attract further abuse from Mother. One of those spiritual directions is a deep, but short term, pass through shamanic traditions, although I do still keep a flame for that teaching alive inside myself.

I went to see a shamanic healer, two in fact, both following recommendations from other people.

One was called 'Crow healer' or something like that. She lays me down on a nest of floor cushions and rugs, then covers me with some beautiful woven blankets, and asks me to keep my eyes closed while she makes contact with my spirit guides. She starts a slow gentle rhythm of drumming and then starts to add some chanting to it. It is very soothing. I lie there and feel a lot of pulling and fumbling sensation deep in my belly, warm and comforting but also like they are tearing me open, moving things around, taking things out.

When it is finished and I'm asked to sit up, she tells me a few interesting things. I have never forgotten them.

She tells me two senior male shaman spirit guides came to her calling, and one knew me well. Apparently, he'd spent several years coming to me in dreams, teaching me to conquer my fear and not be overcome by it. He has come back to see how I've got on and apparently is pleased with my progress thus far; I am on track for whatever it is I'm heading for, why I am still here.

They both leave and then a woman healer guide comes in to help heal my belly from all the sexual abuse and damage done in teen and early adult years. She pulled out of my womb all the negative energy and emotional scarring that has built up there. They leave me with two power animals, the mountain lion so I would walk fearlessly alone through my life, and the badger who can see ways through the darkness and find the hidden truths.

I had told her nothing – just that I'd been recommended to her and I'd come to see how or if she might offer me healing. We all need healing, so I told her nothing specific, just that, like so many people, I'd lived a tough life and was now trying to find a spiritual path through it for myself. I didn't even realise how much sexual abuse I'd experienced in life until many years later on when the 'Me Too' narrative allowed me to recognise what had happened to me in earlier years. But I realised she was talking to me about this dream, which by that age I'd completely forgotten about, but there it was again anyway. And suddenly a few things fall into place and I start to open, blossoming with this intuitive psychic side to my experience of life. I start to embrace parts of myself I had lost.

I drive home, feeling very contemplative and profoundly moved but unsure where this will lead me next.

I get home and stay seated in my car for a few moments, still digesting what has happened. Through the window I see one of my cats, Saffy, lying across the top of the TV, basking in the concentrated heat of the sunshine. I want to go and hold her suddenly, a strong urge. I lock the car and go indoors. She is kind of my favourite but also the most annoyingly independent and occasionally disruptive cat I have ever shared my life with. As I walk into the sitting room, she lifts her head and looks me straight in the eye and I hear these words in my head, very clearly 'now you know who I am'. I realise she is my power animal, my mountain lion, my fearless feline, my independent feisty loner soulmate.

I have recently separated from someone at this point, just before I meet David, and am re- evaluating my whole life. The 'ex' returns to the house and goes to stroke Saffy. She turns on him, spits and hisses like nobody's business, even though she'd been a kitten when he'd arrived and had more or less grown up with him. But she knows he means no good at all, she reads his energy and she is right too.

Saffy is fiercely letting him know he is not welcome any more. I read her message in that hiss and know she is also warning me, rightly so. Soon after he proves her point for himself admirably.

Some five years later I travel with my eldest son to Brighton to see another recommended shaman healer. The second shaman tells me he sees the shadow of a fierce, cruel woman standing over me, although I will break free of her energy. Then he shifts some energy, which I feel physically as a kind of pulling movement and tells me I will have to do the emotional work too. Interesting but less connected with my dream life. I had told him nothing, though he had accurately just described that early mother standing over me, the opposite of the paradigm of the good loving maternal mother.

Back to my story at this pre-teen age range. Things were certainly weird for me, happening on all sorts of other levels, apart from dreams, and mostly at night.

I have a lot of flying dreams in-between nightmares and I love them. In them I can soar above everything that is happening in my life and just look down on it, detached and indifferent. I have freedom in those dreams, I'm invincible and talented and wise and independent. I know this is a portent of what is to come, and I grow increasingly more impatient for my adult life to begin. But it seems an impossible number of years ahead still.

Sometimes those flying dreams went to different places. One that occurs occasionally is that I just lift out of my body and fly around the house. I remember once I fly downstairs and the living room door is just open. Inside my parents are eating dinner on trays and watching TV. I stay and watch their TV for a while. Then return to my body.

In the morning I tell Mother I watched their TV while I was asleep. They don't believe that I was out of bodying with them, they only believe I was creeping around the house at night when I should be asleep in my bed. I don't get punished but I think I spook them because they hadn't heard or sensed me as they would have done if I had actually crept downstairs, which they wanted to insist was true.

I learn not to tell them about my dreams and psychic experiences, but they continue. Another regular experience I have is again out of body travelling into a house that is inside the walls of this house that we live in. A sort of parallel universe which is identical but different. There doesn't seem to be any fear pervading this other house, it is a parallel existence with everything just slightly different, happiness, laughter, warmth.

These dreams give me so much to think about, however you want to interpret it all, and they often occupy my thoughts at school too.

Friday Mornings

No window in this gallery through which I may peek
where I sit happily, as steward, once a week.
Not like school, where I always chose a window seat,
and struggle to focus, my school work to complete.

I watched the world outside with far greater fascination
than the one I was supposed to attend to, the English lesson.
How my dreams and thoughts flew,
from the windows their inspiration drew.

In front of me, imaginings of others are flaunted
while my own tender offerings feel daunted.
Poetry comes in a gentle flooding
of words, patterns of thoughts, delicately woven inspiration.

Should I attempt to dam this gift with intellectual endeavour,
artificial word selection, amaze with brilliance, my metaphor
or metre.
My goal, to gently lead the reader by the hand,
to offer a share of my world, a place to understand.

Simple lines may enthral more for my poetic knowledge,
yet leave you bereft of raw emotions felt from the splutter of
words,
as they waterfall through my thoughts and pencils and slowly
come into view.
I cannot claim these lines, though they are born from my life,
the experiences that inform and shaped me, the joy and the
grief.

11. TWIGGING
WITH MOTHER.

We move to Nottingham in 1964, and things get slightly better for a while. Despite all the seriously traumatic times with my Mother, and although as a child I am always waiting for her to blow again, there are good times. There is some kind of distorted love present in those times too. It never lulls me into a false sense of security but it does echo the memories I must have still, from when I was very little and was in her NPD love bombing stage as her new toy, as a first child, the centre of her universe and all she needed.

It is only after both my parents were dead that I 'feel safe in the world' again and am able to reflect, without defensive fear, and consider what those good times have been and how they felt through my frozen defensive carapace of childhood. This is one of those memories.

Mother wants to be perceived as 'the good Mother' so occasionally she does try to do things that are fun and educational, and which suit her sense of her family's superiority over other local families.

We are living in rural Nottinghamshire, in a village called Radcliffe on Trent. Along the back of our house runs public parkland and a cliff path that stands over the banks of the River Trent, in those days a deeply polluted smelly toxic river which turned into mounds of stinking, detergent-like yellow foam at the foot of the weir close by. At the base of the cliff are a few large lily ponds which are mostly invisible and filled with irises and rushes of various sorts. The amphibian wildlife in them is prolific despite the nearby pollution.

The house we live in backs onto this cliff, with a gate in the hedge which allows free access. It is my haven, my sanctuary and I utterly love my moments of escape from family dynamics. It is also a hugely liberating contrast to suburban outer south east London. From those times I develop what is already an innate love for and deep feeling of connectedness to the natural world. I fall in love with baby toadlets and froglets.

Twigging, collecting small twiggy specimens from many different trees, is on that list of approved activities since it includes outdoor exercise and education, and it is a shared activity that she can control and make herself the central focus of. Mother takes me, or possibly us, twigging at the near end of winter just as spring's arrival is prescient. We look for signs such as slightly swelling buds on the trees and early spring flowers, snowdrops and crocus coming out in swathes in the lawns of the local park that also back onto this cliff path further down towards the village centre.

Twigging is teaching me so much, but especially close observation of natural growing things. I am still struggling at my new primary school with my ADHD and find my life utterly frustrating much of the time, caught between Mother's mental illness and a school system that does not consider the needs of children individually at all.

For me this activity also ticked all the boxes. Outdoors, physical, active, requiring the close observation which feeds my slightly obsessive nature, and largely not social. I have always found socialising for its own sake utterly pointless.

We take her secateurs and a small bag and set off along the cliff path, taking sample twigs from as many specimens of tree we can find. They are wrapped into damp tissue and placed inside a plastic bag prepared for this exact purpose.

When we get home again the twigs are carefully unwrapped and put into a vase on the kitchen windowsill where they get enough light to continue growing and evolving from stark winter form to lush spring new leaves. I take them down at least once each morning to observe how far they have opened. It is almost a race between the species, which will make it out of bud first, who will swell to fully open first. I don't mind which one wins, I just enjoy watching, observing, curious, noticing deeply.

There are plenty of sycamores which are easy to identify from both bark and bud. But the ones that catch my attention with their brown sticky buds are those of horse chestnut, also the small black triangular buds of ash and the long slightly sticky but delicate pointed buds of beech and hornbeam. I love the catkins of birch, alder and hazel, and occasionally willow too, pussy willows in all their variations. I also love the barks of oak, ridged and rough gnarled, and beech, smooth and grey with little tweedy flecks. Cherry trees too, prunus, with their little horizontal eyelet notches down their trunks.

Leaf shapes vary fascinatingly, some smooth, some crinkled or even almost pleated. I watch, taking mental notes daily, as they swell and transform from bud to full leaf size in just a few short days, each one a little miracle of nature, so fresh and green and alive still even though they are cut from their parent plant.

Looking back now perhaps I am also becoming aware of the teachings around impermanence, that everything must die for something to be born, that the bud must die for the leaf to be born. But whatever it is, it holds my attention closely. Transformation. Am I still just a bud too?

I learn to identify members of the cherry family from bark alone, then oak, then beech and so on. I also spend hours poring over plant identification books and start to pick up their family names in Latin - Prunus, Quercus, Alnus, Fagus, Acer, Salix, Betula etc. Just knowing these names feels heavenly.

My stimulation starved brain absorbs all this as if its survival depends on it. As spring progresses, I want to learn more and more.

Then Mother, on a roll with me, introduces me to the world of wildflower collecting and pressing between sheets of blotting paper under the corners of the carpets. She also has happy memories of pressing wildflowers with her own Grandmother whom she'd loved greatly and always spoke of in her softest voice, called Magga.

Perhaps Magga was my Mother's sanctuary in her own childhood. Perhaps she was giving me the gift of sanctuary at an unconscious level. I now know there was a part of Mother that was hidden but in essence had kindness and generosity in it, but it had been so subsumed by the monster of her NPD and trauma that it rarely came out in any identifiable form. Perhaps I wanted to think that too.

I collect ravenously, identifying and labelling each specimen and noting its family names in Latin as well as the common or local names. I start to understand plant family connections and to make close observations of these differences.

It is to this day one of the very, very few positive memories I have of Mother and for that reason I still collect twigs most springs, now that I once more live in a rural setting.

Those woods though have a more sinister presence in my life.

Once, after a particularly explosive row with Mother, I run away, ignoring her shouting at me to come back, and go into the little wooded play area. There's a horse chestnut there, youngish and still quite easy to climb. I race up its trunk as far as I can get, until I am amongst branches that can barely hold my weight. I look down and see how high I am. Then I swing and sway the tree back as forth as hard as I can, willing it to break under me and bring me crashing to earth, hopefully dead. Inside I am daring God or destiny or whatever that alternative influence in life is to let me die, to prove Mother right, or show me that I must live for whatever reason.

I also at times test the weir out in similar ways, edge myself out along the barrier until the water flow is strong enough to take me with it. I know I will not survive the tumble and the pollution. But something inside me wants to live too, I believe that one day I will be able to break free - to escape, and I never take that last step that would have meant there was no return. There is comfort in that testing though. It proves my courage and suggests that my survival is intended, despite how worth-less I really am.

12. LIVING WILD

Apart from twigging with Mother and not fitting into the new school very well, I remember living in Radcliffe as being one of the happiest periods of my early life. This doesn't mean the abuse isn't ongoing, it is, but it has become normal life. What makes it bearable is the country living. For whatever reason I am allowed a lot more freedom here than I've had before. And a bicycle. It means I get a lot more outdoors time than I've ever known. I love it and I live in the countryside surrounding our small Wates built housing estate, all uniform detached houses with garages and good-sized plots of land, and all totally devoid of any character.

My little Grandmother gradually becomes smaller and smaller, her hair thins down until her scalp, red and scaly, is barely covered by the fine white silken strands of hair she has left. She moves with us of course, having declined into a urine soaked old woman who eventually never leaves her bedroom. She becomes a scary creature to us children and is finally taken into some kind of respite nursing home that seems more like a hospital ward. We visit her once or twice and I make friends with Mrs Gaillard in the bed next to hers. She I kindly and I make friends with her, but on our last visit to Little Grandma she has died. They only tell me she is not well enough for visitors, but I can tell. I am sad.

In this I do have sympathy for my Mother. Looking after an incontinent elderly woman and three children, one of whom is still largely a baby, must be an intolerable load for her and mostly she does it well enough on a practical level, though never without loud complaints and demands that she be more appreciated. It strikes me how hard it is to appreciate people for their positive qualities when we are overwhelmed by their negative ones and I challenge her with this when she demands that consideration. She is finding my growing intelligence more and more difficult to cope with and I know it is around then that my intelligence is also turned into an issue, my curiosity and questioning nature viewed as yet another feature of my temperament to be criticised and suppressed with more cruelty and violence.

One of the rituals we must go through as a family is to entertain and be entertained by my Dad's new boss and his family. He has been moved to be an assistant branch manager with his first company car. I guess now it is some vetting process. The appointed day comes when they are invited to our house for Sunday lunch. We're lined up in the hallway when they arrive, ready to be exhibited. My father opens the door and welcomes them in.

I don't remember the exact words to begin with but the part which has never left me is as follows.

'This is our son, Martin and our middle daughter Hazel, she is a nervous little thing, and our eldest daughter Sylvia. She's quite nice if we give her a sound thrashing once a month to keep her in order.'

I see their faces go from smiling interest to shock and horror. This simply confirms it to me, the truth of my unacceptability. The day passes as slowly as a day like this would do for a nine-year-old girl who wants nothing more than to disappear into her bedroom and submerge herself into her latest book. That is my sanctuary always, the next book.

Sometimes Hazel and I get on OK, as sisters do, and sometimes we annoy each other. Some days my sister sets me up to be told off by moaning to Mother that I am not playing with her. I still mostly want to read if I am in the house. So, I play with my sister and then am admonished for making a mess, overexciting her, and all the usual accusations laid at my feet. This day I've had enough and just say no.

Mother looks at me with shock when I simply repeat myself.

'No'

I stand up to Mother, once more telling her what I think of her but, at this age, with far more maturity and insight than the eating dog pooh comment I'd previously made.

'What do you mean no?' insisted Mother.

'I mean no. I want to read my book and not play with Hazel and then get told off for doing it wrong. If I am reading my book, I can't do anything wrong can I?'

'But I am busy, and your sister needs entertaining. It's your duty as the older sister to play with her without upsetting her.' Mother's voice is increasing in volume, my arguments outsmarting her.

'No, I won't do it. It's too boring, and she doesn't want to do anything I enjoy. Why can't she read a book in her room and I read my book in mine.'

The door bursts open. It's Saturday and Dad has been out cleaning the car, but he walked back in and hears what he thinks is me being insolent again, he calls it causing trouble. He doesn't stop to ask, but just grabs my hair and, as before drags me into the front garden, strips off my lower half and publicly thrashes me once more. As his hands fly down, again and again onto my lower back and buttocks, I put a handout out to stop him. He catches my thumb and it gets wrenched back quite badly. I stop trying to defend myself and let him continue, this time flipping out and watching him as his fury burns itself out.

Mother hops back and forth once more and again I can see my sister behind her. I don't know where my brother is, but he is about two years of age when this happens.

I still clearly remember the daisies on the lawn, how sweet and white they are.

I do not cry once. I have effectively numbed all sensation in that area of my body. I feel no pain, but his hatred and anger I do feel. Physical pain is one thing, but the emotional onslaught is an entirely different thing, I can't stop that getting through to me. Numbness is my only defence.

When he finally stops his thrashing and calms down, I pull my clothes back up and go to my room. My sister tries to join me, but I cannot speak to her or acknowledge her. She leaves me alone, and so does Mother. It is as if I am suddenly invisible. No one knows what to say or do. My thumb aches and throbs for several days after. I think it has been sprained or wrenched in some way, but there is no lasting or visible damage.

About an hour later though, my body reacts in unexpected ways. I go to the bathroom, defecate profusely, vomit and wash myself clean, then get my bicycle from the garage and cycle off. I don't care where I go. I just cycle for a couple of hours along country lanes and footpaths. A few cars pass me, and a large white van comes a little too close and fast for comfort, but it doesn't perturb me. I feel inviolable, impervious to everything the world throws at me. All I am aware of is the sky above me, and my legs pushing the pedals around, as if the bike and my body are part of each other.

Along the lanes I regularly cycle, I often come across occasional roadkill, pheasants and rabbits mainly, hedgehogs too, though an occasional badger, squirrel or fox. I often stop to look at them, fascinated by their stiff silent flattened bodies. This is what death looks like on the outside. I am fascinated. What does it feel like on the inside though?

Today I come across a pheasant that has probably been hit by the white van which had passed me somewhat recklessly earlier. It is injured to the point of not being able to move itself off the road, but not fully dead. I stop my bike and watch it for a few moments as it bounces around in small circles, trying to right itself and move away from me, each attempt getting weaker. I find myself transfixed and watch until the poor bird is unable to move any more. I know it is dying but I'm unable to do anything to help it. I feel helpless. I wonder what would have happened if it had been me and not the pheasant that the van had hit.

I dismount the bike, propping it up against the hedge and attempt to pick up the bird. It is still not fully dead, but it can't struggle against me. I lift it to the side of the road and lay it against the hedgerow. It is soft and warm and heavy in my hands, life ebbing but not yet gone. This process of dying is taking time and I sit with the bird for a little longer, just watching it, being with it, unable to help it.

Eventually, when it shows no more signs of life, I remount my bicycle and continue cycling, but the anger and fire has gone from my legs. I cycle along and notice the birds in the hedgerows, the insects which fly towards me and so much more. I am back in my own body. I end up in Shelford, the next village along. I ride down to the River Trent and watch it flowing past me, swiftly but less so than up near our house. Here it is wider and still brownish in colour, still with a faint smell of detergent but less so than my weir.

I don't know how long it is, but I know I probably have to go home at some point. I don't have anywhere else to go, no one to turn to. I can't tell anybody what is happening to me, so deeply do I believe my parents, that I am indeed this wholly unconscionable child for them to endure.

I cycle slowly and reluctantly back home, wishing that something could happen to make it different, but knowing I just must go back and face whatever comes next. There is a relentlessness to my life now, a cycle or rhythm of violence and unkindness that I am used to. An inevitability to the pretence that we are a happy successful and special family, that my parents do love and care about us as children, and to some extent me too, until it changes once more, until it always changes once more.

I have one recollection from our ordinary life in Nottingham-shire that is not part of the traumatic memories returning. Mother has told me to come and talk to her in the kitchen while she is doing some work and I am to help her. I seem to remember peeling vegetables but cannot be sure. I can visualise myself at the kitchen table while she stands at the sink, with the light behind her from the window.

First, she starts to talk to me about my body and how it will be changing soon. I am around eleven. Then she proceeds to tell me how unacceptable my body is, too thin, my hair too lank and straight, my skin too dark and sallow, my legs too thin, my nose too large, my eyes too small, my feet and hands too large and so on and so on.

Some of that is true, but overall, I am not such a bad looking specimen of female. She makes sure I do not know this and I thus feel quite despicable to look at.

She then starts to tell me more intimate details of her relationship with my father, how he is cold towards her, how mistreated she is and how unkind her life is. I listen and start to feel sorry for her. I start to think my father is indeed this bad husband and father. I have enough reason of my own to think like this anyway. She comes up with list after list of all his failings and deficits and showers contempt upon him. But it isn't being aimed at me for a change and it is as if she is confiding in me and suddenly treating me with respect, as a confidante, someone who has worth. I am drawn into her web of stories and perspectives. I want Dad to take the brunt of her negativity instead of me for a change, and I want to be back on her inner circle.

I now recognise thoroughly this is how NPD works, that people draw you into their circles of influence and make you feel special as part of their power/control/manipulation isolation strategy. Called triangulation, it seeks to draw you into a conspiracy against the other person, to create circles of 'in favour and not in favour'. She'd done it to my sister and I, to Dad and I and now she was doing it to me against Dad.

It is a way of owning someone and controlling them and she had me caught. After all the unkindness years here I am, suddenly one of her inclusive ones, part of her inner zone. My eleven-year old's need to belong draws me back into her webs of deceit. My escape is thwarted for now.

I finish primary school at age eleven, having sat the eleven plus and get an extremely high mark because it is an IQ test which I really enjoy doing. There is a shock wave throughout the school at my scores as I had been deemed to be not very clever by this school. It gets me into a rather exclusive establishment at the time, Nottingham Bluecoat School. It is probably my happiest ever year at school, though even here I feel the outsider and struggle to fit in. I still have no sense of belonging or having any right to belong anywhere. But it is from this year that I'm still in touch with a few very old friends on Facebook.

We move back from Nottingham to our house in West Wickham in the summer of my twelfth year.

. . . .

13. A SLOW AWAKENING

There are a few layers of sexual awakening, as for most people.

First encounters.

Love introduced itself in so many guises
Timothy in primary, who liked to kiss the girls
Chasing around the playgrounds, interrupting
our female communal activity tribes.

We never questioned his rights to pursue
Just ran screaming, enjoying the chase
But not his big soppy lips,
big sloppy kisses on our mouths.

And little Stephen, who, in the cloakroom
Liked to expose himself whilst us girls
In innocence, went with curiosity
And left squealing.

What led those lost souls, seeking love or attention,
Confirmation, approval, who knows
Perhaps they were trying to tell us
All is not well in their world
But in a child's world, it is always a game, until it isn't.

And I, what did I say to those blind, deaf children?
Withdrawn, disconnected, yet so alive
An amoeba still waiting to define a form it can call 'self',

tentacles searching out safe trajectories of travel,
or potential hostilities to retreat from, always on the edges.
Did anybody ever wonder what I was trying to tell the world?

I remember hiding my periods from my Mother. I resent the idea of sharing that intimacy with her, I don't want to give her that part of myself and I am a late developer too, not quite fourteen before they start.

The first one arrives when Hazel and I are staying with two older cousins of my fathers, Ellen and Ann. They are spinster sisters who live together in Surbiton which later becomes famous for 'Tom and Barbara', two urban 'live off the land' people in a sitcom The Good Life.

Ellen, the younger by two years, had been ill in childhood, with rheumatic fever I think and had developed crumbling bones as a result. That is how it was explained to us anyway. We often use to stay with them, and they were each a godmother to Hazel and me. They teach us card games which I love, and canasta becomes a staple of time spent 'entertaining' Hazel for Mother, a shared activity in which we can channel our endless competitiveness with each other.

With the onset of the menarche under way life pretty much continues as before. I am now back in south London, at yet another school where I struggle to find a foothold on the friendship ladders, such are the social hierarchies in institutions. So, I move from group to group, trying to make connections, never really feeling wanted though, just tolerated.

Some people appear to like me but I'm not sure how to relate to that notion still. But one craze that runs through the year and possibly whole school, is the art of levitation. We are all doing it in the playground, and it fascinates me. To begin with I'm only wanted as an extra pair of hands but eventually they realised for some reason I'm particularly good at getting people to lift quite high off the ground. Pretty quickly though the school management closes it all down. But I have now made contact with girls in my all girls grammar school. From there we start to spend time together and conversations arise about the future of sex in our lives, the issues of virginity and pregnancy. Many myths abound.

At home my dream life is getting interesting again.

It starts one night when I'm asleep and dream of someone. I'm not even sure what or who they are but later realise it's a man coming into my bedroom. He just holds me all night. I can't see his face, but this happens more and more regularly. I start to recognise him by smell, a slightly sweet earthy smell with a hint of cinnamon too. I am also getting used to his voice. He talks to me in loving ways. His voice is soft, gentle, soothing, warm. I never know what he says to me but intuitively I hear him, the energy of his intentions towards me, and it is always kindness and tenderness.

I grow to look forward to sleeping, no longer afraid of the nightmares that once filled my nights. I can tell no one of my secret visitor in my dreams, but I don't need to, they are too private anyway.

One night I go to bed in anticipation of his arrival and he comes. Instead of just holding me he begins to stroke my whole body, arousing the fires of passion inside me. Eventually he makes love to me though I don't know if it is intercourse since I am still so utterly naïve about such matters. After such dreams I wake up feeling deeply aroused but innocent of that feeling, of what it is. It fills me with hope and a desperation to be old enough to find that man or a real life equivalent. I start to think this is what love feels like, this is what grownup love feels like. It is many years before I understand the difference between sexual arousal and true loving passion. But I am sure there is love here, between myself and my dream lover.

That initial misunderstanding will lead me into all sorts of problems later in life. But like most young teens, sex is a problem I don't understand, am utterly unequipped to cope with and is another source of confusion and feelings of worthlessness in me for being that innocent.

The previous years have taken their toll on my understanding of my place in the world and especially the value of my body, my sexuality, and relationships. It is all horribly distorted.

For instance, Dad has taught me that my body can be used by men, by him, when he wants to vent his feelings. He is both emotionally and physically abusive in his so-called discipline and he leaves me with a lot to deal with.

I am going to address the whole messed up sex thing in one chapter, skipping ahead to later life too, rather than keep drip feeding it into the narrative. It is too important to be broken down and is an essential part of the story and its consequences.

I write a cautionary tale about fathers who are too dominant in their daughter's lives, who are too authoritarian and patriarchal, just too old-fashioned male! Also, mothers who are not emotionally available or safe for their daughters to turn to for advice and support, for someone to be a guide through these terribly difficult times in anyone's life. I write of how one thing leads to another. Even if you think you are doing the opposite, and for good reasons, why the authoritarian approach to life is utterly destructive. Unfortunately, it is still all too prevalent, both in social political cultural strata, and within some families too.

My dad was an emotionally weak man, not out of innate weakness but because the social norm training in those days, of 'how to be a man', leaves him with few options of self-expression, and also because he lives with my Mother. It was my sister who pointed it out on those terms. 'Dad is an emotional coward'.

Before that I'd never really considered this point of view, and it made sense of how he'd treated me over the decades. He was definitely a maritally and emotionally abused man who could not admit to such and so it got passed down the hierarchy.

My parents were married for about 18 or 19 yrs. I never remember Mother treating him with any kindness either; she treated him appallingly for almost all the time. The trick of NPD is to be just nice enough just often enough to keep you coming back for more, and then the next dump of their issues onto you starts. Mother took no prisoners when she had you in her sights, and Dad and I were her primary targets.

It is well stated that one's relationships with parents will be the foundation of one's relationships with future contemporaries as well as authority figures. This punishment regime, the corporal punishment, this authoritarian approach to parenting and child management, apart from giving me lifelong PTSD to cope with, alongside my ADHD, leaves me very afraid of men, yet desperately wanting their approval, their succour, their protection from the evil Mother matriarch older female figure which is the other archetype I am still working through.

Within a couple of years of my dream lover, I reach adolescence just at the time the pill is available to girls of sixteen and older, without parental consent. They wouldn't have wanted me to take the pill or to have sex. Sex was something 'terrible', you mustn't do it. Yet I am led to believe, by magazines like Cosmopolitan which are just coming out then, that having sex would be good. This awareness of their lack of parental approbation made me want to try it out even more. Even though I am in some part always trying to gain their approval, I'm also a rebel against their regime and certainly have no trust for their judgments about life.

Around this time Mother also likes to show me the semen stains on Dad's bed sheets where he has an emission during the night. I am thirteen and fourteen at the time. Evidence of how cruel he is to her!!!!!!! That is part of her idea of sex and relationship education for me I suppose.

I want love and tenderness and all that I believe is part of a relationship with a potential 'boyfriend'. I want male validation, as women are still often taught. I desperately want someone to make me feel special and wanted and valued and loved, more than anything else, loved. I want a real manifestation of my dream lover. Also, validation, a challenge from another man to my Dad, so he might 'rethink his attitudes to me', I hoped!

I go looking for teenage love. I find rape instead. I don't even know if I have been raped or what, I still don't. All I know is I am being pushed into doing something, that 'No' isn't being listened to and I am too frozen to stop it. His parents come home, and we are interrupted. I flee for home but go to a friend's house instead. I don't feel able to go home. I phone my parents and tell them my date didn't turn up and I am at Pamela's house for the night and will be home the next day, Sunday. That day I mostly stay in my room and read. I am left alone.

At school on Monday my way of coping is to pretend bravado, that I'm no longer a virgin, as if it is some kind of initiation rite I have achieved, and I turn it into a laugh. Pamela is clearly frustrated with me, and unable to understand why I cannot take myself or anything that happens to me seriously. I don't count, not to me I don't, but she doesn't understand this. None of my friends do.

What I don't understand about myself until decades later was that being emotionally frozen from PTSD means you are unable to recognise or respond to any real emotions other than fear. Attention seemed good enough.

Many women who were young teenagers in the early 70's will know this story, of how the pill opened you up to unwanted sexual advances and expectations, coupled with the fear of being labelled frigid, a prick tease and all sorts of other unkind labels. Girls being 'given the choice' actually meant, for many, they had fewer excuses and less choice. Men could have the choices they wanted, with more freedom from possible unwanted outcomes and responsibilities.

Sex comes and goes and mostly I endure its unpleasantness, absorbing the increased feelings of worthlessness and self-hatred that come with those early experiences. My first experience is clearly rape, and a couple of subsequent ones too, but even then, I feel nothing other than the swelling between my legs that lasts three more days. I rarely remember saying yes to much, but am too afraid and frozen to say no, or to feel anything.

#Me Too helped me to recognise how much it had been abusive and coercive sex but how much I was also trained to accept that treatment from males. They wouldn't ever recognise what they had done either. I was fair game to them.

I pretend furiously of course, that it is cool and fun and everything else I have been told it should be. Being used is what I'm used to. But no love and no value and no making up for dad came my way, so in the end I settle for marriage to someone who just doesn't want to be on his own. I am not sure he ever values me, at least it never feels like he does, although I still have a kind of affectionate, old brotherly feeling for him, but we've been apart for decades now and simply share two sons. We had many good times as well and that should never be overlooked. He was a good man, just not available emotionally for me in ways that I desperately needed. He is much the same as before in his approach to life, and I am very much changed in the same number of years.

I try to make friends with men, to make them less scary for myself but that pressure never goes and at times becomes so overpowering that it makes me ill. Also, most men don't seem to be able to do friendship with women without the sexual issue raising its head. I go through a few relationships, always confusing sexual attraction for that love I'd felt in my dreams, until I was so utterly disillusioned by 'love' that I feel it unlikely I could ever trust anybody ever again. I'd had a five-year long relationship with someone who ends up mirroring much of my Mother's behaviours and I recognise in hindsight I am still attracted to that kind of energy and my desire to heal it. But those five years do a lot more damage and I finally make my escape, feeling like a complete screw up and worthless to the nth degree.

There was one man who harassed me about having sex with him at one of my places of work. He repeatedly asked me and then 'why not', endlessly and would not take no for an answer. He was a subordinate in my team and he then went about undermining my authority, such as it was. I tried to go through formal channels but was told unofficially to give it up as it would go against me. One thing led to another and I eventually left teaching altogether as a direct result of this experience. He had even boasted about breaking down my resolve to two colleagues, but they were not allowed to state this as evidence. I walked away from that career and turned my life into another adventure of writing and teaching mindfulness and seeing individual clients.

At least by my early forties I've learned I could survive on my own and make a life for myself. I've travelled all over the place, sometimes alone. I have my own home and a career, though that also crumbles with the demise of that penultimate relationship. I go through a massive spiritual re-awakening. I start to recognise my intuitive nature, start feeling all the old astral travel dream world returning to me. I also start writing seriously.

It is just after this phase, in my early forties I go on to find the soulmate I had dreamed of and gradually heal my abusive relationship with men in general, through one good man in particular. We are about as perfect a complementary match for each other as you can imagine, healing each other, supporting each other and making the second half of both our lives completely different by contrast. He is of course the man in my dream, and I recognised that soon after we first met, even down to his smell and voice.

This brief survey of my experiences and the links I made for myself between my early experiences and later ones. Now I will highlight the specific points of why this kind of parenting is so toxic and harming to all children but especially to girls, at risk of sexual abuse as teenagers and young adults.

A child's body is left vulnerable when violated by parental violence more than any other kind of violence because that is the principal archetype relationship with other male and female energies and supposed to be the first source of support and protection.

My intrinsic bodily sanctity has not been valued and I've not been taught/ learned that either; in my case my body was just my dad's punchbag for his frustration with Mother. Where is the boundary set for my body - there is none? There is no sanctity or 'right to deny access' — to say no — for a child being beaten and there is very little difference between that and most abusive sexual experiences where young men just want to use a woman and play the emotional games until they get what they want. Then they stop pretending and treat you badly until you put a stop to it. If you are strong enough to do so.

Secondly, I was afraid of both sets of adults in my life and as with most children that extrapolates onto most other adults, well probably all of them in fact. So even though I appear now to be like an adult on the outside, I never get to feel like one inside, which gives those other so called adults who are now my peers, a great deal of power over me and I am left powerless.

Hope is a dangerous thing when you are desperate, as I was back then, since hope allows you to get into situation after situation where you think or hope it will be different, but it rarely is. This is because my inside emotional valance is attracting exactly that kind of repetition and will continue to do so until I wake up to it inside and change that sense of self-worth to a positive valence. Then positive stuff starts coming towards me. I feel desperate most of the time and try not to show it but clearly give out red flags.

This information should be included in children's sex education.

Self-respect allows you to state your preferences clearly. That has been stripped from me systematically for my entire life up until that point. I must learn it from scratch for myself because I do not have that 'normal' layer of self-defence to call on.

So many of the #Me Too experience rebuttals have omitted to consider this point of view for women, and vulnerable men too of course. People don't say NO when they don't know how to say it, *so it sounds like they feel they have a choice.*

Feeling perpetually guilty for upsetting your parents leaves you feeling guilty for upsetting anybody in life, if your only value is in making other people happy as a child, then you are not going to suddenly think 'oh no I am not responsible for other people's happiness so I can say 'no thanks' to this person's advances', especially if they are in a position of power over you. You want to placate them, so they do not attack you instead, so you give in. This was a massive lesson to learn but ultimately a very powerful one too.

And I mess up real relationship opportunities because I have gotten too accustomed to being used and abused by default.

I try to take responsibility for my experiences, to own them by pretending it's ok and what I want it to be, but that is bravado, there is nothing true about it at all.

My ability to freeze my body from feeling both emotional and physical experiences is how PTSD often develops. It makes me appear emotionless and uncaring. It is purely defensive but has been the only form of self-protection I've ever been allowed to develop in childhood. Saying no, standing up to people, anything actively defensive is punished and only makes it worse, although I do that sometimes. I don't dare risk it with non-parents, that might turn out with even worse consequences. Who knew? I certainly didn't.

There are thousands of little nuanced ways in which I was trained to be abused as a young adult and I know there are far too many others like me out there, which is why I find comments like Germaine Greer's suggestions that rape or sexual assault be legally downgraded to make it easier to prosecute is so missing the point. The media are not taking the whole story into account and I challenge this.

Some people get over that kind of childhood experience, some more quickly than others. Some are more intelligent so can reason their way out of it more easily and recognise their own value more quickly. They are the luckier ones but not all do. Some simply sink into abusive lifestyles without ever understanding why.

Until I stop, start to look at mindfulness practice and psychology, and listen to the spirit guides who have been helping and directing me. I study psychology through the OU and get my degree, a 2:1 Hons, and I meet my true soulmate.

I'm lucky in so many ways. I did find the Dharma, and Thich Nhat Hanh, and emotional and spiritual literacy. Many people kindly, if unintentionally or unwittingly directed me into the place I am now. I cannot list them all but I do thank them all although so many will not even recognise they are on that list, and some directed me through their unkindness as much as through their kindness too. Some just introduced me to ideas that led me on to explore further, which led to all sorts of forms of self-expression now.

I value what I've learned over the years so highly because I know what it is like to not have any of it. I have a great present moment life on all levels and am deeply happily married to my true soulmate. I don't want to write a self-pity or a kiss and tell item I just want to show how easy it is to groom children to be vulnerable to abusers, and to inform probably relatively decent young men what to look out for too, so they do not add to that abuse. I am sure they do not want that on their conscience later in life.

I know both my parents would have said they wanted me not to have sex until I was married and then to stay married to the one man who would take care of me, but life is not like that nowadays for most people in the western world and elsewhere. There is still far too much abuse and rape of young girls and women in the name of marriage, something that breaks my heart for each and every one of them.

· ·

14. LEAVING THE COUNTRY, NEW PERSPECTIVES AND ALTERNATIVES

In September 1969 Mr Tickle, my grandad, dies. It's a shock, we are all in shock. He's had a sudden stroke, followed by another one immediately after, and the combination takes him. He is only seventy, everyone says, too young to die yet. I am fourteen and have been somewhat estranged from him emotionally for some years now.

A few months later I'm in the kitchen with Mother

'Would you like to go to Austria with Grandma and meet up with the Wisniewski's?'

This is my Aunt Gigi's Polish married name.

'Yes please.'

A week's freedom from parents, even the promise of it is just wonderful.

Mother continues

'You're going because the trip was booked before Grandad died and you can help your Grandmother have a nice week away.'

'OK'

I feel slightly more tentative, not really knowing what that means.

'It means the holiday won't be wasted and you're the only one who is old enough to go with her.'

By now I am getting that I am not especially chosen by Grandma Violet, just the only option. I want to go anyway. I am used to being the bottom of the family pile.

Flavia (Gigi) now appears to me as very elegant, glamorous and adventurous. She still has her incredibly long hair which she winds around her head most of the time. Her exotic husband, Tom, is still officially a refugee from Nazi invaded Poland, leaving at the end of the war. They parent my twin cousins, seven years younger, and both work in education. Every summer they take advantage of this shared freedom for a great alternative experience, equally educational and adventurous, and disappear into Europe for five weeks. My grandparents had been due to travel out and join them and had already booked the train tickets and guest house bookings etc. for two weeks. Following grandad's demise and rather than waste the bookings and lose any money, I am asked.

To say that I'm excited over the intervening months is to understate the situation greatly. I can hardly wait to go away with these family members who'd mostly been, intentionally at least, very kind and generous with me. Grandma and I had been close in younger years but other grandchildren had come along, and we'd grown more estranged. It made me feel special to be going with her, whatever the reason.

I'd had a lot of fun scrumping with my Grandmother in the bombed-out gardens around where she lived in Croydon, exploring the huge gardens of derelict Victorian villas that later become a modern housing estate. We collect plants and fallen fruit, bringing them home as bounty to preserve or plant. I enjoy helping with both. However, a regular reminder from my Mother also stops me from ever being comfortable or relaxed with my family.

Mother reminds me, 'no-one in the family likes you, they're just nice to you because they're nice people, so don't let us all down.'

I've been told this for so many years and almost every time we see family, or I receive a present or card from them. So, it's hardly surprising I journey with both insecurity and anxiety as well as the aforementioned excitement. I want to travel, to explore and have adventures, to see what else out there exists beyond my desperate cage; I think more than anything I want to escape.

This being the background, with my small but arm-wrenchingly heavy old leather suitcase and a few changes of clothes, I went off to the big London station, with my Grandmother, to start the journey across Europe on a sleeper.

I don't remember much about the trip there apart from having to change trains a few times and being quite shell shocked by the cultural novelty of foreign stations and not understanding any language. I do remember however my first and currently only time on a sleeper train; finding it interesting to experience lack of continuous sleep and that crusty, stale early morning feeling it brings. I've always liked the rocking motion of trains and the way they make you doze off so naturally, so I catch up between stops and changes.

We don't talk much on the journey. I don't know what to talk about. I realise I don't know how to relate to my Grandmother anymore, or she me. The intimacy of shared adventures of bombsite scrumping and gardening has gone. I'm not self-aware enough to understand the why of this situation but looking back I can see how uncomfortable we are as travelling companions. Mother's mudslinging has stuck.

My Grandmother also has some crazy notion that I must carry the 'heavy' suitcase and she should have the lighter one, the assumption being that my pubescent young body is stronger than hers, aged about sixty five, to carry the extra weight. She's brought all sorts of tinned foods with her so she can eat her usual diet and not too much foreign food. She'd had an ulcer some time before, so I think that is her motivation.

It makes for an extremely heavy suitcase and I can barely lift it, let alone run between platforms with it as she expects me to do. She scolds me for this. Once more I feel the injustice, and yet she makes me feel very inadequate. Nowadays I am scolded a lot by my family; kindness and praise are a scarce thing in my life.

We are heading for Lienz, not Linz, and must not get them confused between train changes, and then onto an even smaller Tyrolean station on a mountain track.

In this anticipatory but bemused and stunned state, I follow Grandma across western Europe. We're collected by my uncle Tom at the final destination. They've already been there for a week, camping nearby.

He delivers us to the little guest house. It is sweet but smells so different to home. It's late. We are both tired, so more or less go straight to sleep. Grandma snores, a lot, and we're sharing a room. I remember now why Grandma and Grandad always had separate bedrooms, even though they loved each other greatly. I do also remember being awake quite a lot that first night. It's funny how things run in families. I now sometimes snore too, as those who must share with me on retreats and the like will recount to me, as if there is anything one can do about it whilst deeply asleep. David tells me it is when I am distressed or triggered that it happens most.

The following day we're served a breakfast very different to ones I'm used to at home, the English post-war standard porridge or cereal followed by fry-up. Instead I eat interesting and different coloured breads, rubbery cheeses with holes in, and cold meat slices of sausages and hams. It feels so good to be doing something familiar, eating breakfast, but doing it differently, with different food and in a house that smells so very different to my family home. I also desperately want to get on with Grandma, but don't know how to bridge the gulf.

We're collected by Tom a little later on and taken to the mountain lake next to the campsite where my cousins are staying. The lake is surrounded by lush wooded hillsides, which are really the mountains in the Tyrol.

My impressions of our daily routines after this are similar. My uncle rescues me from tedium by playing shuttle cock each day on the lake beachside, non-competitive and lots of 'keeping it going for as long as possible' fun. I love that approach to all sports still. I frequently swim in the lake, jumping off the jetty into deeper water and generally loving the freedom of freshwater swimming. I sleep too. I need a lot of physical activity as an outlet for my body's natural tendency to restlessness.

I start chatting with a girl a year younger than me, also camping with her family. She is sitting out on the jetty when I go to jump in and we swim together, exchanging information. She comes from Wythenshawe, near Manchester. We stay in touch for a few years as pen pals until she comes to London and it becomes clear we have grown up in very different ways and have little in common anymore.

It is the start of a life-long experience. Travel does bring friendships along the way, sometimes some very special ones indeed and often these friendships have lasted me a very long time.

These firsts are always so formative in opening opportunities and expectations and widening perceptions of life and its possibilities.

The other encounter I have is one evening this friend and her brother are going to a night club and ask me to go along with them. I have never done this before, and my aunt and uncle are a lot more relaxed and permissive with me than my own parents would ever be. Tom agrees to meet me at a specific point at 10 pm and I'm going to make sure I'm there exactly on time. I have my first experience of dancing with a young male and feeling sexually aroused by someone who is not my dream lover. We hear the first encounter with Je T'aime Moi Non Plus and I think it is the most amazing song I ever heard. It is not out when I get back to UK, but it arrives a few weeks later here too.

I have no idea what those feelings are at all, being so powerful and both confusing and compelling at the same time. They aren't quite the same as my dream lover.

Tom picks me up as agreed and takes me back to the guest house.

The following day I feel withdrawn, confused by these strange sensations in my body. Also being deeply myopic and refusing to wear glasses, for vanity reasons, I think the same young man walks past me by the lake and I do not see him, but my aunt said someone was waving to me. I don't respond and then punish myself for not being able to see, for being so innocent and confused by it all and wanting to appear so worldly wise as one does at that age.

Anyway, my other recollections are of beautiful mountains in which we take steep and challenging walks and my Grandmother drinking from fresh mountain streams and encouraging me to join her. She really has an exuberance for life about her and mostly for the wild and simple things in life.

I realise much later how alike we are and how we might have been such good friends, or maybe I am like that because of her influences. But Mothers' constant jealousy has made sure that will never be.

I don't understand why my aunt and uncle and cousins don't drink so enthusiastically. Later I realise we are lucky, Grandma and I don't pick up any water borne parasites and it does taste so very, very good, unlike anything I have ever tasted before. It is my first awakening to wild living, in forests and on mountains. Something deeply spiritual and primeval awakening in me on those mountain walks, a deep connection to wilderness and the simpler human ways of life. It has never left me, perhaps a little piece of that dismantled child got put back into place, the beginning of a life-long journey of course.

Some days we spend exploring the surrounding areas. I am curious about the highly superstitious and colourful little catholic shrines everywhere, decorated by flowers, often wildflowers I'd seen on the mountain walks, but always very pretty, kept painted and fresh by local devout Catholics. I still don't know much about them. I guess that living with such harsh winters and the dangers that snow in mountains present, they are saintly offerings bargaining for protection. The pretty Tyrolean houses, their balconies festooned with geraniums, stun me with their brightness, and I wonder what it would be like to live in these houses on these mountains, nestled into these valleys. Heidi was a favourite of mine a few years earlier. I have often noticed how my reading habits have been collaborative influences on experiences, in so many ways.

I breathe in the mountain air, notice its purity and freshness. It gets pretty hot during the days in August but is cool at night and in the early mornings and I love that freshness. Living and growing up mostly in suburbia and rarely travelling elsewhere, apart from seaside towns with their salty air smell, I have never experienced such astonishingly fresh, unsalted air before. It is leaving its mark in my subconscious. I'm really not aware of much of this at the time but sensory experiences rarely leave us and it's only much later in life, through subsequent travels that I recognise those deep impressions.

Mostly, I am a very troubled and intensely self-conscious young girl who feels at odds with her whole world and certainly at home. Being with family but away from parents is its own kind of liberation. They are kind to me, my aunt and uncle, they treat me with respect and try to help me to relax and enjoy myself, not something I find easy, but I do begin to let go and relax. The inner journey was unconsciously beginning alongside the outer travelling life.

The time away ends too soon.

'Are you looking forward to seeing your parents again?'

Flavia is looking at me with curiosity as I am becoming quiet and more withdrawn.

I take a gamble at telling the truth.

'No. I don't want to go home.'

Grandma picks up on it.

'Don't you want to get back to your parents?'

'No, I want to stay here.'

All good things come to an end,' laughs Flavia, but I can't join in her jollity.

'What about your missing your Mother?' asks Grandma

'No, I don't want to see her, she doesn't like me.'

'Of course she does, she's your Mother. What about your Father?'

'Not him either. They don't like me.'

Grandma asks again, 'do you like them?'

'No. They don't love me. I don't want to go home.'

They both look at me, not knowing what to make of this exchange, this revelation. I am uneasy now I've confessed the truth to them. Nothing more is said.

I remember the long train journey back with an ever-increasing sense of dread growing in me. I'm later told how badly I'd behaved and how I'd come across as moody and sulky, being viewed as generally ungrateful for the treat I'd been given. This fitted the description my parents gave of me. No one questioned if there was a reason I changed so much on that last day. It is back to the normal. I am deeply chastised when I get home. Grandma has relayed my revelations to Mother. I have shown her up again of course.

• •

15. LETTING OUT THE DEMONS

On the surface perhaps I'm still coping but so much bleak and hostile energy can only stay hidden for so long. It first emerges in various forms of self-harm.

I still struggle with the remnants of it today in my 65th year. Mostly they are echoes now and I talk to David as soon as I feel them. They are dispersed by exposure.

My original thoughts of suicide are not actually to do with self-harm but with wanting to please my parents and test the hypothesis that I should not be alive.

When you have been told repeatedly, 'if it wasn't for you, then the rest of the family would be happy', and if you loved that family achingly hard, even though those feelings are completely frozen to protect them, it doesn't take too many years to start thinking 'if only I could *not be here* then maybe they could all be happy'. It is a simple logic really. I believe, totally it is somehow 'all my fault'. That is what children do, they believe what they are told.

I've challenged 'God', through nature. Was I supposed to still be here? I discover, apparently, I am. I have thought of and been fascinated by death.

I think about running away to make it easier for them, but I don't know how I would survive and at that point have not considered creating my own death. I don't actually want to die; I want to live but not where I am such a problem. Instead I want to find love and give love. I can remember that quite clearly in my childish and teenaged heart, that aching for wanting to love and be loved and not wanting to inflict myself on my family anymore. By now my Mother has poisoned all my extended family relationships, more or less. I can't turn to anyone there. I can't trust them even if they are nice to me, they're just nice people.

Trees are my first genuine challenge to my right to live, daring them to drop me.

The weir is my other.

Sometimes I go down there alone to read and gain some solitude. Although I always find solitude hard to cope with without a book, I seek it when in the company of my latest best literary friend and escape channel. One of the places I like to go and read is on the small level platform at the foot of a large old beech tree half-way down the steep river cliff. I sit with my back to the tree, feeling its skin against my skin. I feel its wide smooth trunk so strong and stable against my fragile human frame. I feel its solidity and friendship, its connectedness with me and all other living beings. We sit, tree and girl, and I read.

One day I find a dead cat. I'm fascinated once more by its death and return over the next few days to watch its progress, its gradual disintegration, until suddenly it has disappeared. Completely. Perhaps something took it?

Decades later, I realise this is a great Buddhist teaching of wisdom – do not fear death, it is a natural thing, think of your own body decomposing. I never have feared death since then, but I realise on all these occasions I don't actually want to stop living, I just want my hell to end and to find some way of living that means I am not the cause of everything that makes others so unhappy.

When I am twelve, we move back south, to Bromley Borough, and everything changes again, including Mother, who finds new depths to her rage and fury. She resents the move most of all. Even though Dad is now quite senior in his company, a status she always sought, she belittles his accomplishments whenever she can, in public and at home, and talks endlessly about her own matriculation at age sixteen. She has done nothing else with her life since then. This is not a judgment of her but a comparison and 'of the times for women'.

Around the same age as sexual awakening takes hold of my life, a deeply destructive energy develops in response to the high degree of my self-loathing, the accumulation of all the energy my mother has been pouring into me. It is demanding my attention. Beyond my early initial attempts at challenging my right to exist through nature, I now start to take it out on my own body in various ways, quite creatively but with serious intent.

It starts when I am around fourteen, perhaps it is those hormones releasing things in me as I start my periods.

I am at home in the bath. Mother has shown me how to remove hard skin using a pumice stone. I take a pumice stone to my skin and try and scrape away the sense of filth. I want to scrape it all off until my whole body is covered in tiny scabs, my arms and legs and belly and any part that I can reach to scour clean of all that I feel inside, all the self-loathing and self-disgust. I sit in a bath and scrub until it is stinging quite badly, until I am sure I have reached blood. Then I stop.

It feels good to have that sensation on my skin, feeling something that isn't inflicted by others. I have some control over how and who hurts me even if it is myself. The following morning my body is covered in tiny pin prick scabs all over. I do this a few times until I mention it to someone at school who tells me I am stupid to do that and so I stop.

Around this time Mother decides to have a cat as her pet. She loves them but so do Hazel and I, and I think Martin too. Mia is our first, a half Russian blue. She is a soft light grey colour with very thick coat that sheds a lot, and she likes to sleep on my bed. The comfort of having another soft warm small body with me at night is a new experience. Mia is allowed to have kittens and we keep one of those, who turns out to have long black hair. For some reasons Hazel wants to call her Chutney. It is unspoken but we have a cat each then, Hazel and me. Then Chutney has kittens and her beautiful long-haired tortoise shell kitten is kept, whom Hazel calls Mango. These cats become a significant source of comfort and affection for me and possibly for Hazel too.

I also start to steal food and 'secret eat'. I remember eating spoonful's of Bournvita from the tin and once being in the act when someone comes into the kitchen, so I close myself into the cupboard and hope they don't find me. They don't. I continue spooning the sweet chocolatey granules into my mouth.

At the age of fifteen a new girl, Karen, starts at my school. She's been at a selective private school, very unhappy there, so took an overdose to make herself heard. Her parents finally listen and when she arrives in my class, I befriend her, and she tells me all about it. She had never really meant it though – it was a warning shot across their bows. However, the idea of actively killing myself sticks in my mind. I have a choice.

I am already ashamed at my cowardice of not being able to leave them and let them be happy without me, to stop being that terrible burden I am for them. I wonder if I could pluck up the courage to kill myself instead of daring nature to do it for me.

One weekend it is particularly horrendous, and I'm feeling as worthless as it is possible to feel, as far as I can know. I decide this is my day, my way out and I'll do them this favour at the same time. I really don't feel I have any hope of surviving any longer. My father's wrathful outbursts on my body are becoming quite extreme, his anger and desire to kill palpable within the blows he rains down on me. It is never just a smacking. Even he calls it 'a damn good thrashing'. But he has got worse and more frequent, and my Mother has too. This is apparently all my fault. I am rebelling a little and trying to stick up for myself and my siblings. In their eyes that is another heinous crime of course, they could never be wrong, and I've become their automatic whipping boy and scapegoat. Apparently, I am now responsible for all misdoings of my siblings, setting bad examples. Also, now I am turning them against Mother.

I wait until all has gone quiet and then slip down to the kitchen. I know in our larder there's a bottle of poisonous photographic developing fluid on the highest shelf. It is a dilute acid of some sort. I carefully open the larder door and pull a chair across the kitchen, making as little noise as possible. I drink as much as I can manage but it is disgusting. I retch but force myself to swallow more. I soon realise if I swallow anymore, I'll bring it all back up. I just hope it is enough, I believe it will be. Then I go back to bed, leaving the bottle out so they would know I'd drunk it. I'm more relaxed than I've ever felt before and fall to sleep after a while and sleep well all night.

The following morning I'm so deeply disappointed when I wake up again. It had been such a heroic effort and really horrible, but I'd been so determined and so certain. My failure is a huge disappointment to me. I'm still lying in bed wondering what to do next when I hear my Mother shriek and footsteps come running up into my room.

'What have you done?' she is screaming at me but this time with panic in her voice.

'I drank poison and I am supposed to be dead now, but it didn't work'.

I say this coolly, matter of factly.

She calls Dad into my room and tells him what has happened. I watch them. They are both scared but try to hide this with more anger. I am not fooled. By this age I have studied them both so closely, I can tell pretty much how either of them is feeling at any given moment. I know I've shaken them, and it gives me a slight feeling of pleasure.

Then they turn on me and I'm admonished for being so stupid, and sent to school as if nothing has happened, where I proceed to throw up for the rest of the day and the following one too. Even now I still shake my head in amazement that my parents did nothing to make sure I was medically OK in the longer term after drinking that poison. They are too afraid to tell anyone, to call in medical support, so they don't, and I survive. The rest of the bottle is poured down the sink.

I vomit on and off for the next two days as my body attempts to purge itself of the poison. They sort of lay off me for a while after that but can't keep it up. After all what do you do with all that anger when your outlet is closed off to you.

I am still here and still healthy so I assume my body coped and it was not my day to die, then or since then. Apparently.

One day I have a particularly vicious row with Mother, when I am again blamed for ruining all their lives. I decide I really must make my move this time and make sure of it too. My choice, to live or die.

I take another large overdose of aspirin, about sixty I counted, washed down with a lot of vodka. I intend it to be final and conclusive. I leave a note saying I don't want to be part of their family anymore, that I want to be some other family's child. But in my drunken state I get maudlin and phone my school friend, Karen, to meet in Bromley for lunch. I steal a five-pound note from Mother's house-keeping purse and treat us to what I think is my last meal. When it's time for her to go home, I don't want to go back to my house, so I go back to hers with her, and break down on the way and confess what I've done. In retrospect I know how selfish that act was, but I didn't intend to do it like that. I wanted to just pass out and pass away, but the food diluted the drugs and alcohol and my resolve broke down after such a long delay for the desired outcome to take hold.

I am visited in the hospital by some kind of hospital social worker, an almoner. I tell her that my mother doesn't love me or want me. My mother has talked to her already, denies all of it, and the woman tells me I am silly and mistaken and will grow out of it.

I stay with my friend at her house for a while afterwards and am made to go and see the family GP. I put on my 'I'm alright' act and convince him that is the truth. I am never going to admit to a GP what the truth is about my home life, after all my parents speak to him too. Eventually my mother comes over to meet Karen's parents and pick me up.

'Oh, so you're Karen's Mother, nice to meet you, thank you for letting Sylvia stay with you I am Sylvia's Mother and my husband is impotent.'

'Oh well, right, that is ok, not a problem.'

We leave as quickly as I can get her out of the door. I cannot believe she has done this, said this. I just want to get away now.

At age fifteen I am legally allowed to work one day per week, so I find myself a job Saturdays in a local clothes shop in Bromley, a very trendy boutique called Chic. I enjoy working there though at times it is interminably boring, But I have money to buy myself nice things and I do spend most of it on staff discounted clothes from the shop. At some point I am talking to a fellow shop assistant and she says something about her Dad. I mention that my dad hits me, and she starts to question me about it.

'That's illegal, that's not allowed.'

'So, what can I do about it?'

'Go to social services and tell them.'

I do. After school the following week I find the social services offices in Bromley and call in. They seem more bothered about him hitting mother too, but he doesn't. They say they will call me soon.

When I get home I tell mother,

'I went to social services to report Dad for how he hits me.'

'Did you?'

She seems almost gleeful, not what I had expected.

When Dad gets home, she tells him, and he comes to see me in my bedroom.

'I hear you've been trying to cause more trouble for the family again. What have you don't now?'

'I just told social services how you treat me. They're going to phone me back.'

'And did you tell them how awful you are for us? Did you tell them how much trouble you cause?'

I don't respond.

'Because if they come here, I shall tell them all about you, about what we have to put up with having you as a child. Then they'll take you away immediately and put you into an approved school where you're kept behind locked doors and forced to do exactly as you are told. So, when they phone you better tell them it's ok after all, hadn't you? Unless you want that better than your family home?'

He leaves my bedroom and closes the door behind him.

The following day when they phone me after school, I tell them its ok after all. They question me a few more times but I tell them it really is ok, and I don't want to continue with my complaint.

The next time he goes to hit me, in front of mother and immediately after she has made something up, I turn and look him square in the face.

'Go on then, just hit me and get it over and done with, get it out of your system. You never bother to listen to my side of the story, do you?'

He drops his hand and I leave the room. But it doesn't stop for long, maybe a couple of months. I am just waiting anyway.

My parents break up soon after that second equally very genuine suicide attempt. My mother is having an affair with a chap called Dick whom she met whilst on holiday with my Grandmother in Oberammergau for the passion play there. She's secretly meeting him in our house on the afternoons when he changes shifts as a police officer. I guess from the smell of aftershave. It's not the same smell as my Dad's in the house one day, when I come home from school. I challenge her.

'Someone's been here. It stinks of Brut.'

'Does it?'

'Yes, it does, who's been here and why does it smell so much upstairs?'

'I don't know what you mean, it must be your imagination.'

'No mum it stinks of Brut and I know that smell. It's horrible.'

Then she can't help herself and starts grinning with her triumphant kind of gleeful grin that suggests she thinks she is winning something.

'Well your father doesn't love me anymore, won't make love to me anymore, so I found someone else who will.'

I watch her closely to see what she'll do next.

'You mustn't let your father know, you won't, will you?'

'You need to get rid of the evidence then, don't you?'

'Will you help me?'

I look at her with a sense of astonishment. She really expects me to collude with her. But then I think, I kind of hope if I go along with this that Mother will ease up on me. We open windows for a while and when it seems to be all gone close them again. I suggest he better not wear aftershave anymore.

She sort of does, and then doesn't ease up on me. I don't think she can help herself after years of this scapegoating habit.

I stand up to her more and more vociferously because I suddenly have power too and am not afraid to use it against her. By now I have little respect for either of them, or loyalty or affection. Not the best of decisions on my part but who in my position would not take advantage of anything they can?

Mother seems to be falling apart though and is ever more challenging, whining that we should love her, craving our attention, telling us how bad our father is as a husband and generally becoming more and more of a burden.

Eventually my father is away for work and it continues over a weekend. Mother is now becoming completely out of control emotionally. She is shaking us and screaming at us one minute then pleading the next. We are told we must love her, but she is making us all afraid and I cannot protect the other two from this, it is too much for me.

I try to take charge in the only way I know.

I phone Grandma and ask her to take Mother away from us. We can't cope with her anymore and just need a break. She comes and tries to talk us down, but we plead with her, my sister and I, and she eventually takes Mother with her. Just as she is leaving though, she decides that Martin must go too. He cries out he doesn't want to; he struggles to get away from her grasp around his wrist, struggles madly.

'I can look after him and Dad will be home tomorrow to sort it out.'

I am pleading with them too. They are both utterly determined, Mothers face is set grim. That is the worst thing we could have allowed to happen to him but are powerless to stop it.

So, my sister and I, at age eleven and fifteen, are left on our own until Dad gets home. Mother never comes back though it's discussed briefly. Dad asked me after a few days if I wanted her back and I said 'No, please not'.

Later he blames me for breaking up their marriage.

I still wonder at what point was I ever allowed to be a child? Can they ever take responsibility for being the adults and behaving like that to each other or to me at all? I have no memory of that happening ever.

When they are going through the initial separation stages before divorce, I remember pleading with Dad to fight for Martin, that it isn't fair to leave him behind with her. I can still remember his words, their devastating effect on me.

'He's too young, I can't cope with him as well.'

'But I'll look after him', I plead some more, offer to go to court and tell them what she is really like. This idea clearly troubles him greatly and I now wonder if something else might have come out. Perhaps she has stuff on him he is ashamed of.

The agreement is set up that Hazel and I will visit Mother once a month for Sunday and Martin will come to Dad's once a month for a Saturday. It is over a year later before this happens, and Mother has now bought her own maisonette. I'm allowed to drive my stepmother's car to take us over there and back again. On more than one occasion my brother pleads with us to take him back, once hiding behind the front seats lying on the floor, begging me not to give him away. But I am powerless. I resolve not to abandon him forever, though at that point I have no plan and am still at school, aged seventeen.

By the time my parents split, I have been date-raped and am just beginning to allow myself to be used sexually, but within a year it has gotten far worse. Thus, a new form of self-harm is born. A complete abandonment of any self-care for my body! I turn it all into a joke and feigned a devil may care attitude.

Bravado.

I hate every moment of it all.

Stupid childish defensive confused terrified bravado. Don't let the buggers see they are hurting you. I almost believe it myself until I start to notice how much worse it all makes me feel, and

I pile so many additional layers of social judgment on top. I am going further and further down.

About sixteen I also discover the comfort I get from more serious binge eating, but of course what goes with that is weight gain and I hate having a fat body too. In fact, my self-hatred manifests in many forms but this is just the beginning. I secretly cook and eat massive meals of heavily savoury stir fry style rice dishes and then throw up using a fork or spoon handle. I also learn the joys of laxatives too and take overdoses to clear myself out of the toxins. It feels cleansing, emptying.

I seriously feel better for the binge purge cycles and this combines with a resumed habit of more surreptitious skin scraping to allow me some respite from the desire to dispose of myself for a while. I continue this for some months but the same internal voice, that helps me so often, stops me and say's 'why do you hurt your body when there are enough people doing it for you'.

I still struggle sometimes though.

Once Mother and Dad part company things do get slightly better with Dad only at home, for a year, until he meets my stepmother and moves her in with us. But that intervening year has allowed me to see how, without Mother, Dad could indeed become a nicer parent again. He would even give me lifts to the pub and come in and buy my friends drinks sometimes. I genuinely believe the nightmare is over. Mr Nice Guy came out to play.

In the period between Mother and stepmother, Dad is talking to me more openly, and admits he dreaded coming home every day, dreaded having to introduce Lorna to colleagues, dreaded everything about her really. And deep down I think she knew that and was mad as hell about it too, which made it all just far worse for everybody.

One day we are sitting in the living room and sort of talking, when he suddenly turns to me and his voice changes. He looks ashamed, has difficulty in speaking. I feel sorry for him before he even speaks.

'I'm sorry I used to hit you so hard. I wanted to hit your Mother. I knew I couldn't stop if I started hitting her. I might have killed her. So, I hit you instead.'

'That's ok, I understood, I already knew that Dad. Just don't hit me ever again.'

He doesn't respond but there is a slight shift in our relationship. I feel perhaps I might finally get to have a father, the one I once knew, who still lived in my deep past, whose energy still lingers. A dad I barely remember him ever being for me, since even when he was nice it had always been until my monthly thrashing destroyed it all again.

I never tell him how much I felt that wrath and hatred against my body, how I thought it was against me and how utterly terrified I'd grown of both of them, how little respect I had for either of them anymore. Instead I said 'that's ok I understood' because I had seen how horrible she was to him too. I forgave him. I thought it was over. Later I wrote a poem about how it affected me.

Childhood betrayed

It was for my own good
you said, as your hand
fell heavily, leaving red
stains on pink child flesh.

Could I have learned from such violence?
Oh yes, but lessons best forgotten
As the pain strips away fragile dignity

Stabbing deeper than skin should allow.

Through fear I learned to obey
trusting deceit as protection.
You never cowed this spirit,
the flame burned angry for too long.

Yet I am still cowed,
waiting for a hand to fall,
longing to forget.
Why can I forgive you and not myself?

But my self-harming wasn't over and the ability to protect my-self, never having developed, continued to put me in harm's way.

Alongside all this at home I am starting to develop friendships with people both in and out of school, people who really do not value me at all. I must have appeared slightly strange to them somehow. Many of them use me as some sort of commodity, in a few cases a pet clown since my ADHD makes me rather lively and wacky, or someone to boost their own self esteem on by looking slightly down on me. It is subtle, mostly tone of voice or language and attitude used. I only recognise it when I meet up with them some time after I'd been through a huge shift in self-awareness and am no longer able to swallow it. Back then it was just how I expected to be treated.

They are only acting out what I allow them to do though, and mirroring back at me how I feel about myself. I am al-lowing people to use me under the guise of friendship. That becomes evident years later when I start to break out of the whole suppressed emotions which breaks free with the onset of perimenopause. Probably none of it is intentional or cynical in either parties, just where they are and where I am in our emotional development, so no hard feelings here. They have all moved into the past.

Internally my ability to self-harm through putting myself down reaches epic proportions and I know myself to be utterly worthless, that if I could only not be me then life might become bearable but being me is just the worst curse anybody could be born with. Pete Green's song Man of the World becomes a personal anthem. Music plays an increasingly important part in my life. I find I can get lost in it and transport myself away from my own sense of self into other dimensions. It drowns out the manic voices of destruction in my head and vibrates my body to a different pitch. It is very soothing and transforming and I love it, especially when played very loud so it blasts my consciousness clear.

It takes me decades to find out how much and how intensely I find myself repugnant but all that energy from both parents has accumulated and stored up inside me and I have pushed it down further as the only way of protecting myself from the intensity of that pain, and then frozen myself closed around it.

Dad has met someone special. I can see his excitement in his face. We are passing each other in the hallway.

'How would you feel if I meet someone new?'

I don't know what to say. Inside I am immediately and genuinely pleased for him but can't just say that. It leaves me too exposed. I feel my throat closing around the words that might suggest I care about him. That is far too vulnerable to acknowledge here like this.

'I'm glad for you. It will be nice to have someone in your old age, so I don't have to look after you. I can get on with my own life.'

His face drops visibly, I know I have hurt him. He wants support, encouragement, affection, recognition and I cannot give it to him, just as he never gave it to me when I needed it either. I walk away. I know that a special moment has been lost to us both and nothing can repair it.

My stepmother Aileen arrives on the scene just around my age seventeen. She moves in and they live together for the first year or so, though they do later marry once Dad is divorced. They are very ashamed of living together, it is not a respectable thing to do in their eyes and I am admonished for letting people know this is their state of relationship. But I am pleased for him.

I remember the first Christmas they were together. I gave them a shoe box with two white candles and a bottle of wine. It is meant to be a romantic acceptance of their relationship from me and I mean it.

But soon after Aileen moves in with us, the year of respite goes retrograde and I am suddenly treated as a second class citizen once more and judged with a new set of rules with which I yet again am entirely unfamiliar and certainly not in agreement with. By now I am also seventeen and not prepared to be treated like a child once more, or a skivvy either, and Father slowly turns back into the angry thrashing monster I'd previously known, again all my fault for not being what he thought I should be once more.

I really, really hoped she would be a friend (I definitely didn't want another Mother) but suddenly I find I am at fault for everything again. I become afraid of her but in a different way as she is nothing to me. This story has been mirrored back to me in later life and I do now appreciate how hard it must have been for Aileen to cope with a traumatised frozen adolescent who is on the wild side when you have grown up as an only child, very conformist and have no experience of children. I recall my sister once told me Aileen had asked Hazel how she liked having siblings, that she would not have liked to share her parents with anyone else. That applies to Dad too.

I am profoundly disappointed. I want an ally who will keep Dad sweet and off my back.

One night, a weekend, I'm five minutes later than the deadline home because the bus has been late. That gets me thrashed because I should have got the earlier bus to make sure that didn't happen. Aileen hovers in the background just as Mother had done

'I don't think you should hit her that hard John.'

'Don't worry, I'm used to it now,' I retort, numb as usual. Dad finally stops.

What rebellious, depressed, freedom hungry seventeen-year-old will willingly take an earlier bus to make sure they don't miss the deadline by 5 minutes? Well perhaps I should have known better, but I'd started to relax with my new reformed Dad, so this return was a huge shock. Soon after that though I turned eighteen and the next time he went to raise his hand to me I said very quietly, defiantly and determinedly,

'If you ever hit me again, I will do you for assault. I'm now a legal adult and you have no more right to hit me ever again'.

The look on his face is a mixture of confusion and recognition, and he just turns his back on me and walks away. I don't realise the symbolism of his stance though. After that I just cannot get any connection with him at all.

So, I stand up for myself in that way but life with them both at home is pretty oppressive, for them too I am sure. And I carry on allowing myself to be used in the vain dream of finding someone who will actually want me, but not daring to actually hope for it, or believe it could ever be true of course, that is far too risky and exposing.

Until I meet my first husband.

We are hopelessly unsuitable for each other but cling like lonely desperate people do.

Is it self-harm when you know this is not right for you, when you know you are not happy, but the alternatives are too scary to contemplate living with anymore?

I think it is.

I say this without any disregard for my ex-husband who is a kind decent man, who is, like so many men of his generation - emotionally unavailable. He also had his own upbringing to contend with. I did genuinely grow to love him deeply, mostly out of gratitude, but never felt it reciprocated or connected with him at all. We last for nearly fourteen years and have two sons together. Giving birth to my boys starts to melt me and I am looking once more for connection. I am healing but also recognising how hopeless my marriage is, how empty and lonely I feel with in. My sons heal me and blow my life apart once more. They are great teachers in so many ways, so different to each other and I love them both so much.

My rebellious streak blows the suppressed surface calm of married life and once more I am off on a jaunt of self-harm and self-discovery. I find myself being attracted to far too many other men for it to be a one-off thing and I know it is over. Call it learning the hard way, perhaps. At least our parting is as amicable as these things can be, especially for our boy's sake

I think we all self-harm though, in the many ways in which we seek to protect ourselves or fail to value ourselves. Addictions are a form of self-harm, bad relationships are too, lives that leave us unhappy and unfulfilled.

Many sorts of self-harming are promoted as good responsible

life choices but if they do not make your soul sing out, then they are also self-harm at worst, or at least a denial of your own truth, that one is worth more than that, life is worth more than that. Marriage is only one of those.

Before the boys arrive, I try to take my life once more during that marriage and when I am trying not to face how empty it is for me, and then decide to stop failing at that too, it has become embarrassing.

I have one more period of serious suicide consideration, but my protective voices come into play again.

I am walking back from the station feeling desolate. I know home is empty and it leaves me feeling just as worthless as ever. I resolve to make it a serious no returns attempt this time. I begin to think of options. It is summer so I consider taking sleeping pills and going to the coast to swim out until I lose consciousness. I think of a few other scenarios that might prove utterly conclusive. I am walking home from the station, on my way home from work, and have nearly reached the end of my road when I hear a voice from outside my own body. It seems to be coming from a clump of Bamboo in someone's garden.

'Don't kill yourself, you're here for a reason, you're needed.'

I am filled with an amazing energy of light and love. I am being shown my alternatives. I stop for a moment uncertain that I have just had this experienced, but I feel completely different and continue home with a light heart. I resolve to go back to spiritual searching and try an alternative Christian church, non-conformist.

On reflection I realise perhaps how much of a nightmare I was for those living with and around me, the nightmare within me being unconsciously expressed externally because I am unable to think of it in any other way. I am always too busy using all my energy and thought processes to keep that mass of black oozing self-hatred down.

Very disturbed and traumatised people are utterly selfish because they are not able to cope with more than their own inner nightmare. Many become NPD, like Mother and others I know or have known. I am eternally grateful to whatever it was in me that stopped me going to that next level and kept the kindness that is very much part of my true nature alive and in some ways evident. I could so easily have become a drug addict, or alcoholic, or worse.

There is a wonderful teaching amongst the aboriginals of North America. I'm not sure which tradition but it is that a woman going through hormonal changes will not be able to suppress the lies and deceits that are locked in her body. The chemical changes alter her internal balance and throw them to the surface. When in this state, she should be listened to with deep respect.

It is when I started my perimenopause that things start to shift deeply and profoundly in me. I am re-evaluating my life and relationships, as one is ending nastily, just a couple of years before I meet David. I am being prepared for that encounter.

In our culture it is a general desire to continue to suppress these eruptions rather than work with them. By now I'd gone through many shifts in consciousness and am openly working with the spiritual psychologies in shamanism and meditation / Buddhist psychology to self-heal. More of that elsewhere. The point here is that again many so-called friendships fall under the spotlight and I realise I play a large part in allowing myself to be treated less well than perhaps I deserve. Other more intimate relationships I realise have also been using and abusive towards me in many diverse ways and my desperation to be loved has allowed it all.

But it has been all I thought I could ever expect and now I know I am worth more than that. When my responses begin to change, the relationships that have been in a more or less stable equilibrium start to fail. It is upsetting but I understand this is what happens when you change your inner life and match your outer life to your new reality. As the inner so the outer.

I have also started going through all sorts of healing and therapeutic practices, like the shamanism ones, which have opened me up in so many ways and I know I am changing profoundly. I look back and realise how many close escapes I had, when things could have turned far more serious with these routines. It really is as if someone was watching over me.

Life moves on.

• •

16. THE DAY EVERYTHING CHANGES

I think I left my parents when I was about 7 or 8 yrs. old. I just have to wait a long time for my body to catch up.

As soon as I hit adolescence, I have a hunger like none for not being at home. I can sense this whole life out there that I've been deprived of and I'm famished. It is tough waiting though. I just want every day to go faster, every year to speed up. I desperately want to be older and free from them, or so I thought.

I leave them a second time when I begin to reject all their values as nothing to do with me and my life as it would become. I develop socialist political leanings against their true-blue conservatism. It is less a teenage rebellion and more a recognition 'they are not to be trusted and very shallow'. What neighbours think is far more important than real relationship and feelings. That is the norm in the 1970s though.

On my fifteenth birthday my aunt, Mercia, gives me a small paperback book on yoga. What leads her to consider this as a suitable gift, or for me to suddenly find it fascinating, I don't know, but this is another link or stage of my spiritual awakening, though only a glimmer. It is one of those many synchronous moments that will season my life forever.

I start to practice the poses and stretch my body out. It gets me back into my body as a good place to be. It releases some of the tensions and eventually I am doing some yoga on my bedroom floor, often naked or just in underwear, almost every evening I am home. When I start this my parents have yet to separate and my brother later in life confessed how he would spy on me in fascination at a teenage sister's body. He will have been six at that point, not long before our lives were torn apart.

I loved my brother very much back then, his cheekiness made me laugh. I still do though we are now estranged. For now, it is just me doing yoga and trying to make my body more flexible and relaxed. But that is another part of my estrangement from my family, that dividing of the ways, and both parents, but especially Mother, sneer at me for doing 'weird stuff'. When I start to meditate though, I find it extremely hard. I am doing it alone from books. The noise in my head reaches cacophony levels and even though I continue to work at it for another two to three years I find it almost impossible to achieve any sort of mental peace inside myself and eventually give up, but not until I am leaving school and home.

Of course, we rarely understand how hard leaving actually is when we are still very naive about life as an adult. We think it will be easy and everything will just be there for us, like it is or isn't in childhood.

It is not a simple matter of walking out of the door and stepping into a new wonderful life. You take your baggage with you. I carry my overfilled rucksack everywhere I go. I still get abused by other people. New people find new ways to treat me badly and I just let them. I allow it because I wanted to be accepted by these potential peers. I want to wait until they see how great I really am in my heart. But my vulnerability, and probably my PTSD/ADHD combination, made me different. (Even now David says to me 'there could only ever be one of you in the universe'.) People see me as someone to laugh at but not to care about or offer support to in any way. If I do try to talk about feelings, I get shut down very quickly by everyone. My willingness to be that fall guy is just to be included and to feel hip, trendy etc. All of this I allow them to do and they, like most people given the opportunity, make full use of me. There is no reciprocity of care anywhere.

It is a long time before I realise that no return at all means I burn out.

School has finally ended. I am eighteen years and three months old. I sat my very last A level exam on Friday and now this is Sunday. I haven't done that well, I know that – but I have done my best given how hard I find everything to do with studying and learning and exams and being unhappy. I am exhausted and aware that everything is about to change, but I don't know how quickly or how badly.

I come downstairs on Sunday morning, looking for something for breakfast. My stepmother Aileen comes through the kitchen door. I still have my back to her when she starts talking

'Do you think you will go and live with Roger?'

I am very taken by surprise. I don't expect to have such a conversation with her. I don't turn around though, I don't want her to see my face.

'Probably. We haven't talked about it yet. I was still at school 'til two days ago.'

'Your dad and I have talked about it, its ok with us if you do.'

'Oh, OK I'll talk to him about it later.'

'You can borrow my car to move your stuff down if you like.'

It is then I turn around. I want to see her face now, what she really means. She is quite inscrutable though.

I haven't been allowed to borrow her car since I hit a curb when a bus came around a bend over on our side of the road and I pull in hard to avoid being hit. Something in the car chassis buckled and it didn't drive straight, it pulled to the left all the time. I'd hit the curb hard but even then, the bus only just missed us and if I hadn't pulled over it would have hit the car itself and probably me too. I explained this to Dad, but he just said it was probably my fault driving too fast. His annoyance about the car far exceeds any awareness that I might have been at risk myself and I note that deeply. I wonder how he might have reacted if things had turned out differently.

I was driving at thirty miles per hour. I did have a tendency to drive slightly fast, but I have never been a great speeder and disliked it when others drove too fast.

So suddenly I am allowed to use her car again, to move out.

Her next words get to me though.

'Will you be in for dinner tonight?'

Instant freeze, no facial reaction, her meaning is transparent to me.

'No thanks.'

I say it so quickly, a reaction to her sequence of questions and suggestions. I feel utterly unwanted. She is angling to tell me to move out that moment, she can't wait to get rid of me. Dad has agreed. They have agreed how to get rid of me.

Dad is in the garage fixing his car I seem to remember. Her car, a mini, is further down the driveway. I say nothing to him

I phone Roger and explain what has just happened,

'Come right over', he says.

I start to pack her Mini with my clothes, records, books etc and drive the first load over.

About three loads in dad emerges from the garage,

'You're doing a lot of back and forth this morning, what are you up to?'

'Moving out to go and live with Roger.'

His face instantly turns dark.

'You little tart, you whore, who gave you permission to leave home today?'

'Aileen said you did, so I'm going. I know when I'm not wanted. I'm over eighteen years old now.'

I am defying him to deny it and he can't.

He moves to slap me round the side of my head. I stand my ground and I dare him with my eyes. He holds his hand back and storms inside the house instead.

I never find out what is said between them, but a compromise is met. I am to come home one or two nights per week to sleep but that is all. I agree, but it is never comfortable. And it is only for a few weeks as I am due to start at Bath domestic science teacher training college in the September.

I start my summer holiday job in Oxford Street and am with Roger most of the time. He does seem to want to be with me and take some sort of interest in me though there is little evidence of any affection or communication between us. Every so often I lift his arm and put it around my shoulders when we sit and watch TV. I listen to his record collection a lot and merge it with mine. Music is my best escape aside from books now.

But Roger does listen as I spout endlessly about my family and seems to understand or empathise. I find out later that he feels sorry for me and wants to rescue me, so I'll be grateful to him. There is little deep real affection, though that does grow, a lot of dependency and very little companionship in that relationship but we married anyway. I remember thinking this is the best I could ever hope for, that I don't deserve this even and should take the chance while I have it.

In retrospect I realise that we were two lost souls who have little to keep us together, apart from need, which is never a good reason long term.

I start college full of optimism, thinking that life will suddenly all be OK now. I have an arrangement that Roger will phone me every day from work in our lunch breaks, on a payphone that takes incoming calls. My Dad writes to me sometimes too and

Hazel came to stay for a couple of weekends, but as ever I didn't fit in, don't feel I belong and can't settle.

This poem I wrote, more recently, about that time, says it all for me.

Missing letters

I remember now, just now, in this minute just gone,
I remembered something I'd forgotten for decades.
He wrote to me, long ago he wrote to me.
Letters.

When I was at college for just three months
before my confidence collapsed once more.
When all I could think of was to get somewhere
safe. Not home to him though.

I can't remember what he wrote.
I wanted his love—fear kept him out
I cannot recall how he spoke,
the sound of his voice, the look of his face.

I didn't treasure those letters,
until today, when I remembered
wished I'd kept them, so I could read them
now, to see, did he ever really love me?

I think he tried to reach me.
Why else write to a daughter at college
frozen by fear, ice hearted, desperate?

I think he tried to teach me that
Perhaps he would be safe to love again
but then his anger, endless looks of
disappointment would show through.
I could never come out from
behind my fortress igloo.

I wish I could read those letters now
find out who he was, was he kind
funny, interesting, thoughtful?
I don't know this of my father.
His mystery all hidden behind anger and fear
the domestic warfare of life with Mother.

I never knew my father. Did he even
begin to know me though, did he ever look

beyond his own anger, to see the child
he once called pickle poppet, and warmed
her small cold hands with his own?

Was he wise sometimes, insightful?
Experience suggests not, but anger is not all he was,
though it is all I really knew of him.
Just an occasional glimpse of love for a child
so cold with her fear-frozen heart.

I would so love to read those letters now,
allow myself to find my father and to love him
now he is dead, can no longer hurt me.

My father wrote me letters.
When I was at college and failing in everything,
when at eighteen I thought I should
just die. It would be easier for everyone.
Did he know that was what he taught me?
What she taught me? What they co-scribed on my heart.

I wish I had those letters now
perhaps I might find a different story,
perhaps detect a glimpse of love.

My first near breakdown is at college towards the end of the first term. We've been moved around a great deal, a few weeks here and there, very much thrown in the deep end. I am not coping, can't get any kind of emotional footing. One Friday I'm due home for the weekend but supposed to go back and share a meal with my fellow students first and catch a later bus home to be with Roger. I pass through the bus station on my way back from the placement. The early bus is there. I just get on it. I have no clothes with me or anything, but I need to get away.

When I come back on the Sunday night, my student colleagues are really annoyed by my selfishness. I don't blame them. I have nothing with which to respond. I can't say sorry since I'm not, and I try to explain but they can't understand. Why should they? I never let on how low I am, how near to suicidal once more. One of the flatmates, Anne I think she is called, had a father who had committed suicide not that many years before.

It is not a topic we can talk about.

I cope until the end of term, just a week or so more, and come back for Christmas. I find Aileen has been getting rid of the cats, Mia and Mango are both gone and only Chutney is left. I recognise I am no longer at home here; I am not part of my Dad's family anymore. I tell my dad I am leaving college and won't be coming back to him either. He does nothing to help me change my mind or ask why. I guess he is glad to not be paying support and fees anymore too.

I live with Roger. He accepts me and Chutney as a package. A year or so later we get married. I end up collecting cats for the next thirty years, with a maximum of five at one point, and usually named after food.

Prior to this period, Hazel and I are going to see Mother on Sundays, once a month, as per the separation agreement. This particular Sunday we arrive, and both can tell something is not right. Martin asks us to take him to the local Lloyds park and Mother starts shouting immediately about how we come around and let her do all the cooking and not want to sit and talk to her. I explain we also want to spend time with Martin, we will all be back shortly, and will talk to her then. She starts shouting more and more and Hazel agrees to stay behind to pacify her. Martin is desperate to get out of the maisonette for a while, so he and I go to the park for about an hour. Martin and I mooch and muck around, climb trees or something, just walk and talk, until we know we must go back.

When we return, I find Hazel in floods of tears, asking me to take her home immediately. Mother is in frothing mood again. Martin begs us not to go and leave him with Mother. I don't know what to do, but Hazel is really distressed so I do as she asks and give Martin a hug and suggest he stays in his room. He is eight and I find myself feeling furious with Dad for making Martin stay with Mother. His desperation is palpable, tearing me up inside. How can I protect both my siblings from the monster once more? I feel so powerless and recognise I must make a choice, but it eats me inside, though I never show it of course.

On the way home Hazel tells me how Mother has been trying to make out she is dirty and nasty to be living with her father at her age, that she must come and live with Mother instead. She has been attacking her and physically shaking her again.

We get home after only a couple of hours and tell Dad what has happened. Hazel refuses to go back ever again. I agree to support her and am happy to not see Mother anymore. But it means less time with Martin.

They only see Martin once a month at Dad's house on a Saturday when I am at work, so I haven't been seeing him anymore. No one seems to think this matters.

Even though I'm no longer living at home, I do my best to get on with Dad and Aileen. I am often still blamed for things that are beyond my control, as if I have this deep desire to be a problem, when I am trying for all my worth not to be. But I am blamed for things that I am not party to as ever and Dad's rejecting looks towards me do continue to drive deep stakes into my heart every time. The burden of being the chosen one never leaves me.

I've been married for about a year or so when I start to feel bereft of my brother. I'm also curious how Mother might treat me now I am married. Would she be pleased to see me if I got in touch? Would she now value me?

I ask Dad next time I see him.

'It's fine with me as long as Aileen doesn't find out.'

'Are you sure?'

'Yes, … yes, she is your Mother after all. But don't let it get back to Aileen.'

'Thanks Dad.'

The following day I phone Mother up and arrange to go and see her. It goes well.

We arrange to visit her. She seems genuinely pleased to meet Roger and have me back in her life and we appear to get on better than I could ever remember.

I also start to re-engage with my extended family on Mother's side, and most of all my brother. Very soon we are babysitting for him and having him over to our place for weekends. Over the coming years he more or less lives with us at weekends and we take him on holidays camping with us too. Those two aspects of the changes make what happened worth everything, though it cost me dear in so many ways. I have no regrets.

The peace with Mother doesn't last though, of course. A narcissist can never keep up the nice stuff for long.

She first starts nagging me about seeing Hazel. I try and encourage Hazel to come with me, but she is still living with Dad and Aileen though she leaves as soon as she is sixteen and has left school. But she resolutely refuses to see Mother. She sometimes comes and sleeps at our place too, with a friend, if she goes to a night club near where we live, but I see less of her than Martin now.

I warn Mother not to contact Dad about Hazel and tell her it is not him but Hazel who will not come. Mother will not accept that of course. Her internal narrative is that Hazel's evil father is holding her captive away from her loving Mother. It cannot be that we might have a will of our own and make these choices ourselves.

I tell her it will not go well for me or Hazel if she gets in touch, it will delay for far longer the chance of her seeing Hazel again.

In true Lorna ways, she knows best and writes a letter to both of them asking why, if she can see me, can she not see Hazel too? She does not tell me of this letter.

The following weekend Hazel is due to come and stay over. It is on the Sunday morning as they are leaving that she reveals something terrible which she has been holding inside herself since she arrived. She has used our convenient hospitality and waits until now to say it.

'Dad says I can't see you anymore and you're not to contact Dad or Aileen ever again.'

I am floored.

'What why, what have I done.'

'Mum wrote to them and told them all sorts of stuff she isn't supposed to know about.'

'That's not my fault, why are they punishing me.'

'You've been lying to them and they can't trust you anymore. Look don't have a go at me about it, it's not my fault, I just got told to tell you.'

She shows no emotion towards me, no remorse that we are also to be disallowed to see each other anymore. I can see she has also cut me off.

I remonstrate with Hazel not to allow them to control her like that, not to let them bully her. But she is, as always, the good little girl and complies, and that is that. I try and see her at lunch on Saturdays when she is at work but realise there is little point. She has also cut me off and is clearly afraid she will be treated in the same way as I have been by Dad if she goes against his word. Fear dominates everything as it always did in my family and the relationships are broken ever more. Hazel has her sanctuary in the role of being 'the good one'. I can and will break free from being 'the bad one' but hers is a far stronger prison to break out of and find her truth from.

It turns out that everything I have mentioned in passing, in general conversation to Mother about Dad and Aileen has been used as evidence that I am her spy in their midst and Aileen is terrified of her ability to disrupt or destroy. If Mother wanted to destroy my life, she couldn't have done it in any more effective way.

I confront Mother and she denies it is her fault and blames it all on Dad of course. He is the unreasonable one not letting Hazel come and see her.

The rest of the family gets her version which leaves her blameless as usual and there is no point in challenging it. They are not yet able to listen to or hear me.

I don't see my father for another 32 years, until just before he dies.

The plus side is that I now get to see Martin as often as we both want and I am gradually re-integrating with the maternal extended family, though never really feel as if I fully belong. At one point I get a distinct image of myself as the dog lying under the table waiting for the scraps to fall for me. I know I will always be the underdog anyway.

It is at least another two years before Hazel and I find ourselves travelling on the same train to London every morning. I haven't noticed her, I wasn't looking. But she has noticed me and breaks the silence between us. We resume an eternally awkward and conflicted relationship after that, sometimes getting on but always a tension between us.

It is another ten years before Hazel would try and see Lorna again. I facilitate this and check Mother will be in on the Saturday morning, then take Hazel over in my car. On the doorstep Mother asks, 'who is this?' and I have to say, 'it's Hazel, my sister, your daughter.'

There is some confusion all around, but it settles down. Within months, any good footing I have with Mother is now lost. Hazel is back and is once more her favourite 'good daughter'.

At some point during these ensuing years, I have gone to visit Mother when tells me how she used to drive over to our former family house and sit just along from the house, watching. She still sees herself as the tragic betrayed cast-off woman, and probably would be unable to think of herself as a stalker.

'Why did you do that, I mean why would anyone do that?'

'I was in mourning for my family.'

'But you never appreciated it when we were together.'

'I never wanted to be thrown out.'

'You weren't thrown out mum, you were having an affair and that made you even more impossible to live with. No one threw you out, you did it to yourself.'

'You're so cold and unfeeling.'

'No Mum I am not; I am just telling you what it really was. You are not the tragic heroine of a story that you had no control over, you helped to make this story and we all have to just get on with it.'

I leave shortly after that, too frustrated to continue talking with her and she is clearly not happy with me either. In her mind I was supposed to feel empathy with her when she told me that story but instead, I felt more empathy for Aileen. I was not surprised Aileen went crazy when she heard I was seeing mother again. It made more sense. Mother would not have known Dad and Aileen made friends with the couple who lived at the house which mother had parked outside of and without realising it made herself fully visible. I am sure they told Dad and Aileen about mother's little sessions.

What did she hope to gain from it, I will never know other than to play out the role of tragic heroine in her own head?

17. THE GREATEST MYSTERY OF MY LIFE

Dad married Aileen, and I am glad to say this was, as far as anyone could tell, a very happy marriage for him. For that I am deeply grateful. His marriage to my Mother was horrendous for him too. He deserved a happy later life. I wanted him to be happy after Mother. I wanted him to be loved and appreciated by someone. I always was and still am grateful to the woman who did that for him.

Dad has four children in all, three with my Mother and one with my stepmother. I believe his insistence on having another child with Aileen is to refute the impotence claims mother made when their relationship was breaking down. But I also know that he invests less and less emotionally into each child for fear of the repercussions, so my half-sister got the least of him as far as I am told. I don't know her. She is born just before I am cast out and is never interested in meeting me and I am far too afraid of more rejection to show any interest in her either. I do ask both my siblings if she ever shows any interest in me and they say none whatsoever. I am too afraid to put any toes into that ocean.

In some ways I got both the best of him and the worst. He did smack my siblings, that was acceptable in those days, and my brother once or twice rather hard too, but he never never took his anger out on them in quite the same way as he did me. I doubt they ever felt their lives were at threat, but I thought mine was, often. They continue to protect him against my story of child abuse because they still want to protect him, to protect his image, as I did for decades.

I've barely talked about my father except in terms of what he did to me. This is because my father is largely a stranger to me yet is someone who has a massive impact on my life. In my first twenty years or so he utterly dominates everything, and then becomes a huge gaping hole having suddenly and completely cut me off.
This wound slowly closed over and that is it, for over thirty years.

Then, when I am in my fifties, I realise he has now become an old man and I am a middle-aged woman. Time is running out to lay things to rest between us. Time to heal the breach?

That is the best and worst decision I ever made.

His cutting me off was just symptomatic of our deeply dysfunctional, emotionally and physically violent family. There was no redress allowed by him; he was very hard like that. I had tried just after my eldest son was born, had taken Matthew out to show him as a babe in arms, but he wouldn't look at me. That more or less did it for me. A few years later there was a minor attempt at reconciliation.

Hazel was involved though later denied it had happened. She resented the attention on me I realise later.

'Dad's been round to see me. And he spent the whole time talking about you.' She is clearly disgruntled by this. 'He feels badly about how he treated you. I think he want to see you again'

We're in Hazel's kitchen drinking tea after walking her dog in a local park, one of the few activities we both like and can share.

'OK what should I do?'

'I don't know, write to him or something – he didn't say, just sat there full of self-pity.'

She gives me his address and I write saying what Hazel has relayed to me and suggesting we meet up once a year or so, just the two of us for a meal, and leave it at that.

His response is full of garbled messages about not going behind Aileen's back and it has to be all or nothing.

I do and don't want him back in my life. I don't want him hurting us again, and especially not my sons. When he said 'no it has to be whole family stuff', I don't reply to him. I can't. I don't know what to say. I'd given my suggestion and it had been refused. I couldn't risk it. I was not articulate or emotionally literate enough then to understand my reactions, just that I once more froze and could not reply.

That had been over twenty years earlier.

And that is more or less it, until I wonder if my father, who is now nearly eighty years old, might be open to a late reconciliation at least. To lay things to rest and allow us both to feel some sort of closure. I also realise I no longer know what he looks like at all, I have no memory of his face or anything anymore, not even how he had been when I grew up. I had asked Hazel once or twice in the past and was told he looked like Barry Took on TV but that is all. I don't think she ever understood how estrangement makes you lose someone's face over a long period of time.

I decide to make contact with Dad and write a letter suggesting we put the past behind us before it is too late. I receive no response for a few weeks so I send another letter saying I just want him to know about some of what had gone on for me in childhood and how Mother (suffering from Narcissistic Personality Disorder) had so often lied to him about me.

I realise he must know at some level but can't deal with it or face it. I also say I am glad that he has a happy second marriage with Aileen. I truly mean that too, he deserved to be happy. We all do. All I'd ever known was unhappy father or 'putting a brave face on it' father. I have no doubt now that he was a seriously emotionally abused, unhappy man when I did know him. People change. I had massively.

He did not respond to either letter. Silence.
Then things start erupting in me all over again.

My life has stabilised with David and our house project, become loving and peaceful and I love it. But this suddenly takes me over, the kraken awakes, and it won't let me put it to sleep again.

I go on an eight-day trip to Boston, USA, for a week long mindfulness scientists' retreat. Most of my trip there was consumed by this attempt to reach out, being ignored once more, and the extreme anxiety it engendered in me. Anxiety that slowly turned to anger.

That should act as a warning, but it doesn't, and I am drawn inexorably on.

Eventually, some two or more months later, I get a letter from Aileen saying to get on with my life and let them get on with theirs. That felt like a knife in the guts because by then I was much softer inside and less defensive; so much easier to wound again like that.

Aileen writes saying she's read my letter, does not believe me for any of it and I should get on with life. I read it twice, hardly believing her words. In one minute, she seems to be trying to let me down gently and in the next she's being as unkind as possible.

Initially I'm distraught. I recall sitting in my car talking to Hazel on the phone. She seems genuinely sad for me, sorry for me even. I am sobbing deeply while my sister talks with me about it. She is quite sympathetic, and I'm surprised that she cares enough about me to feel that. I recover and decide to try again a while later. Later I realise she is used to seeing me as the underdog and herself as the included one, thus her role as comforter is also one of superiority.

I am so used to living with the physical symptoms of anxiety ruling my life that I've learned to ignore it, and I plough on with my intention to reconcile. I am still in contact with both my brother and sister at this point and I think in their own way they are rooting for me to succeed.

But they are still both dominated by Dad's hold over them and thus caught in a double bind. They have to take sides as they dare not stand up to him. He is a dying man. I am to be the sacrifice to save them from their own nightmares. He'd previously cut them off and rejected them both at various times too, although he had always taken them back. This made sure they would always conform to his wishes.

After the decision not to see me, my sister and brother are still talking to me about Dad quite openly, regularly speaking on the phone. At first my siblings tell me he is unwell, that they are concerned. Then they suddenly stop and fudge, keeping from saying anything with vagaries. I think it's kind of funny but don't pay too much attention to it. I trust them not to let me down. Then they are told not to let me know anything about it, that is when it went silent from them.

One day, out of the blue, I get a letter addressed to just my first name, and inside it a brief note from my stepmother telling me my father is nearly dead from cancer and wants to see me.

My heart goes out to them both. I can only imagine my life without David and think that must be how they both feel. I phone my stepmother on the number she gives me and try to reach out to her. It is about three months later. Dad is dying from oesophageal cancer, has very little time left, and now he wants to see me. I am to phone her on one of two numbers to make the arrangements.

I have a full diary, with someone staying on retreat and no spare days. Why have they put me into this position? I must cancel something. I find a whole day slot and make the appropriate apologies.

I fall for it though.

I call Aileen.

'Hello, its Sylvia.'

Her voice is sharp, I can feel her bristling. 'Hello, your father wants to see you.'

'It's all a bit of a shock though, how are you coping with everything, are you ok?'

'I'm fine thank you. It's been a shock for the whole family.'

Clearly that does not include me and her tone of voice is still sharp, hostile. I feel myself closing down in response to these old echoes and struggle to stay myself.

'It's rather short notice. I'm busy. The only day I can make is Friday.'

'Ok come to the hospice and phone me when you arrive, I'll come out and get you.'

We hang up.

She has reminded me in no uncertain terms that I am not family. I have suggested it must have been a huge shock for her and she replied it was a huge shock for all the family. Obviously not for me though, I was not included in that statement of 'family'. Her voice on the phone, that curt crisp harsh tone, that hostile rejecting phrase that immediately cut me out from any attempts I am making to connect kindly with her. I feel the fear return.

I am in a state. I phone David at work and ask if he can come home. He supports me but agrees I probably have to go. It is my last chance to see Dad alive.

I feel inexorably drawn into this obligation to go through with it now. I also realise my siblings have been lying to me and they have not considered what that would do to me. Neither have my father or Aileen considered what their request would do to my siblings and their relationship with me. I am in deep shock but don't yet realise it, I do feel very apprehensive though. I try to talk to Hazel about how unstable and anxious I feel but she tells me to pull it together and think what is the worst that could happen. She has no idea what that will be. Nor have I. We tend to think in physical terms but I have learned that human psychological warfare is far deadlier.

Apparently, he did not initially want to see me but my brother-in-law, meaning to be kind, has put pressure on him to see me as 'he could not do that to me or my siblings'.

Being judged to be wrong would have done it, would have swayed Dad. Perhaps there is still a part of him that did regret estrangement but could not express it or face it.

I should have known right then not to go any further, but something inside me broke. Hearing her voice like that, rejecting my natural warmth and openness, and my attempts to be kind and friendly and loving towards her, I had once more been frozen completely. Now I am in an emotional lockdown. I just function and appear to feel nothing. I mime the next few days until it is time to go. My request to have support from either sibling is denied, and I am told not to bring David either.

Fortunately for me, David insists coming with me. We cross on the ferry, barely talking.

The water is calm today, the boat barely rocks, just ploughs forwards through the water. But my heart is lurching madly and my stomach feels like it will erupt at any given moment. It doesn't. I stand my ground until we dock and return to our car.

David drives me there to Crawley hospice, to make sure I am safe. He is going to wait for me to go in and then find the café to sit in. I just need to know he is there for me if I need him.

My body does everything it possibly can to stop me going through with it. I feel my heart beating so hard, as if it would break through my chest. But a lifetime of 'feel the fear and do it anyway', for even greater fear of more punishment, I keep walking, and my body does the only thing it can do and makes me faint. If I'd had a weaker heart, I might have had a heart attack. A friend tells me later that what happened is extremely dangerous and never to be recommended, for just this reason.

I lose consciousness and dissolve onto the tarmac in the car park.

David has been watching me walk across the tarmac and realises I've disappeared from sight. Someone on reception also sees me go down, and the next thing I know I am being scooped up into a wheelchair and brought inside. I've never fainted in my life before and never really since though I am much more vulnerable nowadays. David helps the staff get me inside the hospice then leaves me to go and wait in the café.

I have never known such terror in my whole life. The staff are truly kind and let Dad and Aileen know I've arrived and am having a cup of tea before I come in. I am supposed to have phoned Aileen from the car park, and she was to come out and bring me in.

I don't think I am supposed to be known of as a daughter by the hospice staff. I am the offspring that has been expunged from the family story and I no longer exist. No one should know about me. They do now though. I find myself shaking and thanking the attendant repeatedly, telling her I want my Dad to know who I am now, and I don't know how to do that.

I am still shaking and terrified when one of the staff gently supports me down the corridor and directs me to his bed.

I go in and see him on my own. I am not allowed to see him on his own. My stepmother has either insisted she be there, or he has insisted on it, I don't know, but it is two against one and that is exactly how it feels. I am about 4 years old again inside, terrified of both parents, and my stepmother has just replaced my Mother.

He is a stranger to me.

Apart from his cancer, which dramatically changes people's appearance, I still could not recognise him as anyone I'd once known. He is this strange old man, and yet I am still utterly terrified of him. All I can feel is fear.

There is no chair for me, so I stand awkwardly until he tells me to sit on the bed. Aileen doesn't move.

He takes my hand and holds it. I know he is trying to reach out finally, but I am just too afraid of him and I am wooden and awkward and frozen and stilted and nothing of myself at all, although I pretend I am.

I feel my body reverting to behaviours from way back, attitudes and patterns of self-portrayal, that I am no longer connected to. Who I have become? Who I really am? She has vanished.

We try and talk a bit. I can find nothing to say and am clumsy and awkward in what I do say. It doesn't work. It isn't me. I am drowning far out to sea and no one is noticing.

He spills some water. Both Aileen and I move to clear it up, but she is annoyed that I also act. He is her territory now. She shows her hostility, resentment or frustration. Perhaps she thinks I am usurping her place, but I am trying to be helpful, that is all. I cannot stop myself from mopping the water, it is a small sanctuary of activity.

Dad tries to get us to talk to each other, about gardening I seem to remember, but the words are stuck inside me and although I force them out, they are not comfortable. I felt this barrage of hostility endlessly pouring towards me from her direction, an energy field of rejection that I find impossible to withstand and cannot look at her, though I try. It feels as if my face is being pushed away. I try to talk to her, but no words come out of my mouth. My throat is closing up on me.

I flap a hand at some more tissues, and I can only assume she thinks I'm being very rude. Then he mouths 'I love you' to her and looks away from me completely. I want to run out but cannot move.

I cannot physically move. I cannot stand up and walk away and say sorry this was a mistake. I cannot stick up for myself or be myself or be anything other than a whipped dog, cowering, waiting for a chance to say something, to grasp that last opportunity to put something, some little itsy bitsy thing right.

I turn to my stepmother and ask if I could talk to her for a minute. Her reply is full of contempt and hostility. Her words, 'I would not waste a moment of my time with you when I can spend it with the man I love in the time he has left'.

I am left utterly defeated and lost.

A meal assistant comes in and my stepmother is asked questions about Dad's lunch, so she must move away. I try to get a word out, permission to return on my own, but he says, with cold hard hostile eyes and dull voice, 'Don't hurry back', his final rejection.

My only aim has been for Dad to finally get to know me as I really am, before it is too late for us both. But the family agendas have come piling back on and I am crushed into submission. I feel like I am struggling against a prison of invisible chains, hitting walls of terror and wading through a solid mass of impossible assumptions and stories and histories too fucked up to ever be resolved now. I have failed totally.

My sense of failure impacts upon all the thousands of previous times I have been a failure for him and Mother, my terror at his responses still there as if I am again four years old.

I stumble out of there as fast as my legs can carry me. I nearly pass out again, just outside his door and stand against the wall for a while to regain my balance. I take deep breaths. I don't know how I stay upright and make my feet move. I find David waiting for me in the canteen. A nurse has previously told him it was going well because she'd seen Dad holding my hand, but she'd not noticed the terror in my eyes. When I say what has just happened, he wants to get me out of there as fast as possible.

We call in on some family friends who live nearby, and I try to be normal. I tell them what has just happened, and they are appalled. I try and pretend it is ok with me. I try and get on with my life.

Something inside me is now broken, seriously broken.

Turns out I have been gestating a monster for my whole life. And now it has broken free from all my cages and controls.

I struggle for the following few months to keep it all together but slowly, slowly and inexorably I start to go into labour. The waters break and that is it, I am giving birth to the monster which has lain dormant inside me, frozen away into recesses and deprived of light and oxygen until my Stepmother and father's last words to me tear me apart.

Just like childbirth, it takes over and dictates every moment of its own progress. Once delivered, it engulfs my life in its entirety, as infants do. Day and night it storms and rampages through every part of me, releasing every last buried memory, every traumatised moment, every unkind word and violent action, every bit of suffering and anger and fear that the child, who was once me, had lived through.

It takes six years for that unravelling to stop. In the end it is a blessed relief, but I would not have made it through alive without having the most amazing husband in the world who just held me.

David never met Dad, but he had met Mother and did know how bad my childhood had been, that I never made any of it up. That I had developed Post Traumatic Stress Disorder at around four years old is now clear evidence of just how bad it had been.

Dad dies about two weeks later. From time to time I had been ringing the hospice for updates, so I know it is close. It is around 1 am and we are both asleep when the phone rings. It is my brother, now determined to keep me in the loop, telling me. But he wants me to ask sensible questions and I can't. I have just been woken from a deep sleep and all I can think of is in my head the words ' he can never hurt me again', round and round they go, like a self-formatting mantra.

'Don't you want to know how he went?'

'Yes, yes tell me.'

'He went very peacefully.'

'Good, thanks for telling me.'

I hang up and try to go back to sleep.

I discover a few days later that my stepmother Aileen will not countenance me going to his funeral. Perhaps my attendance would take too much explaining that she doesn't want to face, I don't know. Perhaps she can't face me again. Perhaps she has reflected on her words to me and seen how harsh she has been. I don't know if I could have made it anyway, but I don't go. It is over. Or so I thought!

Thanks for everything Dad.

I am sorry your words of regret got stuck in your throat and ate you away.

I am sorry that it had to kill you like that.

I am so sorry we never got to know each other. I think you missed out badly. xxx

18. DARKNESS TAKES OVER, THEN COMES THE LIGHT

It takes several months for the breakdown and trauma to take me over completely. To begin with I try to pretend I'm ok, everything is normal again. That I can swallow this and get on with my life as instructed.

I continue to see one or two therapy/ mindfulness clients each week and see my supervisor monthly. He does his best to support me, but events start to show themselves as they do, and I decide to stop seeing people.

I am also in the middle of a PhD looking at the neuroscience of ADHD and mindfulness. I have a full grant and a great professor to work with. It is my life's greatest dream to do this research. But I can't continue. My GP writes me a letter of resignation support. I feel dreadful for the sponsors, but I really am unable to concentrate, study, or do any of the things you need for a PhD. All the belts and braces in the world are not going to keep this inside and my attempts to do so are becoming all engulfing and still failing. I am completely falling apart, taken over by fear, rage, nightmares and physical pain.

Let me begin with the night terrors. I barely sleep at all. Most nights I fall asleep out of physical desperation, for an hour or so. If I get into bed it might last a little longer, maybe three hours. Then I am woken with shrieks of terror coming out of my body, locking my muscles rigid. I try to suppress the cries, not to disturb David, and go downstairs. I watch TV recordings and try and release my muscles. I take betablockers, the only meds I will take. I know I cannot allow any more suppression from anti-depressants and the like – this must come out, all of it. No tears are ever able to seep through, my grief is totally dry and locked down.

I spend much of my time repeating mantras – it is ok for me to live, I am allowed to live and am wanted and loved, this too will pass, this is not who I am but what was done to me. My wrists throb with asking me to slash them, my mind is screaming end this now, once and for all. I resist this. I am determined to make it through. I have a wonderful man upstairs who wants me to make it through alive.

The dreams and flashbacks come back with a new piece of the puzzle each night, sometimes during the day too when my body starts convulsing and a new memory is released, a new part of the puzzle of my buried childhood. The colours are so vivid, the smells, the sounds. I can smell Mother's apple blossom fragrance, Dad's sometimes acrid BO. Even the food cooking, my little Grandmothers urine soaked armchair and her breath smelling of Murray mints.

It all comes back in such vivid detail, as if someone kept a film recording of it all and is only now allowing me to see this footage, this time with no censorship in place.

Sometimes there are repetitions and sometimes just slightly more of each experience. Each one leaves me exhausted, hollowed out, feeling as if death really is the only answer. It is what I should do to release myself and everybody else from the misery of my existence, but I hang on for dear life, for my wonderful husband and sons. I am determined this will not take me with it.

My physical body goes rigid during these sessions. Every muscle in me is locked solid and hurts more than words can say. The worst parts are across my lower back and my neck and shoulders, my jaw and my hands. My fingers can hardly unlock enough to hold a drink if I make myself one. I take strong painkillers, but they barely work, just taking a tinge off only.

Sometimes I cannot stop myself howling, from a place so deep inside I do not know it. It is a sort of wailing keening noise. Sometimes huge sobs emerge, dry, from some part of me so deeply hidden; they shake my entire body as they leave. I am powerless to stop them or slow them and know I must let them all go. I am surrendering to the process of letting it go. I keep reminding myself this is not about me; this is not who I am, this is what happened to me.

Sometimes the rage makes me go into fantasies. I want to murder my Stepmother and then kill myself, I want to smash the hospice up, I want to make some huge unmistakeable deed that leaves no one in any doubt what I went through, what I am now going through. I allow it all to pass through me and relate it to David so that I know I cannot act on it, just in case I lose that last vestige of control.

During the days I am like a zombie from exhaustion. I have enough energy to complete one or two domestic tasks, then I am exhausted again and must simply sit and consume endless mindless TV which seems to distract my mind long enough for me to relax slightly. I am obsessive with things like sudoku and knitting, with all sorts of things. When I can I go outside into my garden, my sanctuary, my inspiration, and work until my body feels it will break, but some of the pain subsides into the soil and it slowly helps to heal me; soothes me too. My back problems are increasing massively, my lower spine in constant pain, dull aches that every so often go into total spasm and I am crying out from that pain too. We buy a hand-held massager and David works my body over almost every night. It helps to release the muscles for a while.

Living like this continues more or less unabated for months; we have little or no life outside of our home. David has recently taken early retirement on the basis I have my research grant coming in, but that has now gone. I need him to care for me daily anyway. I am helpless much of the time.

He realises I cannot move to a new house, can't cope with the upheaval that entails.

We will run out of money soon enough.

He starts converting our huge retreat centre dream house into two letting units for holiday makers. Sometimes I manage to pull it together for a few days, to put on a show for people, even my brother and family come to stay. David works like a trojan to get this done so we don't run out of money and are forced to sell up before I am well enough to cope. It takes a huge toll on his body though and he develops terrible tendonitis in his Achilles and elsewhere, repetitive strain injuries. I try to help him with painting but the fumes from the paint make me feel faint, nauseous, and weak in the arms. I can manage no more than half an hour. I start to develop a strong dull aching in my limb muscles and back. I am useless. He is left with the rest. He makes it happen by some miracle and we start to find agencies to represent us. Even that seems chaotic at first but eventually we are happy settled with an agency and the bookings come in. We are still afloat and still in the house which is my total safe space. Some people who come are lovely and others are quite unkind. They trigger me. But we cope for about six years until the triggering get too much for me and we must move on. It is changing. People have started to make demands for refunds and complaints about made up things and the dishonesty and unkindness of it deeply affects me.

No one in my family asks how we are doing. They know I am ill, but they never phone once.

Never a single phone call to David to ask how he is coping nor how I am doing.

Apart from one or two visits early on, when we pretend it is ok, no one ever thinks to ask if we are ok.

David keeps me safe. He holds me when I can countenance being loved, the possibility of being wanted, and leaves me alone when I cannot bear being touched, when I push him away, when the terror of trusting him to come close is too much for me. I am unworthy of him. I am despicable, I am the most disgusting specimen of humanity that ever lives.

After about two years at this pitch, it starts to slow down, comes in waves when I am bad and then times when I am almost normal again, except I still don't sleep much and feel the terror almost all the time, just not so sharply. David has to sleep elsewhere as my nights have become too disrupted for him and he needs to sleep, to cope with it all. Then if I awake, I am able to read and stay in bed. That's slightly better for me. I'm becoming able to find ways to calm and soothe myself.

Sometimes I can even read myself back to sleep. Books that have easy stories and happy endings, books about love and families. My favourite author becomes Alexander McCall Smith as his books are gentle and humorous and intelligent and insightful about the human condition. Being able to read again is a great luxury.

But I so miss David at night, the comfort of his body warmth next to me. I do my best not to push him away and he is amazing at just holding me when I feel able to let him and letting me be when not. He never raises his voice to me or gets frustrated with me once, though I know he must feel it, despair too sometimes. That becomes another source of self-loathing and self-rejection. I am convinced that soon enough he will leave me, find me impossible as had my Mother once so many years ago. I am working as hard as I can to keep myself moving forward into a positive future and he knows I can only do what I am doing. I do some yoga but mostly the mindfulness mantras keep me sane and stop me from being taken completely under. Only just though.

I know undoubtedly and with full deep knowledge I will not

make it through without David. He is perfect for me and to me and, as long as I live, I can never say thank you or love him enough to repay that generosity and compassion shown to me, even when I was rejecting him.

I become more and more agoraphobic, unable to leave the house without David and only able to go from home to another 'safe place'. Safe is my desperate search, finding the inside of my own mind so desperately unsafe I am looking for safe in my material world, even though I know that can only be an illusion, but I need that for now. Eventually I realise I need to find something to get me out of the house. We get a dog, Lola, a lovely collie cross lurcher. She is part of a friendship share and David does not want her, does not want any more burdens. She almost deserves a whole chapter to herself, but we have her for two years. Things go wrong everywhere. She takes on my mental fragility and becomes too dominant and aggressive. She is an overly sensitive dog and has a lot of hunter in her. She starts biting other dogs and then people who come to the house. She chases anything that moves. The police start to get in touch about complaints and though we try to manage it, it is closing me down terribly once more. I am afraid of all the people I once thought were new friends as dogwalkers. I was going backwards. Finally, the police say we must keep her muzzled and never off the lead. I cannot do this to her. She loves to run for long distances, she loves to hunt, she is fast, an athlete, and I am now afraid of her too, not that she will bite me but of what she will bring to me. We make the terrible decision to have her put down. Her quality of life would be seriously compromised, and I can't cope any more. We call the mobile vet and he comes and puts her to sleep in our house with us all loving and stroking her.

I can cry.

I cry buckets for Lola, for the tragedy of her life, for what we did to her, for what my illness did to her, for her own confusion and increasing unhappiness. I cry for nearly three months. I cry for everything sad in my life, all the losses, the heartbreak, the sadness of the whole story. I barely stop crying and gradually it is healing me a little more.

Once that subsides though I realise I am still terrified, more so and of everything still, but especially people.

It takes me six years in total, from dad dying and the beginning of break down until the time that terror releases me from its grip.

The healing takes several deeply significant stages.

My first attempt to get help is a disaster. A psychiatrist I know offers to help me and gives me a single session where he makes me shout at an empty chair that represents my father.

'Go on shout at him, tell him how terrible he was to treat you that way. He should never have hit you, shout, never have rejected you.' And so on.

But I can't get it out of me at first. I have a huge reluctance to confront Dad, even metaphorically. I still blame Mother for everything. He keeps on and on at me, that my Father was a disgrace and should never have treated me like that.

He makes me feel pathetic and stupid if I cannot get angry, ridiculous not to place the blame at Dad's door. In the end I feel bullied into complying and something inside shifts. It is a start, but it releases a terrible energy in me.

I walk out to the car where David is waiting for me. I am not safe to drive during this time, I cannot concentrate. I feel strange, lost, in a new world.

That night is terrible, the terrors are now released. This is the start of more night misery. Too much has been released and I have no strategies to cope with it. It is too fast, too huge, and eventually also utterly misguided. So much in one go, with no strategies to manage it. He offers to see me again, but I am too traumatised by the single session to risk going back.

Unfortunately this makes things worse for a while and I end up venting most of that rage onto my brother and sister for colluding with Dad and Aileen to keep me in the dark and then put me in that position, to set me up to be broke down. I keep telling them I need them to say this or do that to make me feel safe again. They don't understand and are overwhelmed by the pressure I am putting on them. I have no way of coping other than what I am doing. Hazel has become close to Aileen and tells her it doesn't matter to her how she treated me, then relays that to me. I am devastated. It is as if a torturer is now more valued by my sister than I ever was or would be. My grief is doubled. I am utterly powerless to cope with it. I can feel myself completely fragmented inside, utterly broken into pieces, utterly betrayed. My brother and sister think I am utterly unreasonable. Communication has now completely broken down, so has trust.

Even now, I am still afraid of them both. They will carry the family paradigm about me, the family energy and that is now utterly toxic to me. I know they find me too impossible to cope with. I am now like Mother's raging foaming monster myself. We are triggering each other deeply over our respective traumas without anybody understanding what that means. That is a hard lesson to live with over the future years, until I do find peace and forgiveness within myself, and then gratitude.

Next, I have some great counselling. That gets me so far, but it can't stop me getting re-traumatised often and badly, so I'm plunged even deeper back into the worst of the trauma. Then I have EMDR.

But I am a people pleaser at heart, and it doesn't work, though I want it to. The therapist says I just have to sit there and follow the little blue light while we chat about Desperate Housewives and other such things. She is convinced of that and I now know we should have been exploring the terrors so the light could break them up. But I manage to keep them safe from her and the treatment, still unaware at this early stage of quite how much I am holding on trying to stay in one piece and not yet remotely aware of what is to come.

The storm breaks for a second time, more massively than before even. I try to get more help but the NHS only allows you so many sessions and I've had more than my official allocation already. I am deemed better after the first year, and indeed I do have a brief period of relative calm when it seems to be over. At this point I am still managing to hang onto my relationships with my siblings. But I have a lot more to let go of and things conspired to retraumatise me even more deeply, and even more easily this time since I have no defences left anyway.

Mother dies four years after Dad, in 2012.

I am too ill to go to her funeral, and still too locked into my self-revealing traumas. Through the various stages of revelation and physical manifestation of the trauma locked deep within me, I begin to notice parallels between myself and my Mother. For my whole life up until that point, if you want to upset me the most just say I am like my Mother in any small way at all. It makes my skin crawl at the very thought. And now I am seeing it for myself.

I feel the grief and sense of isolation, the darkness and desolation too, and I realise they all came from her energy. She has poured them into me because she had no way of telling anyone what happened to her in her life that gave her this darkness to carry too. She gave it to me to tell the story of it, to tell her story through my story. The story must end here with me telling it out loud.

I start to feel forgiveness and compassion for her in her own life, to consider the pain of having three children and knowing she has driven them away herself, of knowing that no one ever really liked her, they were just nice people, her family didn't really like her either. Everything she'd told me about myself I now realise was a projection of her own inner feelings onto me. The piggy eyes and overlarge feet and hands, the lank hair and everything else. If it hadn't been for her, we might have had a happy family. It was never me. It was always her she'd been talking about. My poor sad lonely devastated Mother.

This really begins the healing changes inside me. But there is still a long way to go.

The buddha teaches us that to understand all is to forgive all. This is the first stage for me. My heart is suddenly beginning to ache with sadness for Mother and mentally I imagine holding her tenderly and saying how sad I am for her.

I physically feel the release of forgiveness in me, a real shedding and lightening within me, a letting go. I have let my anger go, my fear too. Forgiveness doesn't mean any of it was ok, it just means I have stopped taking it personally. That is my healing point. It is liberating but not the end of the story just yet.

David is brilliant. He gets me back into yoga, which he has done more or less daily for roughly fifty years now. He helps me, encourages me to stretch out my back and generally looks for ways in which I can let go. We share some of our meditation techniques but I am still unable to access this approach just yet beyond affirmations.

He perseveres. He identified I had PTSD in the first place, and I passed that onto the counsellors, hence the extra treatments. But despite this realisation we are left wondering where to go next, and I am just not getting properly better. Apparently there is more to go.

David does some more research and finds MDMA has been developed to help people in deep trauma to feel safe, like me, but because it had been used recreationally and had some related deaths due to lack of understanding of how the drug works physically, it had become illegal and is not available to me medically. All official medical research has stopped.

We get hold of some anyway and I take the first lot. I feel ok but nothing much. Then I persuade David to take some with me and come to bed to survive it together. We know we have to drink enough but not too much, and we take the journey.

I don't know what makes me suggest this, but it comes spontaneously as all the best ideas often do.

It is amazing.

All fear leaves me, all pain, my muscles unlock and we lay in each other arms for hours with only the awareness of how deeply and profoundly we are connected, that our love is far greater than either of us have ever realised before. It makes complete sense of the escalator experience I'd had when we first got together. We are swimming in sweat and a deep, deep sense of release from all fear and pain. Our defences are completely down for the first time ever for us both. Here we are in our cocoon and we find we were as close as is possible on some deeply spiritual emotional level which neither of us knew existed, but it is tangible and wonderful and so so healing for us both. After four or five hours we come down and I feel exhausted but free from fear. Again, I think that is it.

Within a few days though my terrified body locks up again and I feel rigid mentally emotionally and physically once more.

We decide to try again.

Although the effect is less spectacular than the first time, we got back into that place and can tell each other things neither of us could ever have shared before, even with each other.

Instead of just laying together and experiencing the journey, we decide to work it. Layers of shame and bullying, of grief and fear drop away from us both. We allow our inner children to meet up and let them play together, to end the loneliness and confusion we both went through in childhood. It is less about me and more about both of us this time. We send messages back to our younger selves, as if on MDMA we can actually reach them, that time is not linear but circular and all at the same time. I wonder if the dreams I'd had of my mysterious teen dream lover come from this moment, when we went back and told our teen selves to hang on and we would meet up in the future and make it all ok for each other.

On another trip we share how lonely we'd both been during our childhoods and we set our young children, me at four and him at six, playing in a stream together damming it up with stones and paddling, chasing sticks and generally just mooching around. We feel the companionship of that time in the stream as a real and tangible thing, as if it had once really happened. Perhaps in another life or perhaps we are making it happen in circular time in this life and this existence. Who knows! It doesn't matter. What matters is that our inner children are suddenly not isolated and alone anymore. We are looking after each other back then and now too, we are equals holding each other tenderly. It is the end of any shame or guilt about anything between us and we have never looked back.

I still go back to my stream with the two of us in it when I am feeling low and uncertain. We bought a house with a stream at the end and I love to go and watch the water in it, fast flowing and gently singing to me.

But like all good things there are down sides.

We take that journey a total of six times, working through different layers each time, being raped and sexually abused, being less than our perfect ideal selves. Each time I think it is ended but a few days later the traumatised body is back, the mental and emotional lockdown too, albeit slightly longer before it returns each time. Something is shifting but not enough.

The MDMA come down is getting harder for me, making me feel wasted and worn out. My chronic fatigue is struggling to cope. It is taking me days, up to a week before I feel well again, so I say no more.

We turn to cannabis and find that helps too, eating it in cookie form, for a while. It helps with the muscle unlocking. By this time my lower back is in constant acute pain. But eventually I must stop that too, it only helps up to a certain point, then everything comes back. Temporary moments of relief keep me hopeful though. I am being shown breakthroughs.

One particularly hard period of night terrors, when the PTSD is still ebbing and flowing, the flashbacks are still coming, though less and less hard, and I still cannot leave the house alone, I feel a sense of hopelessness creeping up on me. I turn to David next to me on the sofa.

'I'm not sure how much more of this I can take.'

'I know, I understand how hard this is on you.'

'On both of us. You've had to carry so much to get me this far through. But I just can't bear the thought of never really being able to sleep through, and feel free to come and go as my body still allows me to, to live a life.'

'Ok, I understand.' David take my hand and smiles tenderly, 'hopefully we can get you through this though eh!'

'Maybe, but if one day or night I go, you will forgive me? You won't take it personally?'

'No, I won't take it personally, I'll understand.'

It is a profound moment of understanding between us, then I melt.

'I don't want to leave you. I want to get well again. I want to be your wife again.'

I continue talking with David about how hard I still find it. It is an endurance and though we've made progress, I cannot imagine surviving living like this for the rest of my life. I tell him how grateful I am and how much I love him. Gratitude has increasingly become part of my outlook on life. I am utterly humbled and broken, and gratitude for anything simply filled my emptiness up. I resolve to keep working on it with all the skills and energy I can muster.

I know how the meditation and mindfulness background has kept me going so well, even though I find it too intense to practice any specific meditation. I return again and again to the healing Dharma truths. These help me get through the darkest moments, always just getting me through them.

I decide to give that a go with full immersion. I book myself on four retreats with the Thich Nhat Hanh community in UK and Plum village in France and embark on four intensive healing retreats.

Each one lifts a little more, but when I come back from the final one at Plum village something has truly shifted in me. I have reached bliss.

It is astonishing but I gradually notice all the back chat and noise in my head has gone silent. That I have no sense of I, or me or an independent separate self-identity. I feel as if I am part of the flow of everything. I can watch my body go through the motions of any task and there is no agenda attached to it, I am observing my body doing whatever it is doing, and it is not 'me' anymore. I have let go so completely that I have let go of myself too.

It feels amazing. I think that is it, it's over forever, I'm healed. I feel invincible, reborn and astonished.

This is once more very challenging for David since I seem to have no attachments of any kind, not even to him, the wonderful husband who has helped me get through it all, who has encouraged my trips to meditate and heal and who is now being left behind. But I know I still love him and want to be with him, but it will be different, for now at least, there is no dependency or attachment, just love and a decision to make for the future of this selfless body.

I have written about this experience elsewhere and call it my 'golden pond period' since it feels as if I am floating in this limitless abyss of golden lit lagoon where I am part of everything. There are no sides or edges, no bottom or top. I am simply there in perfect balance and harmony, in pure consciousness, floating through incarnate life, and nothing really matters

Except it does and after roughly five months, life conspires to bring me back to earth, but without the trauma anymore. I really do think 'that is it' then, my new normal is established.

I have that zen moment of realisation, quietly and gently I realise that this is it. Life with all its messy annoying devastating experiences and all its deep joy and tenderness too – this is what it is all about. Not just one without the other, but all of it. It feels complete. Life made sense. The purpose of this life is just for the experience, nothing more and nothing less than that. Getting too caught up in the material reality or the details misses that point completely. I feel remarkably free and liberated and wonder if I've achieved 'some kind of enlightenment'.

I haven't of course, but I have woken up to a new way of looking at everything from an experiential instead of a theoretical position, and I love it deeply. I notice I still love everyone else deeply too. I think 'now I am healed – now I can get on with life'.

And I naively think that is the truth.

Not quite!
When I was ill.

When my levees broke no one could see the broken mosaic of my heart, or the darkness pouring from me.

You thought that was mine? Yet I have been holding it for the world, for my entire life, keeping it safe.

Nobody said it wasn't mine to keep. I kept it hidden, to protect you. That you will never understand is ok.

It finally flooded out of me, to release me, it was never me. Vitriol, hers and his, not mine.

Fury, fear and hatred lined up to take their turns, to jump ship and fly free, taking me with them where they could, to continue their legacy, until I unshackled my own broken body from their demon grip.

Then turning around to look behind at what remained of me, finding even deeper buried, the love inside myself, forgiveness, gratitude. These are my gifts, in return for those I once had.

When I was ill it was invisible. So many told me to pull it together, just like before, but this time it was too big and too ferocious and everything just broke me, again and again and again, until I could barely move or breathe or sleep.

Fear governed my every moment, freezing me into a time long past yet ever present, forever haunting.

Hunted, tortured and twisted, waiting until the storm would pass, trusting that this was not the ending.

None of this was ever me, just a legacy, a lesson in darkness, journey to hell, to know what that place feels like, to know what heaven meant, what love felt like,

What gratitude for every minute of life would give, for knowing what it means to truly surrender all, and wait 'til the storm passes.

When I was broken, no one could see the suppurating wounds inside the child's body or understand the effort it took to 'cheer up'.

I wanted to be cheerful but the poisonous hatred, contempt and derision they poured into my child's-frame soured all potential, extinguishing the light in my heart, the joy from my spirit, filling my mind with such thoughts of self-destruct.

When I was broken no one could see how jagged the edges of my heart became, how ragged they were where they were torn from me again and again, when all I wanted was to love and be loved.

Any child will ache for just that.

When I was ill, the expectations from those who could or would not see my invisible gaping holes, became unbearable burdens, their weight beyond me.

How they shouted, judged, or silently condemned me from their lofty palaces of being whole, and thought, really thought, it was all me, the real me, and threw me away once more on trash-piles of their ignorance.

When I was frozen, when no feelings could disturb me, I appeared sub human, uncaring, unmoved by the tragedies of my own life or of someone else's, but I kept myself on ice, preserved for a future feast, one in which I would not be the main course to be devoured, dissected and disallowed.

I still see the looks and judgements of those days now I am come back to the warmth, ready to open to love once more. To life. To living in this precious moment.

Now I am come back who will join me, who can I allow?

Those whose energy reflects that which took me down, no not them, I am not a welcoming mirror for them, though I feel their sadness, their lostness, their neediness, I have nothing for them.

Those who held me close and allowed me to be broken

Those who saw me, not their own judgements and delusions

Those who come to me with their own vulnerability

I will embrace them, I will embrace the broken and the wounded, I will share my own gentle nature and loving with them, to lead them to where I now dwell.

Healing, when it came, was pure. It was existence in love, in joy, in amazing grace. That took time. That too is invisible. It takes time, to build, to rebuild, to remain broken open, and yet strong enough to take your respective hells on once more.

When I am healed, when I am strong once more, when I can stand still and not be moved by the hurricanes of your darkness, when I can feel that hell once more and laugh in its face, when I know I am invincible, when I know my love is greater than your power, greater than your games and darknesses.

Only then can I turn to the whole world and say, 'Now I am yours'.

19. TRIGGERING THE DARK NIGHT OF THE SOUL

I awoke at 2.30 again this morning. It is now 3 am and I am struggling to get on top of the ritual thought trains that haunt me when I'm triggered. Currently my wrists are throbbing, asking me to slice them open and a narrative is forming in my head in the form of a simple prayer. This is five years after my release from the interminable trauma of PTSD, and it is still happening, though not constantly. In between I am fine and happy, and life is exceptionally good.

But I have learned that my nervous system was adversely affected in those early years and I have too sensitive stress reactions to be normal. Some things just upset me, and I am upset but fine, but some things trigger the PTSD back into my body.

'Dear God, please let me go soon. Please send me a condition that ends it for me now so that I don't have to give into my wrists and hurt those who love me, for whatever reason they find appropriate, since I deeply know how much they are mistaken and have not yet woken up to my basic unlove-ableness and unworthiness to exist'.

I know this routine so well. It is exhausting to go through it yet again, being triggered into this cycle by thoughtlessness, carelessness, emotional illiteracy and general human fallibility. I know I should be able to rise above it and see it for what it is, a stupid mistake. I want to shrug it off and say it doesn't matter.

But, for now I must go through this cycle one more time, yet again. Trying to find ways of reducing its power and unwrapping its stranglehold on my life.

It doesn't matter what caused it. What matters is that it has crushed me again, sucking the joy out of me like a leak in my spacesuit of personal defences.

Since my breakdown I have no defences in place anymore. They were all maladaptive from a childhood of abuse and thus served me ill anyway. They all went so I could be free of trauma. They have left me wide open and raw, emotionally stripped back and experiencing life in its immediacy. Most of the time this is a joyful and wonderful connectedness to the exact present moment. I wouldn't give up on it for anything. It makes every moment into a 'this is it' moment, that zen moment of pure realisation of joy right here in this breath.

It also keeps me humble, open, honest, insightful and intuitive to levels I did not know possible. It keeps me grateful, compassionate, generous with what I have. I am more open to being wrong, less defensive. I can re-evaluate my opinions and recognise how desperately wrong our judgments of each other are, to understand how much everyone is suffering. I am more aware of the interconnectedness of everything, that suffering elsewhere is caused by poor decisions made of ignorance in one's own life. I can feel the suffering energy of the planet but also the love.

We can't have everything. I have this wonderful gift of freedom from illusion.

Except when I get triggered!

Is it to remind me of where I came from, to keep me humbled and in place? Or perhaps to challenge me to release myself from this once more, to make sure I am not complacent in my newly found liberation? Perhaps a reminder of what life feels like for most, still burdened by their defences against the injustices of this world, from which I am largely protected by privilege and having my wish granted of 'just enough' materially to live without fear in that quarter? Can one ever live without fear anyway?

Is this just the form my fear must or will now take in life? Surely my greatest fear is that I will for some reason lose my beloved ones, my sons and grandson and most of all my soulmate? It seems strange that my greatest fear is that I must continue to live for now. That my prayers are to go now, to be done with this life, to let me finally say 'I did my best and I am too tired to fight this anymore'.

What am I tired of? Triggering, cruelty of political systems and ideologies that ruin people's lives, and so much more. It exhausts me. But alongside there is the joy I feel in my life too. They are both extreme ends of the spectrum. It seems I'm not allowed to waddle comfortably somewhere in the middle of the joy/despair spectrum. Life after all is just a series of spectrums, happy/ sad, sick /well, and we are all at some point along each of them, rather like my ADHD and other spectrum disorders.

Life is a spectrum disorder.

Ha-ha that has made me laugh at this idea and myself.

Perhaps this is the breaking through point for me with this occurrence of triggering. But will I be able to go back into the scenario which triggered it. I doubt it. What happens is that my body says, 'ok you're safe here at home writing about this, but I won't let you go back in case they trigger you again'.

This has curtailed so much of my life. I have withdrawn from many of the interest groups I used to frequent and enjoy. There are certain people who are utterly toxic to me, especially aforementioned psychiatrist, and a few others who have just pushed me too far a few times too often. I can barely look them in the face when I run into them. It is a small island, only two degrees of separation here. Members of my own family are included.

If I ignore it, try to pretend nothing happened, return to normal and carry on, it just triggers me again, which means emotional lockdown and physical rigidity to pain levels that are quite high, even though I am used to them.

If I fight against it, I pay with that lockdown and must medicate, or not and sit it out anyway, wait for it to pass. Which means I am out of action for other things too.

If I give into it, my life shrinks a little more than it already has done.

If I do what I am doing now and explore it, get it out into the open and say to it 'is this really how you think I should live, be and feel?' If I do this act of exposure often enough, will it eventually decide to agree with me and stop trying to control me?

'Shine light on your trauma and it will dissolve.'

This is the summit of advice from all quarters, and it's true, it does dissolve, slowly. But this last stage is taking forever and stands out as more painful in contrast to the joy I feel most of the time.

Stop whingeing perhaps, be glad for the joy I feel and accept this last level of burden of trauma from the past.

I consider Tonglen, a Tibetan meditative practice where I absorb the suffering of the world and breathe out that very joy in its place. I practice this against the injustices of the world, the petty cruelties of wealth and corruption and damaged souls being given power they do not deserve or know how to use wisely, only self-servingly.

I ache for the raw suffering of others and the causal thoughtless cruelty that causes it.

I weep for a world that is destroying itself and cheer for those who would act to wake the rest of us up. I do, daily.

I challenge that world and the sadness it sows in me for others. I challenge those damaged parental voices too. I do it through my writing. I do it in my meditation. I do it in my approach to life. I do my best though I know it is inadequate. I try to stop berating myself for that too.

I work at being fearless, courageous, brave. Even just to go and talk to people, I am being all those things, though they will never know that. It is easier for me to stand on stage and give a lecture or performance than it is for me to talk to people in a more intimate way, especially in public or in groups. One on one with trusted people is OK though. I have enough of them in my life.

What I really want is to live in a bubble of safety with my soul-mate and my sons, to have nothing more touch any of us. We have all struggled with those legacies. What I really want is an end to the terrors of my childhood being re-enacted again and again through my traumatised nervous system. What I want is for this to end! Either by ending life or by ending the triggering process.

I know by the end of writing this I will have become determined once again to get through it and live on.

I know by the end of this I will have shifted the vice grip of this process, this routine my body deems it necessary to put me through once again.

I know that the love I feel for my family and my soulmate husband will prove the stronger force in the end.

I know that if I return to my bed my husband will wrap his sleepy arms around me and hold me until I can cry it out of me and let it go.

I know that writing this and publishing it is my way of saying 'hang on in there' to myself and to others who may feel like this but also to say do not judge others, if you are not experiencing triggering like this do not judge others who may be, you cannot tell from the outside. It is an invisible injury that we carry all the time.

This too will pass, eventually!

But will I ever be able to go back again? To any of the long list of triggering events, locations and situations?

A close friend triggers me when I see her, not that often. Do I stop seeing her, talk to her, avoid her for now? It is just her lack of understanding and her sense of her own self-importance and priorities in her life. She makes me feel like an after-thought but then expects me to fit into her schedule, friendship as commodity rather than valued company. Another has a go at me for something minor on facebook. I withdraw from her too.

It is not about me, just like everything Mother and Dad did to me was never about me. Yet I was traumatised then and still get triggered now, by even small echoes of that family paradigm. I honestly prefer not to socialise, but people expect me to and made demands of me. I refuse much of them but not all. I am not churlish, but I cannot help some people to understand how hard it is for me still.

Every day I leave my house without my husband is a huge act of courage, but I am determined to do it, to keep going.

What my poor nervous system needs more than anything is to be soothed. Apparently, David is healing my brain, my amygdala, the emotional processing part of my brain, with his gentleness, this is how it happens. The more I can live life without being triggered, the more quickly that damaged nervous system can re-grow into a neurologically stable one. Thank heavens for neuroplasticity. But I read another study led by my old professor which shows that neuroplasticity cannot fix it completely. That children deprived in early years do have smaller brains than those given emotionally stimulating and happy healthy environments.

Will I ever be completely free of it, would that be a good thing anyway? Who knows? Is it worth even trying? My home island holds many trigger points now. Perhaps I should just move on again instead, or is that running away still, is that why I ask for the end, to avoid that? Perhaps this is the turning point when I stand my ground and say, 'no I will not run and will not be triggered any more'? Can I do that, can any of us who have been deeply traumatised in our pasts fully achieve that, or have I got as far as it is possible to do so. Who knows? But I think I just gave myself the reason to keep going today this time, and to return to my bed and claim my cuddle.

After Trauma

Will I crumble into dust

If I dismount the horse of fear,
Depart the wild hunt of insanity
Take control of my mind, emotions, life.

But who is the controller?
It shape shifts, sometimes strong,
fiercely demonic, crazy wild,
Often it cowers, over-whelmed by all.

Thunder bullies my nights, banishing
all respite of sleep, rampaging through
the dark hours of wakefulness,
leaving me exhausted for the restoration of the light.

Oh, that I were a wolf child
running free and fearless through night forest,
alive by moon, eyes piercing darkness
welcoming it's caul of concealment

A fragile girl lies curled in pools, her own blood,
endless seeping wounds that cannot heal,
pecked at incessantly, the two ravens of thought and memory,
persecutors of those who would seek peace.

Moonstones, misted solidified tears shed alone at night
Reflecting blue, grey, white,
moods of shadow and light
dancing on my face.

Whatever I am given I have learned not to trust,
Your motives, are they for me,
or your own edification? You cannot buy me,
I am priceless, too fragile to own, too fierce.

I look timid, soft spoken, pliable to your demands,
yet I will turn, a fire breathing dragon
defending my fears and myself, will I ever know love?
a flow of give and take, of acceptance and compassion?

I'm OK now. Being broken open has its positives and without my spiritual meditative practice I would not have made it through but with that, and my totally amazing beloved, I am now able to write it out of myself.

Sometimes my inner child is pre-emptive of a possible attack, but only when a pre-existing experience suggests it will re-occur. Sometimes her pre-emptive self-defence is quite mal-adaptive and has a certain kind of sneaky quality to it. That is how I can tell it is not rational adult Sylvia but frightened child Sylvia. Sometimes I feel deeply ashamed by her actions and must work hard to have compassion instead for her ongoing struggles. I also must keep working on helping child Sylvia to let me deal with adult life, to trust whom she has become. Then perhaps the triggering will stop and my poor over wrought amygdala can finally rest. The final editing of this book is being done during the Coronavirus lockdown and thus I am only with David in our home, as safe as it is possible to be. We have each other to ourselves, though are keeping in touch with the people we know and love too.

20. FURTHER REFLECTIONS ON MY PARENTS AND THEIR STORIES

This chapter is full of reflections and snippets that do not fit into the narrative, but I feel deserve some attention.

My father remains so much of a stranger to me, but I've managed to piece together much of the story of my relationship with him, and to answer the question 'WHY' to fit my own experience of events as they happened. The traumatic events of endless nights of flashback and night terrors have shown me much of what happened, as if it was only just there right now. It was so vivid, not 're-membered memory' as in 'put together over time from recall', but traumatic memories finally released. There's a huge difference between the two.

But it wouldn't lay to rest for me, and I couldn't let it go.

Then something occurred in another sphere of my life, which troubled me greatly, caused me some sleeplessness and a slight and unexpected, unplanned, change of direction in my activities. Such is life! In the midst of that turmoil I began to see my father in a new light; this enabled me to complete the story and close it, from my point of view at least, with understanding all and thus forgiving all.

The dynamic between my parents has already started when I am born, as far as I can piece together from snippets I have been told over the years and deductions from my own experiences in answering the great question why? Why had all the abuse that occurred during my childhood mostly been aimed at me exclusively? What caused my extended family's inability to see the truth about my Mother and her mental illness, which was almost certainly Narcissistic Personality Disorder (NPD) with psychopathic overtones. Why were they in such denial that she was ill, and so afraid to challenge her, placating her instead, which made her so much worse?

I think most people who have been through something traumatic want to know why? It is that great unanswerable question in the end but exploring can help one to let go, it did me.

My Mother is insanely jealous of the initial loving bond between my father and me. I sense there is something off about her from the start and Dad is not like that, his energy feels better to be close to. He is a relief from her at the end of each day and at weekends. Early on at least that is true.

My parents meet at the Young Conservatives club and start dating. Little Grandma is described to me, more than once, as a snob, (by Dad), and she likes John dating an 'Ife girl' as they are seen as a catch or something. Grandma and Grandad Ife want to get Lorna married and off their hands. She is difficult. And in those days what else do you do with daughters. Mother has a good job in a French bank because of her dual linguistic skills, but that is not considered in the long term for women. I believe both my parents have their doubts about each other but are pushed together. Mother certainly says that to me in one of her little confidential cosy kitchen chats about Dad's impossible imperfections.

Before they get married, Lorna is the charming side of Narcissistic Personality Disorder. It's called love bombing and it's very convincing. 'You are the best thing ever, the most amazing, the only one who can make me happy' etc. Dad would have loved that, lapped it up. He is one for social approval and validation, and is a social climber, at least when I know him, he is.

Lorna has always lived in a fantasy world where she is some kind of princess or goddess. Perhaps this comes from being made to stand in circles of adults and perform her French language as a child, but the image fits. She expects some rosy Cinderella castle and fairy tale ending to her story after marriage.

Dad cannot provide this. It is post war era and there is little spare money around. They are to live with his mother in her house. She is now widowed.

When they get married, or soon after, it will start, the other side of NPD, the cruelty and derision and blame for all her distress and disappointment. Her lack of fairy tale castle and feted lifestyle. Marriage means a certain amount of drudgery and she must give up her job now she is married. Married women do not work out of the home, their job is to look after their husband.

Not that long ago and before the dementia takes her away, my aunt Mercia confirms to me that she still remembers how publicly critical and unkind Mother was to Dad from the beginning. Her tactic is 'this wasn't right and if he just did this then she will be happy again and all will be well'. The hoops to jump through are impossible though and her derision at his inability to wave magic wands and meet her demands is ever more vocal and public. The trouble with NPD is that there is never an end to 'what is upsetting me', and it is never their responsibility.

In fact, this is the opposite of what is true. Over time I have learned that no one is responsible for upsetting others, it is a joint activity, one doing the upsetting of course but the other one taking it personally. And her demands are outrageous. That any external event is as distressing as we allow it to be, would never be accepted by her for her whole life. My father is to blame for everything that troubles her in the first few years and the list is endless. Having a baby will make it all ok for her. I am sure my Grandmother told her that on more than one occasion.

I am conceived and being pregnant makes Lorna the centre of attention, so she is happy. The hormones help too.

Then I fall out of grace and join that list with even more crimes against her wellbeing. I become what is causing the family to be unhappy, then I become to blame for absolutely every bad day either of them has.

When Mother is upset, she is not a nice person and her vicious tongue will use any intimacy, any piece of information she has about anyone, consciously or unconsciously; she will use it against you to make you feel utterly worthless and useless and contemptible and any other such term you can think of. She is devastatingly accurate in her criticisms and powerful in her denigrations of Dad and I feel his suffering as much as I do my own. My father is not a very strong man emotionally; he is scared of her, like the rest of her family, that much I now realise is true, that is why he also rejects me once I hit adulthood.

However much I am not like my Mother, I am her daughter and thus a reminder of her to him. I know this difficulty from my many friends and my own children and their divorced parental 'other halves'. My sons play computer games. This is a large part of what divided me from my first husband, not that I have any regret and neither does he. But I must accept it with them now and not allow it to colour our relationship with them in any way. This is so common and is often behind family estrangements.

One of the saddest things for Dad is that he is then afraid to connect with any of his other children, never allowing himself to form deep relationships or close emotional bonds. That is something I know my siblings will recognise too. He wants children but cannot show any interest in them, and the fact that I once had this bond with him means that my relationship is quite different with him than any of theirs. For better or for worse.

All my father ever wants is a quiet and happy life, social ease, and comfort, to be valued and appreciated; all that most people want out of life really.

What I have realised in life; this goal takes a lot of effort to achieve and will never result from a position of defensive victimhood or inaction. I have finally achieved a life of little conflict and have done that by working extremely hard on what causes conflict from within; the power of the Dharma is the key to that little life skill.

I don't know where his 'weakness' came from and in fact I don't think it is a weakness of the individual, of my father, but the cruelty of the stereotypes of gender behaviour in those times. 'Men behave like this and women like that and woe betide if you can't live up to it'. This applies to both of course. But like many men in that era he must appear to be strong, however vulnerable he feels inside, and, like all men, not allowed to show sadness or other 'weak' emotions from early childhood.

I have no doubt that he was a deeply emotional man, but my Mother uses his deeper emotional nature against him, as she does mine against me. That is how she operates. That is NPD in action. That is why he only has one method of looking strong and decisive and being the authority, that of violence. I doubt that side of him ever showed its face again, it is not his intrinsic behaviour other than under extreme duress.

Violence is never the answer, we all know that, and yet humans' resort to it again and again in all areas of life. Look at the violence involved with war. My family was an emotional war zone. Violence succeeds through oppression and fear or through escalation, until the recipient is finally broken into acquiescence. It didn't work with me, but it might have done.

Neither of them knew I had ADHD and my 'misdemeanours' are as random as my Mother's decisions to find me annoying and unacceptable from one day to another. They see it as evidence of my wilfulness.

That is why I bore the brunt of my parent's inability to form a healthy emotional alliance as a married couple. That is why I became the chosen one for both of them. 'If it wasn't for you we would all be happy', 'why do you deliberately upset your Mother all the time', and other such questions, none of which I could answer except that I didn't mean it, ever, any of it. I wish they could have understood and believed me.

I often tried to get Dad especially to tell me what it was he wanted from me, but he could never reply. Once I wrote a note to Dad and Aileen and left it on their car windscreen in the morning - what would make me acceptable and would they explain what it is that I get wrong, and other such despairing and imploring questions which I put to them both endlessly and which they could not respond to, because there is no answer to it.

Both parents needed me to fulfil this specific role for them, to be their scapegoat, so they could avoid facing the truth about their own relationship, which was that it was abusive. It became the true story in their minds, and nothing would change that. I have learned not to trust the stories we each have in our minds. They may be deeply mistaken. I learn this from Quakers, and also from Thich Nhat Hanh. I have a postcard on my kitchen dresser which is sent by a friend, 'Are you sure?' I try to remember that always.

I realise now, my estrangement from Dad is a protection for me, not a punishment. I am free from his judgments of me, from his permanent sense of disappointment and disapproval, which would have devastated me just as much, if not far more, than the way it panned out.

I read somewhere, and cannot find the quote now, that life is like a well-crafted novel in hindsight, that everything falls into place at just the right time as if there was some kind of master plan to the whole plot. It is only living through it forwards that makes it feel so confusing and challenging. Or maybe I thought that up – I don't know now as it doesn't appear when I search for it, though snippets of it do.

I meet David when I need to, when he needs me too, for both our next stages of emotional development. I know, when I am not in self-doubt frame of mind, I have been as much value to him in numerous ways as he has to me. We both give each other a life we could never have envisaged before and would never swop for anything.

I never ever remember my Mother being nice to my father unless he had 'punished me' for my purported misdemeanours. Then she would act all 'unintentional' and supplicatory towards him, simpering and flirtatious even. His redemption would not last for too long though, a few days, a couple of weeks.

I believe this is what toxic masculinity is about, not allowing men to become fully emotionally literate, to be healthy happy individuals and be able to express their softer side without fear of scorn and rejection. I want this to change. If my husband were a traditional male, he would have had me sectioned and I would never have recovered properly, not as I have done, not as the full and real me, vulnerabilities and all.

And Mothers, the sacred Mother paradigm, please don't get me started about how wrong that is too and the nonsense that a Mother is always the best parent to have a child in custody after divorce. My brother has never forgiven the law for that one.

Mental health affects most people at some point in their life, so can we please stop being afraid of it and get it out in the open. That is why I am writing this book, to scream it from the roof tops, open your mind world, open your eyes to the unnecessary suffering caused by such blindness and closed-down self-centred thinking.

Confidentiality just breeds more shame and distrust, more ignorance, more unkindness and cover-ups. Hello – I am Sylvia and I have PTSD and ADHD. Nice to meet you. XX

Listening to others is such a simple thing to do, and it might mean the world becomes a better place with fewer traumatised people in it. Because as far as I can see nearly half the world population will be traumatised soon. And that is the real tragedy.

I was terrorised for the first few years of my life. I have lived the rest of it coping and surviving and even thriving, but still dominated by it. Some people never make it out though.

Perhaps triggering is the motivation for me writing this all out now, twelve years after Dad died and this blew me out of the water.

21. MOTHERS PARTING SHOTS

I mention that several other massively triggering events occurred during my long slow and complete breakdown and one of those is Mothers parting gifts.

Mother is obsessed with making money on the stock exchange and it is often a source of our disagreements. I have strong beliefs about not doing harm and not colluding with harm being done to others. Gambling is a huge problem in our society with so many families brought to breakdown. She likes to invest in gambling companies because they bring her good returns. She doesn't approve of gambling and considers those who do it are fair game for her financial gain, not worthy of her consideration or compassion. Where are her Christian principles, her manic Sunday church attendances desperately seeking redemption when during the week self-interest and the Great God Profit win her loyalty even more strongly?

Her principle point of great pride and superiority is that she had become a rich woman from an initial small inheritance sum of £50, a millionaire in shares terms, and because she has no self-esteem or true self-worth at all, she boasts about this as a basis for her superiority over others.

After her second husband Douglas dies from cancer, Mother is befriended by a builder who has done work on their bungalow. She becomes obsessed with him, though he is married and the same age group as us, her children, but nevertheless she becomes utterly dependent upon him, especially emotionally.

I get early warning intuitions almost immediately that this means trouble and mention it to Hazel. She then tells Martin who goes rushing over there in true Martin style and confronts him. He denies all wrongdoing and convinces my brother he is just looking out for her, that he is happily married with a family and has no untoward intentions with my Mother at all. Martin is convinced and ridicules me for my intuitions. I know it was not going to be ok but am now silenced within the family and not well enough to do anything further. The builder becomes actively involved with Mother financially, doing a lot of work on her bungalow for very high prices, which she always pays in cash.

There is one occasion which seriously raises our suspicions. Mother has been charged £5K for a job painting the outside of her bungalow. That this was too much was already an issue. But then she went to the bank to collect cash, brought it home, went to the supermarket and when she was out in those few moments was burgled of £5K. There was little sign of any forced entry, but it was possible a tiny bathroom window had been left open. Later someone says they saw a young man running away from her front door. I have my suspicions of course. We all do. But Mother is insistent that it's a random burglary and couldn't possibly be anything else. I have been burgled. They trash the house looking for what they might find. Her house is not trashed, and they find the money easily and without much trouble apparently.

Who knows the truth?

We never shall and it no longer matters, but at the time this is becoming a huge source of distress for us. If the builder hadn't asked for cash, there wouldn't have been cash in the house and might not have been a burglary.

Mother's involvement with the builder grows and grows. He claims Douglas asked him to keep an eye out for Lorna when he died. Again, who knows, but why Douglas would ask a builder who did occasional work for them and my aunt, to look after Mother once he has gone, I do not know.

Finally, Mother is angry with us because we don't go and see her often enough, all three of us, either individually or collectively. Her weapon of choice after her tongue is always her money. I have been in and out of her will like a yoyo. Both my siblings have been threatened with disinheritance if they do not involve themselves more in her life. None of us can bear it though. We have all struggled really hard and done our best but it is pretty much a constant nightmare.

On one occasion we go to see Mother in hospital. We are at Martin's for the weekend so David and I agree to keep him company. He tries to take his two daughters, but they are crying, and pleading not to go. They are terrified of her too, as my sons were. The three of us go alone and get through it by supporting each other.

Mother announces that she has changed her will in favour of her friend. He will inherit her house and we can have what is left over. At first glance this seems fair enough. She only owns half the house since the other half is owned by Douglas's children as their inheritance from his death. My brother and sister try to enforce the power of attorney that Mother has previously installed with them but she overrules that and replaces them with her friend, now listed as her brother in hospital records, in control of all her finances as she becomes slightly more frail. There are many confusions and arguments around this whole thing. We try to stick together as siblings over it, but we don't trust each other, cannot listen to each other with respect and are so divided against each other, mostly an alliance of Hazel and Martin against me, that I just step back. It is triggering me very badly. Some days my heart is racing so fast it feels almost as bad as outside the hospice just before seeing Dad for the last time. It gives me a huge setback and is another basis for my rage with them. They just cannot listen to me or respect my intuitive way of living and the wisdom that comes with it. They despise me for it. We lose control of it all, then we all agree to walk away from her completely.

In 2011, I am still unwell but trying to function normally as much as possible, I have started to come to terms with everything by then, gone through forgiveness into gratitude and I want Mother to go in peace with me at least. I travel up from the island to visit her in Croydon by train, alone, walk to her house and arrive unannounced. The carer lets me in and leaves me alone with her, turning the TV off.

'You came to see me.'

'Yes, I did, all the way up on the train just to see you.'

Mother is clearly pleased to see me. She is much more mellow now since her age and decline have weakened her rages. I feel encouraged. I try to talk to her properly, not demanding anything from her but actually wanting to absolve her.

'I always loved you, in spite of it all.'

She starts shouting immediately to her carer

'Come and put the TV back on… I want the television back on, I'm missing my programme.'

She can't stand it and is shouting loudly for the carer. It is so loud.

Out of the blue, the carer starts telling me Mother is justified in leaving her money to whoever she wants.

I assume she thinks that is my motivation for coming, to challenge Mother to change her will back. That is how Mother will have portrayed us all, though that is her motivation never mine. It is as far from that as is possible.

It really upsets me. I end up shouting that she has abused me so much over the length of my life and I have serious mental health issues because of it. The carer goes quiet and said she doesn't know that. I then go to leave.

Mother says, 'Don't go, don't go, you've only just got here.'

'What is the point of me being here when you don't even want to talk to me!'

I go anyway.

I travel home on the train to Portsmouth, shaking with stress for most of the time home but get back and am able to calm down. Once on the boat I feel safer again.

By the time Mother dies in 2012 there is almost no money left. It has all gone in her private care needs, which is fair enough. What we do discover though is that the builder friend has organised the pay out of Douglas' children so he can have the whole house, free of any encumbrances or costs.

I don't go to her funeral. I am just too ill.

The last time I see my siblings together is at her house, a few weeks after her funeral, when I hold myself together enough to go with David to all meet up and take what we are allowed. I find myself feeling sentimental and take a few items of her jewellery and even now I wear them with memories of her and how much she suffered herself, for the damage done to us all. Emotionally I am as resilient as wet tissue paper and can only function at all because David is with me.

At one point David tries to talk to Martin and Hazel, but they make it clear they don't want to know, tutting and turning away from him and me. I asked him to leave it and let it be. It is clear to me they no longer want to know me, and I am not sure I would ever feel safe with either of them again. And that is that. The end of any relationships with any of my family in any direction. I can see why my siblings were just as afraid of Dad, that they could not go against his word as a dying man in case they caused his displeasure. But they are still only able to blame me and not him for putting them into that position of betrayal of my trust in them. I have stopped protecting Dad, but I do have enormous compassion for what he went through and realise how limited he was. It has helped me to understand how traditional masculinity disables men so badly that they so often cannot cope without anger or violence if things are not 'going their way'. I have come to understand how impossible it was for my siblings to stand up to him and say no to his demand that they not tell me he was ill. I understand that his wife did not want to hear another story about a darker side of the man whom she had placed on a pedestal for over thirty years and that he was still afraid of that part of himself and his guilt that he could never face how he had treated me.

I remember another dream I've had in the past, and it suddenly makes sense.

I am at a party in a house like an Escher drawing, with turrets and staircases that go all over the place. My whole family is there, all the cousins and everyone. They are all congregated in the lower rooms and as the outsider I explore the higher turrets. I discover I have the magic power of flight. I can fly between the turrets and feel astonishingly free. I can soar above the house too and look down on them all. They look so far away. But I know that I must not be seen by them or I will lose my power immediately and crash to earth and be broken beyond repair. I work carefully, gliding from balcony to balustrade and land-ings. I realise it is getting dangerous, so I go back downstairs, just as they are all leaving and have started looking for me. They do not notice where I have been, so my secret talent is still safe with me. Then the dream ends.

I realise now I am free from all the burdens of the family agendas and stories about me. I can write my own story away from them all. I can be myself and find out what that looks like, who I am, what I might become. The breakdown is the final clearing pro-cess of all the debris. I am free of family.

Except a few weeks later my eldest first cousin, Emma writes me a letter saying she cannot imagine how I must be feeling, and she does not want to lose touch with me. Gradually over time we start to see each other and grow closer, talking more and more about our memories of that time. I tell her how I was warned by my mother and grandmother not to get involved with her in case I turn her like my siblings, being such a negative influence on anyone I meet. Emma is indignant.

'Do they think I was not capable of making my own life messes and outcomes?'

We laugh at it now.

Emma gets to know me as I am, and confides she was also always afraid of my Dad, as she was Lorna, her aunt. We share a few more stories and it helps and heals us both and brings us closer too. She and I have much more in common than she or I would ever have with my siblings, more to share and talk about. As Emma said to me once,

'I still channel more of my inner hippy.'

Although she has her biological sister with whom she is close, we are also now like sisters. I am her older sister as she said she once looked up to me when we were children. I am so grateful for that friendship too. It has encouraged me, not stopped me flying at all.

22. REVISITING FAMILY STORIES

It is a beautiful Sunday morning in December. I am staying at my cousin Emma's house for a couple of nights to catch up with each other, but also to catch up with other family. Emma had previously arranged for the both of us to visit Aunt Flavia and Tom, sixty years of marriage next July, 2020. I have very faint memories of sitting for a family meal at my grandparent's house in Croydon and meeting Tom for the first time. I must have been about three or four then. I remember him being very witty and making the adults around me laugh but I remember little else about that. I am not even sure if my sister had been born yet or not. I remember a joke he told us. What is yellow and goes round at 33 RPM, answer a long playing omelette? It is strange what one remembers from so long ago.

Emma has driven us expertly to Elephant and Castle and found a parking slot easily enough in a side street. It is now over twenty years since I lived in London and had this kind of knowledge and confidence within me, but I am too used to country lanes on the island and am in awe of her management of London traffic which seems overwhelming to my country mouse ways. We take the underground across to West London and emerge into calm, thin winter sunshine, gently warming and bright compared to fierce midsummer sunshine.

Ealing Broadway is busy, full of people with their lives closely compacted, cars and traffic probably not as busy as weekdays but still pretty hectic. Travelling underground on a Sunday morning means seats, space. Emerging into such bustle, with people passing each other by and not acknowledging each other has become alien to me now. Even strangers in our village acknowledge each other. I have in the past felt a sense of invasion, of noseyness and gossip about this culture but there is also a recognition of humanity within it. I thought I missed the anonymity of living in outer London but now realise I have adjusted to a rural life and all its foibles too. I feel both lost and at home in both places, unsettled, uncertain where I belong anymore. It's a strange feeling. I am aware of how dependent I feel on Emma's presence to get me around, to know the ropes which I also once knew so well and have since lost so completely.

We stop to buy a coffee and I take a loo stop, my anxiety making my bladder seem ever more sensitive. I am sure my aunt is equally nervous as I am at meeting up with her properly after so many decades of awkwardness between us. We follow Emma's direction app which takes us slightly around the houses, but we talk as we walk happily along, reminding each other of the snippets of family history we each have and filling in gaps where we're able to, wondering which versions will be confirmed by our aunt.

We arrive and my uncle greets us at the stairs and welcomes us into their flat. We take our coats off and hand them to Tom and I pass over a bouquet of Christmas colours which Emma organized to bring.

Then I find myself being unexpectedly embraced. I don't feel any desire to resist as I would normally do, distrustful of human contact except with very few.

Flavia holds me very tightly in a hug, whispering 'I've been wanting to do that for a very long time', into my ear.'

I can feel both of us melting into this embrace, my fear dissolving in seconds. A connection, that has been severed so long ago by my Mother's involvements in our lives, is re-establishing itself, a connection that had once been deep and important to us both.

Tom generously organizes drinks for us all and we sit down to explore these old family stories that go back beyond our own times. Flavia has always been a good raconteur and we listen as she starts with our great grandfather. This account is however fleshed out in accurate dates and details by my own research on ancestry websites where I am studying our family tree. I have got back to 1768 on the Ife family line but far further back, to 1445 on the Southam line. There is a village named after the family still in Warwickshire and the church records hold details back to very early on. I plan to go and visit some-day but for now I use the online availabilities. The research into the Clare family has not proved so successful and I am stuck at my great grandfather Clare in name only.

Grandad and great grandad

Charles Ernest Ife, our great grandad, was born in 1873 in Monmouth Wales, to Benjamin W Ife and Susan Maria Ife. He was one of eight children, and the second to youngest. He was a very romantic and passionate man by all accounts. Emma has a letter he wrote to his wife when they were apart, and he does not hold back on expressing his affections for her, which is slightly surprising given the Victorian attitude to emotions at that time being one of stiff upper lip for men and emotions are those things that only weak women have.

As Charles Ernest grew up, he wanted to be an artistic creative person, that was his self-image. He made several attempts at both musical composition and writing but was not deemed 'good enough' to make a career out of it. Flavia remembers his work being spread out over tables when she was younger but not being impressed by any of it. He was encouraged to make a successful career elsewhere to provide for his future family. My cousin Damian, Flavia, and Tom's second twin son, has a copy of the only surviving compositions he made but he'd had ambitions of wanting to create grand operas and such like. He also wanted to be a song writer and writer generally, but again managed to produce nothing much of merit. On the way home both Emma and I comment on 'who was to judge'. It is my own experience that writers may be born with an urge to write but they still have to develop their voice and talent and approach to whatever they are writing, and some people come to that place of knowing their skill and also their limits earlier than others. There is a tendency in our family to look down on those who do not reach the 'top' however that is measured. It has taken me decades to accept 'good enough' is all you need to be and deep happiness in your life is the real measure of success.

My own writing has improved greatly since I stopped trying and started letting it flow through me. And it is evolving still of course. I am an eternal student and enjoy taking this approach to life on all fronts. I am deeply happy. I feel as successful as I need to be. I find myself feeling sad for my great grandfather, and this deepens as Flavia continues.

Having apparently failed at his creative endeavours, Charles married Mary Eleanor Southam against her family's wishes. She was 12 years older than him, born in 1861

They married in Clapham Holy Trinity church on the 14th June 1892. She was thirty-one when they married, and he was just nineteen years of age but looked older due to a beard which covered his youthful skin and gave him an appearance of some gravitas.

He becomes an industrial chemist and they live, and he works in Belgium for many years. She has an early miscarriage but is glad that it signifies she is still fertile. Then in 1899 at age 38 she managed to carry and give birth to Alan Ernest, whilst they are still living in Belgium. He is the pride of their lives.

Eleanor, as she prefers to be called, is a multi-linguist, speaking fluent French and German, so also loves living in Belgium, and their little family, against much criticism and doubt, was flourishing well.

Meanwhile the organisation which Charles worked for asked him to professionally and scientifically endorse a product as safe when he knew it wasn't. He was put into an intolerable position of moral and professional conflict, damned if he did and damned if he didn't. The latter seemed the lesser of the two evils though and he refused to follow instructions. Defensively and heartlessly, they sacked Charles Ernest Ife without reference or papers, thus giving him no future and no chances to be a whistle blower since the response would be his 'revenge motivation'. It was a position of intolerable unkindness and dishonesty but life and profit/greed traits in businessmen is ever thus, personal moral courage taken as worthless compared to the profit-making potential of a short term situation.

They must pack up their home in Belgium, a rented home, and sell up the belongings that are too costly to bring back with them. They return to Britain, to withstand the cruelties of those judgmental family relatives on the Southam side who had so disapproved of the marriage in the first place. They were not taken in together by family though. Charles Ernest got digs back in Brixton and Eleanor takes refuge with her family and must endure their criticisms, the unkindness of the 'told you so' attitudes.

He tries and tries to get work but is endlessly unsuccessful and eventually commits suicide with a massive overdose in July 1905, aged only 32, having sunk into a deep despair and depression. My granddad is only six years old when his father dies, and life is about to get a whole lot worse for him. Eleanor is a widow and single parent at 44.

The coroner at Great grandad's inquest was a kindly wise man and listened to the whole story as it was. He took pity and put it down as an accidental death due to his depression and Ernest losing track of how much medication he had taken. Thus, it was recorded as a mistake that he had forgotten how many tablets he'd taken and took too many. Charles Ernest, who prefers to be called Ernest, can be given a proper burial as a result.

Eleanor is not able to remain with family any longer. She takes the hard decision to train as a teacher, but with no money at all her own, she is unable to take care of Alan as well. There are no facilities or understanding of the needs of young children in those emotionally brutal days.

Eleanor gets herself accepted onto a teaching diploma course and then puts Alan into an orphanage school while she trains. She condenses the course into two years instead of three, but it means no time off to visit Alan either.

She'd told him to be very brave, but Flavia remembers him having tears in his eyes when talking to her about those years of bullying and isolation, when his Mother could not visit him due to her own schedule of study and work commitment. Other family members did visit him and a family friend visited him every holiday (Mrs Peacock), but one wonders how hard it was for a young child with very myopic eyes (we all have his very strong myopia in my family but some worse than others). It breaks my heart to think of his trauma, but I am beginning to understand what unfolded over the years.

Once Eleanor has completed her training, she is almost 50 but she gets a teaching post, brings Alan back home and quickly rises to become school deputy head.

Alan was an intelligent boy, like his parents, and he worked hard and got himself a scholarship into Oxbridge and I believe achieved a first. Then he had a very junior and limited career in the foreign office. Great success and something to be proud of indeed on one level but thwarted in achieving that full potential. Emotional literacy has now been shown to have more effect on people's future life success than any educational achievements, yet we still insist on pursuing the latter at the expense of the former. Again, another ideological madness that I just cannot guess at the motivation behind, beyond stupidity and the fear of an emotionally literate workforce.

Sadly, it had all left a mark on Alan. Emotionally he was traumatised, his natural emotional development interrupted and distorted so that he had not grown up with the interpersonal skills to have a career with progression. Instead he made a considerable amount of money on the stock exchange and that was his claim to fame within the family. He taught Lorna her share gambling skills too, it was a bond between them both. He was also one of the first people to recognise the value of buying your own home when they were, relatively speaking, cheap as chips. This had made them 'something'.

The Ife family eventually live at 1 Tierney Road, Streatham, where Violet Heaps, my beloved big Grandma also lives when she married Alan in 1928. Grandma and Grandad meet on the running track of the civil service and they just get on very well, even though he is 6 years older than her. Apparently, Violet's exceedingly long legs are a big attraction. She is tall for a woman of that time, five foot nine inches, the same as myself before my spine started to collapse.

Violet finds living with her Mother-in-law very trying as Mary Eleanor is reputedly very dominating, but she's had to be so strong through her life, and it would be hard to relinquish her only son to another woman. Nevertheless, they are still living with Eleanor until after Lorna is born, in 1929.

Two years after Lorna is born, my grandmother has an ectopic pregnancy which nearly kills her. The GP could not work out what was wrong with her and why she was in so much constant pain, until one day he works it out and runs to my grandfather's house telling him to take Violet immediately to a hospital for emergency surgery. In roughly 1931, there is no real anaesthetic and surgery was very crude compared to nowadays. I have a strong insight into how my grandmother felt then.

In 1977 I also had an ectopic pregnancy, not recognised until about three months old, and I also started to haemorrhage badly, and lost all feeling below my waist where nerves were being cut off, before they worked it out and saved my life. But in my case the foetus was deformed by its constrictions and had adhered itself to much of my internal abdomen, bowels etc. It took the surgeon a long time to detach it everywhere and the adhesions I lived with for the following two years were horrendous. I survived thanks to more modern anaesthetics, antibiotics, and surgery skills, but still shudder at the recollection. Even so I would rather go through the extreme physical pain than the emotional experiences I had during my break down, it was a walk in the park by comparison.

But I am presently relating to my grandmother deeply too. She must have suffered terribly and been quite traumatised by her experiences. The only anaesthetic she has is ether, I remember her telling me.

She then gets pregnant with my aunt Mercia, Emma's Mother.

Meanwhile Eleanor wanted Lorna to excel in languages, as she herself had done and more or less coerces, or bullies my grandparents into sending Lorna aged nearly four, to stay with some French friends, and much against Violet's better judgment.

From here I recall my Mother's own account of that time. Grandad did not tell her where they were going or what they were doing, he just took her on a long journey by train to where his friends lived, put her to bed, and left very early the following morning to return home, to avoid any distress for him that Lorna might make at his departure. Perhaps he was remembering his own distress when he was taken to the orphanage school, but for whatever reason he did not want to cope with that, and I assume didn't consider how that would affect my Mother emotionally, since that was an unthought of consideration from which so many terrible injustices arose in that period of time. I am both shocked and horrified for my Mother and strive to be understanding of the times they lived in and what was considered normal. The notion of children 'seen but not heard' was still dominant and a deeply distressed child should be even less seen or heard.

This is where I believe Lorna's trauma originates and her abuse starting on me at the same age was her only way of telling her story too, vicariously, by acting it out on me. Lorna was not born evil; she was deeply traumatised, and this solidified into Narcissistic Personality Disorder which she never got diagnosed or healed from. No one understood that kind of thing back then. I remember Mercia once telling me how Lorna's rages were astonishing when she was growing up, and no one knew how to deal with them other than to work to assuage them, which more or less meant giving into them to keep the peace. She was disliked, avoided, placated, punished perhaps even, for that aspect of her personality as it was forming.

Flavia then told us that Lorna was deeply affected by the heat in France that summer and had to come home early. She came home to a new baby sister, Mercia.

'You are not the child I wanted, so I have had another one now to take your place.'

I can see exactly how those words came from Lorna, formed in her mind as an interpretation of what had happened to her, and were then projected onto me.

When she arrived back in England, she could speak fluent French, and no English, a party piece to show off to friends and acquaintances, and Lorna was asked to perform accordingly from time to time. A child serving as an appendage to her parents' status and boasting potentials.

When she started school, a few months later, she couldn't talk to the other children or understand what was being said to her. The traumatised child had given up on her own language to enable her to survive with this French family, and then expected to come home and carry on as normal but just with fluent French. Flavia did say that Violet had said no repeatedly to the idea until her husband, keen to please his Mother, wore her down.

My poor Mother!

My heart goes out to that sense of desolation and confusion she must have felt, and the anger subsequently she felt and was unable to articulate. No wonder she became a monster. Somewhere inside the monster was a normal person, I think a highly sensitive individual actually, though apparently only to her own needs. Everyone else had been shut out and eventually she got stuck as the narcissist personality disorder with psychopathic tendencies that she was. It still makes me so sad to think of how she had to live her life 'til the end. She had three children and seven grandchildren and none of them could stand her. She alienated everyone and eventually was left with someone who was, perhaps unintentionally or unwittingly, a groomer. How tragic. But he filled a need in her and she in him and I genuinely think they had a sort of functional relationship that worked for them both, even though it was based on some deeply misguided foundations. After Lorna's death and the sharing out of the remains of her life, we all agreed that the builder had in fact been paid to look after her for the last ten years and that was sort of fair enough. It enables us to let go and move on ourselves. I am glad for any comfort she could find since her own mind was so filled with those taunting inner voices that necessitated the loud TV on all the time.

Flavia then hands me a package of letters going back sometime between herself, Lorna, and Mercia, the three sisters.

It's clear that at some point, when Flavia and I were not in touch, she had also had a breakdown of some kind and that related back to her own childhood. Lorna had coerced Mercia into an alliance of bullies against Flavia, younger by nine years to my Mother, and the same age gaps as between myself and my siblings.

Mercia changed though, apologised, and made it up to Flavia over the years. But these traumas don't go away do they, I know that so well. Sorry doesn't make it ok, it is never enough.

Flavia told me that Grandma Violet said they both knew what was going on with the bullying but left them to get on with it as sisters. My grandparents were avid bridge players, achieving some national status I believe, and my Mother was often left in charge of her sisters when they went out.

Even now I could hug my aunt Flavia forever, I know what she went through, I know what Mother is capable of.

Tom makes us another drink all round and starts reminiscing.

'Do you remember Austria when you came on holiday with us?'

'Yes, I do, clearly.'

'You were so good with us then, no problem at all.'

Flavia chirps in, 'Yes we allowed you to go out with those friends and you were so good and did exactly what was agreed without any argument.'

It makes me smile to think that the story my mother came back at me with is not how it was after all, maybe apart from Grandma though.

Emma and I are both curious now and want to know more about Tom and his love of travelling and camping through Europe every year.

As he relates his story, I realise ever more deeply how many people face trauma in their lives, and how differently it plays out for each of them.

I am so lucky. I might have gone through hell in childhood, but it made me a deeper wiser person with a desire to heal and live as authentically as I possibly can. I can be brutally honest with people but also with myself, and I believe we should all evolve constantly to become a better person daily, incrementally, as life shows us.

I am so deeply grateful for my whole story. I do my best to live up to that belief.

When we get back to Emma's house, we go in the afternoon to see my other aunt, Emma's mum, Mercia who is now in a dementia care home. She has declined beyond recognising people now and I feel like voyeur visiting her. It will be the last time.

Coming back to Emma's I recall a previous visit a couple of years earlier when she still knew who I was, just.

When I had arrived for that previous visit we had gone for a walk around the gardens of her home. She repeated her walking rhyme, 'now we go off with our left, off with our left and now we go off with our right, off with our right', and reminisces how she would take school parties on day trips. We see a young fox in the wild corner of the garden lazing in the afternoon sun, before it spots us and moves off.

Then I am sitting in Mercia's room with her looking at photos of family and going through who they all are.

'How is Lorna?' she asks brightly.

'Dead', I reply rather bluntly.

'Oh good,' says Mercia, 'she always was a bit of a problem, always causing trouble.'

And that is the last time we talk of my mother, her older sister. I wrote a poem of that last visit.

To my fading Aunt

I am lost from your view now,
my face a faint recognition
unplaceable, my prompts
do not make the connections for you.

I miss your cheerful outlook
your delight to see me,
your joy at still remembering
who I am. Just a niece.

Nothing more, but I have known
you for my whole life,
sought your approvals, your smiles.
And now the cruel disease takes
all from you and you from all of us
as you sink into oblivion.

Soon you will not know your own
children, grandchildren, people
who loved you, all fading into some mist,
a mental fug of forgetfulness.

Your body, aging but still sprightly.
You conduct the music being played
blithe and joyful in your present moment.

If I visit- do I intrude upon your world?
Do I confuse and confound you into
seeking memories no longer there.
A struggle to place me in the catalogue
of your life, already being deleted
page by page. Is it selfish
to want to see you once again
to walk with you in the garden?

'Off with the left, off with the left,
and now we go off with the right,
off with the right', your walking chant,
so dear and familiar, playful,
like the child you are becoming,
that day when we did the pathways,
circuits to exercise along, and saw
a young fox basking in autumn sun.

We shared a wonderful intimate moment with that fox
and then you turned to me and said
'you realise I won't remember any of this once you leave',
And you hung onto my arm a little longer.
I go home feeling sad, thoughtful, yet uplifted too.

APPENDICES

I wanted to share some more factual and technical information about NPD but didn't want it to halt the flow of my narrative. The following chapters include information about family estrangement, more clinical detail about NPD and a section on the toll and struggle to write this story down.

23. WRITING THIS BOOK

"Until you make the unconscious conscious, it will direct your life and you will call it fate."–C.G. Jung

For my entire life, everything I have done, one way or another, has been to challenge these early experiences and to survive them; to cleanse them from our family energy system as far as I am able myself alone. Certainly to heal myself and my sons from them and to live freely. Healing was the biggest challenge and still is but daily I can feel small transformations occurring, steps forwards and steps backwards too.

It has dominated my entire life, either coping and understanding, or moving on and letting go.

The three most significant tools I have used are firstly mindfulness, secondly self-awareness which grows out of mindfulness - of my own spiritual and psychological nature, and through that I have developed and used the concept of reality, and thirdly the skills of forgiveness and gratitude.

Writing comes easily to me since my break down. Although I'd written and published a few books around the time I met David first of all, I had more or less stopped writing beyond course and teaching material, all along the same lines but not for publication.

But I have been trying to tell this story for nearly thirty years, not realising the story was not yet ready to be written, not yet complete, and that is why I could not get it out or down, before now.

But now is the time. I feel that most strongly, most intuitively.

What I find interesting is that earlier, none of what I wrote worked, but this has flowed well, been its own birthing doula and I am merely the channel. I simply know it must be written, not for my own sake but for whom it might help.

Writing as catharsis

Writing this has been the toughest thing to do emotionally, but I have read many memoirs and they all go to places that are excruciatingly painful to revisit at some point or another. That is what makes them good memoirs. As Mary Karr writes 'any family is a dysfunctional family if it has more than one person in it'. Can writing about it help you?

I've gone through most of the traumatic flashbacks and healed them individually, but I need to heal the whole story, fragments are not enough. And then put it to bed.

I have found my own experiences become less traumatic when I can use them to help others move on with their own traumas. That is the hard part though, delving into those individual incidents and placing them within a whole narrative that heals, allows me to make sense of it all. I have now completed that process with this book. It was a challenging delivery.

I have encountered huge internal resistance to writing and editing certain chapters that expose me at my own lowest or my family at their worst. They are the hardest. I find I am playing a lot of card games on my laptop instead of completing the writing or editing. I've had red 'screen eyes' for the last month as a result. I've also found other displacement activities born of that resistance. I have recognised the pull back into self-harming and self-rejection too, and I know I must pursue them and flush them out fully, so they lose any final influence they have over me. These consist of secret eating of foods that are bad for me, not being able to care for my body by keeping up my yoga, flossing my teeth, caring for my disintegrating spine etc. The worst offender is going back into self-rejecting thought patterns. 'How can David possibly really love me when he knows all this, and he has had to put up with so much from me.' Perhaps these are their death throes though.

It is a relief to get it all written too. This thing has been pursuing me for so long and now it is near completion and I feel a sense of lightness and release.

Therefore I am still here, to tell this story, to tell Mother's story and help others.

This fits in with my experience of 'self' nowadays anyway, since my 'golden pond' experience. But in this process, I discover who my family really are as people through these stories and I still love everyone – utterly. I am also able to feel softer towards them, more compassionate and accepting of their struggles as the background to my own. There are no perpetrators, no baddies, simply people struggling and messing it up too. We can all do that.

Like most family stories, they start way back, and I must take that journey into the past to really understand what happened to my Mother to make her the nightmare parent she was. As the buddha says, to understand all is to forgive all. That is exactly what's happening to me. Once I grasp the enormity of the family story over generations, my fear and anger fall away. You realise it is impossible to blame anybody anymore.

Grandad and Great Grandma unwittingly chose my Mother to pass their suffering from that orphanage school period of his life on to and she, also unable to speak her truth, chose me in turn.

I now speak it out for all of them on their behalf and to try and stop it recurring in other people's lives.

When you see the whole story, you begin to understand how the unconscious psyche manipulates us into re-enactments, repeating them until they are recognised and ended. Then we find ways to re-tell a story that makes us look better, called cognitive dissonance. This memoir has worked hard to get past all that and to find the true stories as I experienced them. I understand the self-justification of everyone involved, including myself and have worked hard to be honest throughout, without exaggeration or self-pity, since I feel none. This is just what happened to me, as those memories showed, with a clarity brighter than any full screen Imax cinema could reproduce.

When Lorna is brought home from France, she finds herself 're-placed' by a new baby sister. Her perspective is utter confusion and a sense of rejection and anger that will have no outlet ever, so it is all turned inwards against herself. That ruins her own life and takes down many others in varying degrees. I have hundreds of snippets of evidence of how much Lorna was universally disliked by her family, all of them without any exceptions, even those who superficially stood by her. That support was out of fear of the consequences, or duty, but never love. She was tolerated socially too, hence her projected words onto me, 'they are just nice people'.

There are several stages in separation anxiety that are recorded in young children. First there is distress when a child protests loudly. If this achieves nothing, the child seems to get over it and goes quiet, but the harm is going deeper. Then a child will go into compliance, and work with their new caregivers. The final stage is rejection of the original carers. When the child is picked up by the parents later, they are often rejected initially, as if the child is happy playing in their new surroundings, but they no longer feel able to trust you. This is where a deep insecurity has occurred and it will heal over time but takes a lot of patience and perseverance. Separation rarely causes any problems in short terms, i.e. a few hours and with good loving parenting is a natural phase in child development, to learn to be away from parents for periods of time safely.

Over a week or more or, as in Mothers case, many months, it does damage. A child will gradually learn to cope, but over a longer period it leads to deep trauma and frozen fear. This turned out to be utterly the case throughout Mother's life, but like Grandad she projects it onto other people, so it is not about her and again she has done nothing wrong, nor have her family. Neither Grandad nor Mother can ever embrace any form of criticism and take it as personal rejection for which you are in the wrong as the accuser.

Keep your enemies closer - she makes an ally of this second sister and is as good to her as she can be, reading stories to her and other sisterly activities, which Mercia recalls to me from time to time as the reason why she supports her.

But when a third sister comes along, she enlists my aunt to help her make sure this new sister is made to feel unwanted and between them they bully her mercilessly. Neither parent do anything to help their youngest though they know what is happening. But Mercia regrets her cruelty and turns it around into being a great sister. The damage is done, and Flavia also suffers, and still does, with some of the after effects of that kind of early damage. She has once told me how she also failed at school and was rebelling in ways that are self-harm when understood from this perspective. She has a breakdown in later life and some of my letters about mother start to show her how manipulative Lorna still is, game playing and lying about everything. That helps her a little.

Mercia and I have some sort of bond too, in adulthood, which I never really understand but do value. There are times when she turns against me and is influenced negatively towards me by my Mother's jealous words. But she and her husband Uncle Colin see something in me that is more than that and it wins out. She is also just not nasty like Mother, possibly because she has been the favourite daughter who makes everyone laugh endlessly and was never traumatised so completely.

Nevertheless, she has the same very sharp critical tendencies as Mother, which can be quite hard to be 'told by'. I experience it on more than one occasion. Violet my grandmother has that too. No one is ever allowed to criticise Violet or Alan though.

They are 'paragons of virtue to be revered and respected utterly without question. We are a great family of great successful people. We are lucky to belong to such a family'. This is the family story.

One other interesting thing that Mercia tells me, several years before she is also claimed by Alzheimer's, are some stories of how Grandad treated her and Lorna when they were little. This is the one that stands out in my mind most of all and echoes Mother's treatment of me.

Alan has taken both older daughters out shopping, before the youngest is born. They are about 3/4 and 7/8yrs at the time. They are in a large department store and he gets my Mother to hide, with him, from Mercia – 'to see how she reacts'. Note the age again. TO NOTE HOW SHE REACTED TO BEING ABANDONED.

Grandad wanted to watch someone else go through what he went through, and he stops my Mother going to comfort her desperately afraid and crying sister until he has his fill. Then they re-appear and make light of it. He trains my Mother to watch, with curiosity, some-one else suffering, knowing that he is unnecessarily causing it and knowing he can stop it immediately and not wanting to do that, immediately. I suspect this is where her psychopathic tendencies come from.

I am the next link in the chain, that is all.

I've talked much of this through with Emma and we both agree that Grandad meant no harm, he probably thought it was a practical joke of some sort. He might have also had some kind of autism issues since he was not very good at social interactions, but, like Lorna and myself, he was just carrying the trauma inside himself and it made him rigid with trapped fear and confusion. Nothing more than that.

The fallout on me though. Well I am still sifting through that and probably will be doing so until the day I die. I still find I am apologising for a lot more than necessary but nowadays I am able to turn that into a more compassionate 'sorry you are suffering this', not 'sorry, I am to blame, even if it is nothing to do with me'. I still feel over responsible for other people's issues and am learning slowly not to beat myself up for things way beyond my remit in life. The plus side is that I have no trouble in genuinely taking responsibility for what I am responsible for. We can only be responsible for how we think, feel, and behave in this present moment. Everything else is beyond our control or power to change. I've shed the burdens of guilt and shame at being me over time and now am open about when I make mistakes and when it is not my stuff. Learning these lessons in life can take a long time but in the end they are some of the most valuable ones you can have. They come with honesty and humility, two other dimensions I did not always have as I struggled to defend my internally defensive child-self.

I recognise how many people never take responsibility and just deny deny deny. My Mother did this, they both did but she was astonishing about it. She would say something one minute and then the next deny it completely. It was a completely impossible permanent double bind position to be in and this has been linked closely with various mental health issues in later life such as bipolar. I'm lucky I avoided that one, but I know people who haven't.

Drawing lines, creating boundaries, and saying no.

This is almost impossible with an NPD parent, both in childhood and later in adult hood. They have no respect for any such thing, let alone your attempts to establish any self-protection. You are their source of whatever they want to use you for and thus have no rights whatsoever. So, you become either a people pleaser or a rebellious people dis-pleaser. You can meet their needs either way, as victim of your appalling behaviour or as supplier of adoration.

I did both.

In childhood I would consciously say to my inner self, 'this person wants me to do such and such so I shall do the opposite', especially when it is linked with pleasing them at my own expense. Many adults expect children to meet their emotional needs even in little ways without giving a thought to the child. I rebelled. That gets me into more trouble, but it also keeps me sane and stops me becoming completely overwhelmed. I make my own inner boundaries in the only way possible, which is to refuse to be charmed or give gratification to attempts to extract that from me. Probably not such a nice trait to have but if it keeps me sane then I'm happy with that part of my childhood self.

Learning to say no takes me years, like all the rest of it. Those early understandings and lessons take down my first marriage and several other things in life but heals me from the endless tendencies to self-abuse and allowing others to use and abuse me too. There is no point beating yourself up about something you did once but would not do again because you're a completely different person.

We all need to learn from experience. We all need someone to give us that experience in the first place. We need to learn compassion, forgiveness, and humility. I do too.

The other problem I had was that I often over volunteered or offered to help. I wanted to show people how kind and willing I really was and overextended myself in the process, which led to a few exhaustions, which meant I did not perform as well as I wanted to and thus fed back into my 'I am completely useless' self-view. I am learning to unpick that set of behaviours too and say yes when I know it is a good idea and not say anything when I know it might prove too much. Nearly there.

Slowly I reclaim my life story and change trajectory.

The body I live in now, the cells that make up this body are no longer anything to do with that earlier body. Nothing remains of her, not even a few odd cells hidden deep inside. I feel cleansed by that knowledge and love the life I have now with my adorable and adored husband.

I am still willing to please and help others, but from free will and choice, never from duty. I also know that this is a far greater gift than I could ever give before. Nothing extracted from emotional abuse is worth anything compared to a freely given gift from the heart. No one will ever manipulate me into anything again. If I get even a whiff of it, the burden of someone's expectations can still trigger my PTSD responses to them, but I stand my ground and smile as sweetly as I'm able to, and continue to make my own choices.

Intuitive self-belief.

I have alluded to this deeply spiritual intuitive dimension to my nature. This also helps to keep me sane, even now. My dreams, stories and passionate love of reading allow me to escape the living hell of reality and find other places and other ways to think and experience life. I know it is all fucked up big time and I remember trying sooo very hard to get my Dad to listen, that he 'could not love me if he used it as a weapon to withdraw it from me every time I got something wrong'.

I've always known things at a deeper intuitive level of wisdom beyond myself, as if I can dip my toes into a well of wisdom from ancient times, eternal perspectives that never become obsolete. When I read or hear or recognise such wisdom, it affects my body in peculiar ways, as if I am sinking into something utterly original and natural. I've learned to accept and embrace these insights

I just knew Mother was beyond reaching. I'd seen her joy at watching me suffer emotionally when she hurt me, and I knew I simply had to survive her. But Dad should have been my salvation and he wasn't, he just added to it all, except every so often I glimpsed the love I'd known as a little girl. I think he was a great softie who did love very much until my Mother's jealousy took it away from us both.

Over the years this inner knowing system has alerted me to other people with NPD tendencies, sooner or later. Although I am initially drawn to their familiar energy. I am also aware of how destructive they are. I have been burnt a few times by ignoring my intuitions, but that intuitive voice has also helped me get out of it and know my own reality strongly enough to stay sane. Again, I can happily state that without it I probably would not have made it.

My dream people helped me get through, though other people have widely ridiculed me for this approach to life. I know it is my reality and continues to be my sanity.

Insecurity in relationships.

This is the biggest thing I have had to struggle with. As you know, I once called myself

<u>'old wobbly feelings thingy twit head'</u>

because I had just so much uncertainty and distrust in any relationship I was in and needed constant re-assurance. That can be a drag for the other person, a constant demand for them to say how they feel.

I've never been able to fully heal that particular wound (yet) so tend to select people who are quite open and demonstrative as good friends. I need to feel a physical energy connection to people before I can trust them or relate to them properly and if that is not there, I cannot trust them or myself. It means I can seem elusive and unfriendly at times, but it is just my self-protect buttons on in that sense.

David remains open to telling me how much he loves me and letting me pour out my love and gratitude to him on a daily basis. He is incredibly open and loving and is equally pleased to find someone who values him for himself. I think we have been soulmates for an exceedingly long time.

However even when he spontaneously tells me how much he loves me and gives me a huge energetically connected hug, a little voice inside whispers, 'really, still, you haven't realised your mistake yet'. I now voice that inner dialogue to him, and by slowly confronting it, that old programme is becoming weaker and weaker.

What I have done over time though is to gradually learn who are the people I want to spend my time with. Rather than always seeing myself as a commodity to meet other people's needs and then be discarded, I now value my contribution to a relationship, and theirs to me. I am no longer always waiting for the discard, which is how I used to operate, and then usually when I think there is a hint of it, getting out fast, first if possible.

Nowadays I truly value my close friends and life travellers, more than I can say. I also consider myself more than a commodity in their lives but as someone who they want to spend time with and would enjoy contact from me.

Reading the signs - defensively

I am an expert for noticing the slightest signs or symptoms on other people of a change of heart or attitude. Towards me of course, mostly only towards me, and my own contributions to their lives. I see things that other people don't' notice and have been told many times that I am imagining it, but I know I am not. This highly attuned, extremely sensitive signal awareness is real. It comes from a combination of the need to be hyper-vigilant for the next outburst from Mother and my innately intuitive being.

David is sitting next to me watching TV or a film or listening to a talk online and I will suddenly feel his energy change and ask him 'what did you just think – I felt you change?' He is always astonished at how accurate this sense of mine is with those I am close to, although he is getting used to it and now both respects and believes it. I can read his energy more accurately than his expressed words and luckily he is as open and honest emotionally with me as I am with him.

My sons learned about my intuitive powers growing up when they realised they couldn't get much past me either. We are all very blunt and up front with each other too. It works for us.

Can you imagine my joy at finally being loved more for these weird innate aspects of what it is that makes me?

This is a hard path to travel, and I know I am alone on it even if there are others like me. We are in a minority and I don't know anybody else quite like me.

Do I enjoy being a 'one off'?

Sometimes I confess I do, and sometimes it feels like a curse. But what I have learned is that there are people who are ready to judge you on an instant and others who will embrace your difference and enjoy you for it whilst still not seeing you as a commodity. I have been people's pet clowns in the past for my eccentricity and I cannot blame it all on Mother and Dad or all on my ADHD /PTSD challenges in life. There is, in me, a natural rebel. I really don't want to conform to anything ever. If you start to categorise me, I will just walk away. My history and psychological make-up mean I am not that straightforward even though I am incredibly open and honest. Mother and Dad just did not understand me, they wanted me to conform to their expectations and needs, to make them socially acceptable. I get that I was hard for them to comprehend, a challenge that they knew no other way to manage with their own emotional deficiencies.

Learning how to trust

This has been my biggest challengeand is still also a challenge for me, even now, in my 7th decade.

I must list it here as part of the fallout of surviving narcissistic parents, recognising trust takes time to build, is easily broken and almost impossible to repair without humility, total honesty, and acceptance of responsibility. These are such important life lessons I have learned, and they have made all my relationships better than I thought possible. I still take a very long time to trust people though reading their energy helps me greatly

The other problem is trusting too easily and having what are called porous boundaries. These issues are ongoing issues for me but the more I release those childhood traumas the more I am learning how to manage this deeply important dimension to all relationships on which they flourish or founder. The gift in this lesson has been to examine trust closely and to understand how it works, how valuable it is and how irreparable it can be once broken.

Fear of natural disharmonies of life.

Even in the best relationships there are times when there is disharmony, disagreement and even anger and rage or hurt and tears.

I know them, they are familiar and thus I know how to deal with them. What I don't know is how to feel safe with them. They are still a threat to my integral safety and wellbeing. They make me want to run and yet to cling harder, both responses I had to my parents at different times. To learn to deal with this I also had to overcome the deep rages that once flamed within me.

David won me over with his chat up line 'I have no anger'. It turned out he hadn't completely lost all his anger, but it showed me that he was working on it, which was what I was also doing at that time.

We have spent the last twenty plus years working on that and many more issues together using our mindfulness and Buddhist psychology as our guide. We rarely have a heated disagreement, but we sometimes squabble playfully if there is a disagreement, and then one or other gives way. Nothing is more important than the harmony in our life. We never have the same issue more than one or twice, we talk it out when we are not annoyed, and it gets resolved somehow with both of our needs being met.

Away from home and family, I am still triggered by extreme anger in people, along with dependency and expectations. Sometimes that anger is not even expressed as rage, but I can sense it with this super sense, my survival technique and life skill. I'm working on it still, using compassion meditation for those who have that stored anger in them. It does them more harm than it can do to me now, except triggering me.

Although for many years I was almost completely emotionally frozen, giving birth first starts to unfreeze me and gradually the emotions within me rise to the surface. I would like to say I managed them with aplomb but of course I did not. They led me into all sort of regrettable incidents, and I hurt myself as much as other people as their fury seeped out of me. I am not that person anymore. I never really was but carried so much suffering inside; it came out in many twisted and distorted ways, as it does for all people.

The more obviously empty and damaged someone is on the outside the more I feel compassion for them inside, even if I cannot cope with them yet myself. Yet another work in progress.

Writing this book has been a final stage catharsis. I thought I might not be able to go back and write dispassionately about who I used to be and what that little girl went through and how she coped. It is disturbing my sleep and churning things up, so that I am uncomfortable and forced to face them for another layer of clearance. Just enough. Too much and I'm not able to simply explore, write down and then let go. Without my spiritual practice and meditation, without being able to fully and finally embrace all that I am and have been I could not do that. I am not afraid of that child and younger woman. I am not ashamed of her either, well mostly not. She suffered greatly for me to understand what I understand now and to her I shall ever be in deep gratitude. I salute my former self for all her faults and failings, how do you learn if not by getting it wrong? How can you be successful without learning to fail?

Once we can identify our emotions and understand how they developed we can let them go and heal those old wounds and damaging experiences, turn them into positives for ourselves and find true happiness. Learning to be authentically yourself is very liberating.

The importance of tears

Tears have rolled down my cheeks from time to time

Or been blocked in my heart, my throat, my head.

Tears, unshed, will clog you up, but you must have permission to cry them out, your own of course, but of those around you also. I had no such permissions in childhood, they were taken from me. I gave my sons permission to cry but society tried to stop them anyway. I am delighted to see the occasional tear in my husband's eyes. I know he is healing too.

In adulthood I remember the day I deny myself the right to cry at all for myself.

It is after my first marriage broke down. I want to find out how life would work out on my own, but am also terrified. I know if I start crying I will falter, collapse, and fail to function. I tell myself firmly 'no one to cry for now, you're on your own, so get on with it'. And I do.

I learned a lot of very tough lessons through that time but my tears were frozen, and that inability to release emotions broke me for a second time. I was deeply anxious too, all symptoms of the PTSD that is lurking deeply within my body. I learned that betablockers cut the anxiety and allow me to continue as if all is fine with me. Just occasionally I used to wake at night with an emptiness so deep it is horrific, and tears wrenched themselves from my frame. That is soon replaced by dreams, the red girl dream most of all.

In this dream I am following a long dark red lit tunnel into a small room which is very hot airless and claustrophobic. I am reluctant to go down this tunnel but feel inexorably drawn in anyway. I reach the room at the end of the corridor. In it is a girl, wrapped from head to toe in bandages, and bleeding from a million tiny cuts all over her body. She looks at me expressing deep sorrow with her eyes but cannot speak to me. Her mouth is bound too. I cannot reach her. Something stops me touching or speaking to her, and I am always forced to leave her to her suffering, just turning my back and walking away from her. I feel a strong ache to reach her and simultaneously a revulsion of her. This dream came often during my thirties.

I never feel safe in my life. I read Stevie Smiths poem Not Waving but Drowning, and it speaks so much to me. I start to read poetry again from volition, not school curriculum. The PTSD is influencing my psyche without my understanding or recognizing it.

I try crying. I imagine little scenarios of myself being all alone and forlorn, sitting reading once my sons are both in bed. But the reality is that my life is pretty good, just that I can't access that feeling very often.

I remember once when I am alone in that first 'home of my own', and the boys are with their dad. I am decorating my bathroom and kitchen, cutting and fixing tiles, building an airing cupboard using old doors I've salvaged from the original kitchen. I'm so engrossed in my work that I feel blissful and I eventually notice it. It is of course another recognition of mindful activity but I still don't know the term yet. But in those hours, the anxiety has dissolved, and I am perfectly peaceful. Later that evening I meet an old friend Clare, nicknamed CG, and we go off to see some European film, something we often do together. The following day I will be studying my open university degree work. It is a perfect weekend, one of many, only made so by accidentally discovering mindful activity, by finding my bliss in those moments. On Sunday evenings the boys come home from their Dad's and all joyful and loving chaos returns of course. It is a simple time in my life and a good one. But I still can't cry.

What started this journey of discovery into the heart of my own story?

I remembered meditating once, just after I had met David and we were developing our meditation experiences together. I knew something was tying me up inside and thought maybe I could just ask for it to be shown to me so I could let it go. I thought it would be a simple thing. I'd already done so much therapeutic work on myself, read endlessly all sorts of books that gave me hope of how to live with stability and happiness and it had really been working, ideas of how I should value myself. I'd been changing over time, so I thought I was making good progress.

I had another think coming. Life has a habit of showing you how you cannot assume anything and that nothing is permanent. Events conspired to take me down once more and spectacularly badly too.

But it has all been worth it in the end.

24. WHEN FAMILIES BECOME ESTRANGED.

How to survive when love cannot heal.

I can only begin to remember the good bits about either parent because they are both dead, because it is now safe to do so, and only now.

I had to harden myself against them both so often just to survive myself emotionally- to keep my own self intact - either while I was in touch or when I was estranged from them. It was defensive and heart-breaking at the same time. I longed to be loved by them, but I couldn't begin to trust either of them for one second. I learned that incredibly early on.

That they brought out the very worst in each other is in no doubt; that they took that out on me mostly is also not a secret though the narrative is that somehow - in their own distorted logic - I always deserved it. Other family members embraced that narrative and interpreted me in that frame from then on. I was the problem for all to see. Except that I wasn't.

Well that is the lie I want to debunk with this book. No child deserves what I went through. Even though I know plenty of people go through worse, it is not a competition. This damaged my whole life but also makes me who I am now.

I have a huge sadness that it was like this for us all, for what we all lost out on with each other, for the damage done to all concerned, not just myself. But not sadness that it is over now, not sadness that they are both dead and not sadness that I am now writing it down for all to read and understand. I want this story told not for revenge or anything else but so that those going through it might find this book and read it and be re-assured and encouraged to live their own life and walk away from abusive families, if that is their only safe option.

Families are designed for survival, possibly biologically evolved to be a self-supporting unit, a group of people who will somehow be there for each other and make sure each is ok, through thick and thin. To love, despite foibles and idiosyncrasies, to be able to absorb the whole load of human variations in an acceptance of 'difference' and a collective of blood and history.

Yet amongst the people I know this is less the norm and more the exception, even among people who to me are thoughtful, wise, kind, loving people, it seems that extended family life is often not possible or at best a real struggle.

In each case there is a point when it breaks off, but that point will have started a long time earlier, the final straw is rarely the real reason for the break down.

It usually starts through damaged communications systems that fail to resolve conflicts.

Often in families there is a reluctance to talk things through. There is a lingering fear that if we reveal our inner self too much to family then we are left vulnerable and exposed. Too often families are filled with judgemental attitudes of each other. Certainly it was that way in my family and in the families of most of those I know where there is break down.

I remember, when training as a family therapist, the lecturer on systemic family theory described the family structure as a child's mobile where every individual is placed on their own arm of the family structure and in a specific position. If everyone stays exactly in the right position, then the family balances out. In healthy families there is wiggle room, and everyone can adjust well.

In unhealthy families there is none. The whole family will put pressure on each other to not change the balance because that threatens each of them as much as anything. If your position on the mobile is an unhappy one, your need to challenge the existing layout is only seen as a disruption and not as a potential for healing old wounds, not as an intrinsic need for personal growth and development.

Some families are more able than others to shuffle in tandem and to allow change and growth over time and still maintain balance, but the more damaged a family is, the more rigidly reluctant it is in facing its own dark corners and skeletons. Yet those dark spaces damage and eat away at any shared bonds there might be. Refusing to deal with issues, and grow together through them, is the most common cause of any relationship breakdown. Thus, the individual who is being hurt by that family layout, and their designated role within it, has little option than walk away.

They are punished on every level for this. Punished initially by being the underdog in the family or being the one upon whom too much pressure is being put. However, that family structure is hurting each other, the individual upon whom most rests is the one who is most hurt. Some stay and prefer their role to isolation but many leave, or are pushed out even, so they can continue to be the role holder in absence. The empty chair on the family mobile which is still holding the place for others but only has an occupant in symbol, not in reality. They can still be identified as the problem though in absentia.

I remember a story I was told that has stayed with me forever and been a strongly guiding influence on me. It is about growth and choices within family.

There is an old woman who goes for a walk one day and falls down a great big hole. To be honest the hole is not that big, but she is afraid to climb out and so walks around that hole looking for an easy way out instead of taking a risk. The hole gets deeper as a result.

At home, her three daughters start to wonder where their Mother is. The first daughter goes looking and eventually hears her Mother calling for help. She follows the voice, finds her Mother, and reaches down into the hole to offer her Mother a hand up. But the Mother declines the hand proclaiming it will bring the sides of the hole in upon her head and suggests instead that the daughter comes down into the hole with her and they can both call for help more loudly. So, the first daughter comes down into the hole and joins her Mother in calling for help. The hole gets deeper.

After a while, the second daughter wonders where her sister and Mother are, goes looking and finds them. She sits at the top of the hole and discusses the options with her Mother and sister, 'Come down with us and call for help'. The middle sister say's 'but I have come to help and you're not accepting my help.' And they continue to argue indefinitely, both unable to see the point of view of the other. Finally, the younger sister realises that no one has come back and goes off to see what has happened. She hears the arguing and calling and follows the sound until she finds her Mother and sisters. She stands looking down into the hole and comments that it is not so deep really. She looks at the sister sitting at the edge and realises she is not making any progress either. She suggests there is little point in joining in as they have all bases covered and walks off to get on with her own life, leaving those stuck positions behind.

We all have that choice. Do we stay, and fight, argue or struggle to create change or do we finally accept defeat and walk away to live our own life. You cannot change others. You can only change yourself. Once you have offered your help and it is rejected there is little point entering an argument about it.

One thing that has occurred to me, and I know I am not the only one-

In a toxic family system, the problem member in a family may

be the only one who can see through everyone else's bullshit.

In other words, being the outcast might just mean you are the sane one, thus being the problem can be a blessing or compliment, if unintended.

The breaking up of family ties is a long slow drawn out process of gradual disillusionment and hurt. The final blows are a death and can be felt as a genuine bereavement for those involved.

Relief can be the more unexpected emotional response to leaving family behind when you think you will feel loss and sadness. Relief means you are doing the right thing, you are honouring your own life over the demands of others, you are being true to yourself and your own story instead of inhabiting someone else's. Relief may come immediately or after the bereavement process is completed. It may arrive suddenly and be complete or it may be a gradual dawning recognition that life is actually better now.

What I learned from my own experience is that they will fill the space you leave with their own projections of you into that place, like a film version of you that is not real, but completes their version of real, as they want you to continue to be, to complete their story. Then gradually they can fade you out as they retell their own stories over time, just leaving you in reserve as evidence of your wrongness, and their rightness.

Just to show that you are not alone in this, if this is your family situation, then just contemplate this 2015 piece of research, done by a charity called Stand Alone, which shows nearly 20 percent or twelve million people in Britain are part of an estranged family. That is an awful lot of people in families that are unable to communicate and balance with each other.

Families like this are not a small minority and an awful lot more people are part of intact families that are deeply dysfunctional. It is sometimes 'family' which is an abusive structure and sometimes it is that the estranged one is the damaged disruptive one. This is not about laying blame for anything or on anyone, but just a recognition of how many people are damaged in and being damaged by families though.

Fear of being alone is what keeps most people stuck on the inside of a destructive family system. Kicking the crutches away and standing alone can be a daunting prospect – until you have done it – and then you realise how liberating that place is. There are so many reasons why people must move away from families but the most common are religious abuse, sexual, physical, and emotional abuse, addiction, and mental health or personality disorders.

Family abandonments are not usually taken lightly and frequently come with their own burdens of guilt, shame and regret along with that feeling of worthlessness that often accompanies the causes that led to this.

Perhaps that is why family breakdowns are so rarely discussed compared to open discussion about divorce and couples breaking up. We are often happy to say, 'I am divorced' or 'on my second marriage' but not to say, 'I no longer have a viable relationship with my Mother or sibling'. And reactions differ hugely too. For instance, if I say I am in my second and incredibly happy marriage, people just nod and accept. But if I say that I no longer see any of my birth family apart from one first cousin and a few more distant cousins, they make comments that are less accepting, especially when I used to say this about my parents.

People who have close and fully functional birth family units are few are far between, but most people rub along with not too much friction though there may be falling out and difficulties that lie undisclosed within family circles. They will be the subject of conversation with friends. This is where we feel safer to let off steam about conflicts we may have, but still in the context of an ongoing relationship. When you say there is a rift people will always ask or suggest that it might be resolvable one day and 'you never know' and 'time heals all' and other such platitudes. This may be true in a very few cases, but it fails to acknowledge the damaging effects that led to the break. The last thing someone wants, having broken free, is going back to try again.

The reason I am not in contact with my family is because although individually they are a pretty nice bunch, no one is perfect. They don't like talking about things openly, having feathers ruffled and being faced with things they don't want to think about. I am one of those who does just this, not intentionally but mostly I think because I have ADHD and am a very open person who likes to be clear about things. I also need to tell my story and they have a right not to want to hear it. I can let things go completely once it is resolved but I cannot brush things under any carpets. I am also politically and ideologically at the opposite ends of the spectrum and most of my interactions with them were them silencing me anyway.

Put that into the mix of a very dysfunctional and abusive family paradigm about me and I am clearly better off out of there. It was a mutually comfortable decision in the end. I can honestly say that I deeply love my family, all of them, but I have no desire to spend time with them or get involved ever again. I can love them, wish them the absolute best, and let them go.

My father was the one who refused to speak to me for 33 years and it was only during my breakdown from PTSD from family issues that I realise that was a spiritual protection put in place for me - not a punishment of me but a safeguarding position in which I could develop my own intended destiny. Not that I am a believer in determinism, but I do feel strongly that we are all here to complete something, a task or a development in our spiritual existence, a contribution to the greater good perhaps.

I cut Mother off a few times but always went back, always hoping she would start to value me, and it is only after they both died that I realise that could never have happened because to do that would be to admit they had been wrong in the first place and that would never occur.

If you are in the yo yo phase, probably it is time to reconsider the value of putting yourself through it any more at all.

We all want to be loved and valued by our families. It is tough to realise that will never happen. It can lead to many forms of depression and mental health issues and this is one reason why this conversation needs to come out into the open and be as acceptable as divorce relationship breakdown is mostly nowadays. Whether it's your choice or thrust on you, try to reframe that context for yourself and see that it might be your salvation.

Being cast adrift can make you resilient, self-reliant, resourceful. Growing up in my family gave me that since even as a child I was not cared for or nurtured in any recognisable way either physically or emotionally.

It is easier to leave when you are the underdog, it is harder when you are a 'preferred, perfect cannot do anything wrong one', the replacement that arrives because you're not what they wanted or expected. It is easier to challenge that you are worthless than that you are the good one who got it right. In so many ways I feel luckier than my siblings now because I have cleared out all family issues and can write about them for others to benefit from. I doubt they can even talk about them anymore than they could decades ago when I last tried.

For me in my second marriage, without family baggage, I can be happier than I ever knew possible.

- I now know the people who really like me and not just go through the routines for family reasons.
- I am secure in my sense of being who I am and can share my story without too many stirred up emotions, it all happened to someone I used to be.
- I feel free to express myself as I choose and as comes naturally
- I can clearly see how hard my journey was and how awesome it is to be finally free of it

- I can love others with my whole heart and know that I can survive if they hurt me in ways that are barely survivable, I've already done it.
- I can stand alone when necessary
- I am good enough as I am, and family is a construct that is not always functionally viable
- I have learned the lessons necessary to have good relationships with both my own sons, David, and many friends too.

Is family breakdown a failure, a form of self-preservation, or a very sad fact of modern life? Should we judge those involved in it as somehow slacking in their effort to make it work, and not being tolerant enough or should we be compassionate and recognise that for some like myself it is pure self-preservation. It always was, maybe with desperate attempts to make something change thrown in. for most people that would also be true. No one has a perfect family, but some are just far more damaging to others and sometimes not to all family members, just the few who get caught up at the bottom of the heap.

We all want to project the perfect family story and friends for whom that story is real can be very insensitive to those for whom it is not real, for many reasons. Hurts get passed on whether we intend it or not. Until we're fully healed, we cannot help it, it is just what happens. But in the end being able to talk about it openly and lovingly with those you do choose to have in your life in the present can make it far easier to cope with longer term. The vacuum never seems to go away completely but it is wise to be very wary of what might fill it. I tried to heal that vacuum in my own life, and it led to a ten-year illness and many losses. Although I have come through that and am better for it, indeed grateful for it, I was lucky. I have an amazing husband who got me through it. Some may not have that support in place and may not recover. As they say let sleeping dogs lie. Going to see someone just before they die may not be the cathartic healing opportunity you hope for, they may never see your point of view as it clashes with their story, and we all have our own cherished story which is our reality, but not true for everyone.

Going to a funeral may seem like a way of drawing a line and giving closure but it can be just another torment when you have already said goodbye a thousand times.

25. WHAT IS NARCISSISM AND NPD

Narcissism is a complex disorder which is difficult to diagnose and yet once you know someone has this condition, or perspective on life you can see quite clearly that they are NPD. There are several types of NPD, usually about five which are clearly identifiable, but some people will be a mixture of two or even more in their various shades of expression

Types of narcissism

Grandiose narcissism - attention seeking - look at me - don't listen to anybody else – I am definitely the most interesting and important person in the room, I know more than anyone else and am smarter than anyone else

Malignant - all the same above but really nasty with it, taking things out on other people, mean and really bad things- almost a little psychopathic – cheat steal etc lie, consciously hurt others and then deny responsibility

Covert – secret – butter wouldn't melt – misunderstood, put upon victim, still *feel* grandiose about how great they are but not recognised – may seem like depression but don't get better – woe is me, hyper sensitive to criticism – cold and distant if rejected. World doesn't get their greatness. World hasn't been fair to them

Stealth – every day is 'woe is me' – nice you got that thing lucky for you - not so easy for me. Check out how much of a victim they are and how much they say they want to change but don't –

won't take responsibility – not my fault - everybody else made me do it. A complete victim of circumstances and unfair treatment by others.

Communal – 'off to feed homeless today' – all about them and intend well but cannot give back in reality – lack of empathy and compassion – validation for all their good works needed - do it to appear good rather than to genuinely want to help others silently – can't do good quietly. Trumpet their own contributions.

Just to make it clear – we ALL have some of this from time to time but if this is all we have then we have probably got NPD and if not then you are just human and can work on it

There are various specific behaviours within these categories which show us more. Having at least part of the questions answered for my own interest, I take several diagnostic check-lists and questionnaires, and work through them, point by point, to consider how Mother matches the items on that list.

For a person to be diagnosed with narcissistic personality disorder (NPD) they must meet five or more of the following symptoms:

- Has a grandiose sense of self-importance (e.g., exaggerates achievements and talents, expects to be recognized as superior without commensurate achievements).
- Is preoccupied with fantasies of unlimited success, power, brilliance, beauty, or ideal love.
- Believes that he or she is "special" and unique and can only be understood by, or should associate with, other special or high-status people (or institutions).
- Requires excessive admiration
- Has a very strong sense of entitlement, e.g., unreasonable expectations of especially favourable treatment or automatic compliance with his or her expectations. They get first choice of chair, room, office, out-

ing destination etc.

- Is exploitative of others, e.g., takes advantage of others to achieve his or her own ends.
- Lacks empathy, e.g., is unwilling to recognize or identify with the feelings and needs of others.
- Is often envious or jealous of others or believes that others are jealous and envious of him or her. Always wants to muscle in on anything that other people are doing together without them, and if possible take over.
- Regularly shows arrogant, haughty behaviours or attitudes
- When something goes wrong, does he/ she blame everyone but himself or herself? – always.
- Does your partner refuse to be accountable for his or her bad behaviour? (For example, "*You* made me so mad that I couldn't help …")
- Does your partner believe he or she is always right?
- Does your partner do considerate things for you only when others are around to witness that good behaviour?
- Do they seem to carry grudges but never seem to let people go who have moved on from them?
- Can they relate to your children or other people's children, as children instead of seeing them as an audience?
- Do they seem to need to compete with you and find ways to make sure they are superior, or if not then detract from any success or accolade you might win.
- Other tendencies include great social charm and the ability to make you feel very special in the beginning- called the love bombing stage, 'you are the best, the greatest, the only one, if it wasn't for you'. But they are not said in gratitude , rather out of giving you responsibility for their happiness and sense of well-being – so that you are then responsible for when this also fails,

never them.

- Tendency to fly into uncontrollable rages, which 'you' are responsible for. People living with NPD often have to walk on eggshells to try and avert a rage though they will occur anyway.
- Likes to be in control of any given situation and has lot of rules which must not be broken, cannot cope with spontaneity or the unexpected.
- Often let people down or leaves them in limbo, their needs are the only important ones and your time or demands are of no consequences, changes arrangements all the time to suit them rather than fit in to suit you.
- Often lies and keeps secrets. Narcissists are liars, they cannot help it. They want to portray a perfect person so are obliged to distort truths and keep secrets about his or her true thoughts, feelings, or intentions. Individuals with NPD are pathological liars who often actually begin to believe the stories they've created.
- Gaslighting – an extreme form of lying, when they actively tell lies to undermine someone else's sense of reality, a total distortion of perception so that the victim's own sense of self, and any certainty they have in the world is taken away from them. This makes the victim dependent on the NPD gaslighter and gives them control over reality.
- Wants to be the centre of attention, whether in a crowded room, or at home. The narcissist relies on others for fuel - called 'narcissistic supply'. Anyone competition for the spotlight will be quickly discarded or made to look foolish so the narcissist can take over. Ridicule and derision are their favourite weapons
- Narcissists will always try to take credit for the ideas or accomplishments of others. If a narcissist believes another has an original or intriguing plan, they will

take every opportunity to bring it to life *and* to take credit for thinking of it initially. They can be so skilful at manipulation and distortions of reality they can convince everyone it was originally their idea.

- Superiority over service workers, 'you are a mere cleaner I am better then you o you clean up after me while I do important things' Service in a restaurant is never good enough. The tendency is also to exploit the position of service by others to their own needs to be superior.
- Disconnected from reality. So often their view of the world is nothing like the reality most of us live in, however we view that reality since there are so many anyway. They are often confused when away from home turf when their reality can be legitimately challenged.
- Addiction is often a feature as they struggle to maintain their social appearance of bonhomie and generally being wonderful, as well as supressing their own initial trauma which made them NPD in the first place. Some encourage co-dependents to also become addicts.
- Cannot cope with criticism but is very happy to dish it out as advice. Advice can be viewed as covert criticism if it is not an established part of the relationship and a mutual or two-way thing. They will 'give it but not take it'. Even if they themselves behave in similar ways they cannot accept that they are the same as you, that only you are the bad one and there are reasons why they are forced to behave in certain ways which is not their fault. Narcissist injury is a bruise to their narcissistic sense of self, which leads to a sense of humiliation for them, instead of humility at being wrong. Even comments made in jest can lead to such bruising. They will most likely then seek revenge and not stop until it is avenged for them on their terms.

- Disrespects other people's rules and boundaries. Will invade other people's space, go into their possessions without invitation, consider someone else property open to them to use, but this is not reciprocal. .Will break all social rules and make out the rule is the problem, not them
- Have no sense of remorse at hurting others and be more likely to laugh at their distress of gain a sense of power from it.
- Viewing others as an extension of yourself, *my* son <u>husband wife partne</u>r etc. you are a possession not an individual with a life of your own. How the 'other' might behave is also all about the narcissist. You let them down, you show them up, you are responsible for their social standing.

When I read these individual lists and even when I amalgamate them, as I have here, I can see Mother in every single item.

 I am sure reading this, you also get the picture, and easily find many websites on line that will guide you well enough. The crucial thing is that someone who identifies with items on this list is not complacent or in denial about their application to themselves and thus are willing to change grow and learn how to live more compassionately to them self and to others. I know I can raise my hand to some of these items in the past but on the recognition I can then also work to change and not to repeat. That is the difference between someone with NPD and someone who is just learning about life.

What can you do with this list?

Is it helpful to you to self-examine as well as to identify the traits in other people in your life? These lists can be a starting point for you to being a recognition and then to make a decision about your own life. Is it hurting you or are you identifying yourself in the list above.

Some people who are narcissists are quite open about it and say Yes I am, and cannot see anything wrong with it. They are almost proud of it. Many Narcissists get to positions of great power and influence and can do untold harm in the process. There are many examples of leaders of entire countries who are total NPD, both historically and right now in this year as I complete writing and editing this book.

RESOURCES

Some of the books websites and inspiration that helped me get through.

<u>Books</u>

The Miracle of Mindfulness by Thich Nhat Hanh

What the Buddha Taught by Thich Nhat Hanh

Transformation and Healing by Thich Nhat Hanh

The Body Keeps the Score by Bessel Van Der Kolk

When the body says No by Dr Gabor Mate

Daddy's Rules by Rachel Sontag

<u>Web Sites – You Tube</u>

There are absolutely loads of ordinary websites but I found talks the most helpful to listen to – just search NPD and you will find so many and all are helpful, some more so than others. You must find the ones that suit you though.

https://www.youtube.com/watch?v=Zrg43vCxv2Q   Surviving Narcissism and other You tube videos by Dr Les Carter, all extremely helpful, supportive, re-assuring and insightful for self-liberating from and NPD relationship or family.

https://www.youtube.com/watch?v=6dv8zJiggBs&t=457s – Med circle - great video discussions about the links between and differences between narcissism, psychopathy, and sociopathy. More about recognition and less about healing or helping yourself.

https://www.youtube.com/watch?v=53RX2ESIqsM talk by Dr Bessel Van Der Kolk on recognising and healing from trauma.

Also helpful for me is the Plum Village You Tube channel with talks on trauma and love and compassion and healing etc. https://www.youtube.com/watch?v=ljdsTSneYuY a teaching on interbeing which helped me enormously understand my place and my right to exist just as I had been, but there are so many talks on this website and almost anything by Thich Nhat Hanh himself is wonderful.

Printed in Poland
by Amazon Fulfillment
Poland Sp. z o.o., Wrocław

61627483R00167